# WINNERS AND SINNERS

●●●●●●●●●●●●●●●●●●●●●●●●●●●●●●

Instructive and amusing, reliable and readable, *Watch Your Language* has established itself as a standard desk reference, as a school and college text, and as a writer's guide that is a joy to read.

It was developed by Theodore M. Bernstein, assistant managing editor of *The New York Times,* from material that originally appeared in *Winners & Sinners,* "an occasional bulletin of second guessing," written by Mr. Bernstein and distributed to the reporters and editors of *The Times.* These semi-monthly reports on good writing and bad soon became collector's items; and at that point, says Mr. Bernstein, "a book publisher twisted my arm."

The happy result of that brief tussle is *Watch Your Language*—a practical handbook that has also been read for pleasure by a nonprofessional audience of thousands.

●●●●●●●●●●●●●●●●●●●●●●●●●●●●●●

*Watch Your Language* was
originally published at $4.50, by Atheneum.
A Leonard Harris Book

# WATCH
# YOUR
# LANGUAGE

•••••••••••••••••••••••••••••••••

A lively, informal guide to better writing,
emanating from the News Room of
THE NEW YORK TIMES

•••••••••••••••••••••••••••••••••

*Theodore M. Bernstein*

PUBLISHED BY POCKET BOOKS, INC. NEW YORK

WATCH YOUR LANGUAGE

Atheneum edition published July, 1965

A *Pocket Book* edition
1st printing.......December, 1965

This *Pocket Book* edition includes every word
contained in the original, higher-priced edition. It is printed
from brand-new plates made from completely reset, clear, easy-to-read
type. *Pocket Book* editions are published by Pocket Books, Inc., and
are printed and distributed in the U.S.A. by Affiliated Publishers, a
division of Pocket Books, Inc., 630 Fifth Avenue, New York, N.Y. 10020.
Trademark of Pocket Books, Inc., 630 Fifth Avenue,
New York, N.Y. 10020, registered in the United States
and other countries.

L

# Contents

Preface BY JACQUES BARZUN, vii

Introduction, 1

1  Words That Need Watching, 7

2  Storytelling, 55

3  Syntax Sinners, 103

4  Helpful Hints for Hatchet Men, 134

5  Head-Hunting, 161

Appendix: A Handful of News Stories, 181

Index, 204

## TWO ACKNOWLEDGMENTS
## BY THE AUTHOR

*The first is more of a dedication. It is to Beatrice, my wife, who not only feeds me, clothes me, comforts me and buffers me against the world, but also is my most encouraging critic. On top of all this she handed me the title for the present book.*

*The second acknowledgment is to Lewis Jordan, news editor of The New York Times. He is the solid anvil against which much of the Winners & Sinners material is hammered out. It is also he who regularly copy edits W & S and occasionally saves it from falling on its arrogant face. He copy edited the manuscript for this book, too, and his suggestions were always invaluable.*

# Preface
## BY JACQUES BARZUN

Years ago—it feels like a hundred but is probably less—
Mr. Theodore Bernstein was managing editor of a college
newspaper to the news board of which I, a freshman, aspired.
It was one of Mr. Bernstein's pleasant and exalted duties to
mark up every day the issue just published and, by ex-
coriating faults of style, form, and proofreading, to award
demerits whose uneven accumulation on various heads would
in time eliminate the surplus of candidates for positions on
the board.

Having survived this and other ordeals, I now find it my
pleasant and exalted duty to commend Mr. Bernstein for
what he did and has done in the same happy vein during his
distinguished career as journalist.

But I am not inviting the reader to witness a tender of
compliments over what may seem like a mere byproduct of
professional skill. On the contrary, I am drawing attention
to a function which is now neglected by every educated
person in his role as parent, teacher, or employer, quite as
if the older practice of marking up texts and marking down
slovenly writing had had no purpose but to annoy.

The truth is that unless some effort is made to arrest the
black rot that we try to disguise by calling it "the problem
of communication," it will presently bring us to the last stage
of mutual incomprehension—that in which we think we understand one another when we do not even understand ourselves.

The language is unquestionably in a precarious state. You
have only to look in these pages and see the errors that professional writers commit; you have only to read your favorite
authors and the letters of your friends, to listen to public
speakers or to your own voice. Something has happened since
the days when only the half-literate social climbers bought a
dictionary as they now buy a book of etiquette: educated
people knew how to speak and write, and their usage was or
became the language. Today, it is the educated who lead the

way in destruction, it is they who in the name of freedom deny any social obligation to use decently that valuable common property, the mother tongue. No circle or profession is privileged: our lax democratic manners tolerate everything, while literature of every grade uses by preference the language of the gutter, and belles-lettres and scholarship multiply pseudo-jargons as if to run away from responsible assertion.

Perhaps our last bulwark against barbarism is the press, including broadcast journalism and advertising. I have only to name this bulwark to remind the reader that it is paper thin. Yet in journalism alone is some perception left of a common audience, of a public that must be pleased, of people who, whatever they may feel as specialists or readers of fiction and poetry, will be neither flattered nor relieved, but irritated, to find in their daily paper words and sentences they cannot understand.

Lucidity, to be sure, is only one part of good writing, and we discover in Mr. Bernstein's pages at what cost clarity plus a modicum of literacy is achieved. A managing editor is perhaps the last man in western civilization to speak as one having authority over another man's prose. The fact would be awe-inspiring if one did not notice at once how often this potentate tries to humor and cajole while advising and rebuking. His irony and wit, his allusive colloquialism, turn instruction into entertainment, and I am sure that every reviewer recommending the book will tell the public that this guide, with its catalogue of error, is most amusing.

Of course it is amusing! Comedy is the castigation of human failings, and Mr. Bernstein is a comic writer with more material than he can handle. An ordinary issue of the Times is as full of words as a longish novel—about 150,000 words—and the newspaper is usually written in greater haste and under worse pressure. Few books are printed these days without errors that a professional writer should be incapable of making and that a copy editor should catch and eliminate. No wonder, then, that in half a dozen years Mr. Bernstein has been able to collect from the pages of the Times enough examples of modern illiteracy to fill a book.

The sadness of the comedy is that these blunders and barbarisms come from a newspaper dedicated to all the virtues of the mind and which both reflects and influences the speech of its readers. Fortunately, Mr. Bernstein is not willing to accept excuses, whether the journalist's haste or the reader's indifference. He will not and he ought not to be content with his efforts until even the early edition of the Times is literate, as indeed a newspaper should be which can choose its writers from the most experienced talents.

The device Mr. Bernstein uses to insinuate good usage into the columns of the Times and applaud it when found is a bulletin titled *Winners & Sinners*, issued every second or third week, and which comments under several rubrics, upon faults discovered in current issues. In doing this he continues playing his old part of censor of college prose. But nowadays he does not merely mark and circle errors—he philosophizes, or at least explains himself. And it is this reasoning upon words and their uses that gives his book general interest and utility.

At one point in his varied disquisition, Mr. Bernstein throws off a phrase which sums up his teaching: "care and clear thinking." This could serve as the motto of the would-be writer, and indeed of anyone who deals responsibly with words. There is nothing to add by way of general advice. Yet how difficult it is to take care, how arduous a task is clear thinking! No one can notice every part, every relation, in a piece of prose, or analyze his own meaning so completely that it dislodges all but the perfect words in the perfect order. But that is the very reason why habits of exact expression are indispensable: the words themselves rightly used take care of hundreds of relations, they avert as many ambiguities, they direct the mind to still subtler pitfalls or distinctions. In short, precision in writing not only exhibits thought when fully fashioned, but also leads to the discovery of what that thought is.

The daily writer, in business, school, or trade, needs this discipline as much as the journalist or other professional man, and he can begin to acquire it from this book, provided he believes what he reads and acts upon it. Mere assent is not enough. You may come to see the absurdity of saying: "The reason is because . . . ," but recognition will do you no good unless you ostracize that expression from your vocabulary —in speech, in letter writing, and elsewhere: you must end by never thinking it. And so with the rest of the errors and illiteracies dissected in these pages. Mr. Bernstein is a superb mentor who gives not merely rules but principles of self-correction. His mind is joyfully aware of its own workings, and cannot help inducing the same energy and pleasure in the reader who wants to know on what the art of writing depends. It depends on the very skill with which the author turned a series of comments into a genuine book, full of his own wit, charm, and fine intelligence.

This commendation does not mean that I agree with every detail, or even with every tendency, in Mr. Bernstein's uncommon but very practical manual. I dissent from some of his allowances and some of his strictures; for example, he seems to me pedantic in his objection to Frankenstein, misleading in his tagging of certain expressions as clichés to avoid, and insufficient or arbitrary in his discussion of the fused participle and the handling of "and which." Again, in his discursive sections I deplore his concessions to prevailing ideas of color and liveliness in news stories and headlines. But I recognize that he is talking primarily to writers whose professional neurosis is to despair of being attended to and in whom, therefore, a kind of solemn ritual clowning is inevitable.

Mr. Bernstein's tolerance for this does not in any way diminish the solid and systematic wisdom he imparts so abundantly on every page. In the present domestic crisis, when M. Jourdain is dying of dropsy and Mrs. Malaprop has supplanted the rightful heirs, there cannot be too many voices raised in defense of good usage, right idiom, and unmistakable meaning. Differences of opinion on particular points may sharpen debate: they do not divide counsels. Indeed, they add to the pleasure which is the reward of those for whom words share some of the attributes of living beings: beauty and ugliness, character, historical and personal associations, manifest destinies, and—above all—constitutional rights.

# Introduction

What appears between these covers was originally intended to be read by only the 600-odd writers and editors of The New York Times. But it came to the notice of a steadily widening circle of interested persons outside the staff, and at last a book publisher twisted the author's arm.

The material is derived entirely from *Winners & Sinners*, "a bulletin of second-guessing issued occasionally from the southeast corner of The New York Times News Room." "Occasionally" means whenever the manila envelope into which the editor stuffs clippings is overcrowded, and his schedule of editorial and social duties is not. This conjunction of events occurs every two or three weeks.

As a combination of gadfly and know-it-all (in the most objectionable meaning of the term), the author set forth this prospectus in the autumn of 1951:

"The purpose of *Winners & Sinners* is simply stated: To make The Times better—better written, better edited, more interesting, easier to understand. To do this W & S will point to things done well and to things done ill. It is to be expected that the bad things will outnumber the good ones, because to do things properly is normal and even a slight deviation to the bad side is noticeable, whereas a deviation to the good side has to be quite pronounced before it appears to be anything more than normal. We shall not name the doers of the evil deeds because we realize most such things could happen to anyone. But we shall name those responsible for the good ones and we hope they could happen to you."

Sure enough, over the years the sinners have greatly outnumbered the winners, and so they do in this book. This should not create the impression that The Times errs inordinately. It means rather, among other things, that The Times is consciously looking for errors and striving to prevent them. Actually, the number of errors in an average issue is surprisingly small.

It is not only errors, however, that are the concern of W & S. Ways of improving the presentation of news—of making reading swifter, comprehension easier—equally engage its attention. Metropolitan newspapers, and particularly The Times, tend to be voluminous. The news, focusing increasingly on the intricacies of physical science, of economics, of sociology, of psychiatry, becomes increasingly difficult to grasp. And, paradoxically, although readers enjoy more leisure time than they ever did, they do not devote more time to newspaper reading. Other activities—television viewing, for example—have taken up the slack. Therefore it becomes ever more necessary to make newspaper reading quicker, easier and more attractive.

Thirty years ago the formula for the lead, or introduction, of the news story was the five W's—who, what, where, when and why or how. This frequently produced leads running up to a hundred words and forming an indigestible lump that required rechewing before it could be assimilated. Nowadays, although the five W's must still appear near the top of the news story, we favor a concentrated broth that can be easily swallowed, and we do not boggle at introducing a dash of seasoning.

Thirty years ago it was not uncommon for our editors to refuse to print an explanation of, say, a bill in Congress on the ground that "we printed that only six months ago," as if readers maintained a running index of newspaper articles and kept referring to it day by day. Or editors would not define an obscure term because it could be found in the dictionary, as if every commuter train had a Webster's Unabridged installed right opposite the men's room. Or they would not take the space to explain the Malthusian law since "any high school senior knows that." Which was true enough, except that a goodly segment of their readers had not been high school seniors for ten or fifty years, and another segment had not yet reached that station.

Today we think it well to make each issue as nearly self-sufficing as is reasonable, so that the reader does not feel the need for a research staff to help him understand the day's news. Perhaps the best slogan a newspaper could post in its city room would be this: "Keep two readers always in mind: the high school sophomore and the man who has been marooned on a desert island for three months." Both of them, for different reasons, have to be told what it is all about.

Understandable presentation of the news requires more, however, than simplifying, defining and providing background. It also involves language that communicates clearly, and this is a matter of grammar and usage. Here we find ourselves on a well-trampled battleground. On one side are the stiff-necked grammarians, brandishing rigid rules, which they wield whether or not the rules are supported by history, idiom or certificates of convenience and necessity. On the other side are the soothing champions of the masses, with their battle cry, "Whatever the people say is okay by me; the people speak real good."

This wordmonger refuses to join either camp; he takes up his position a trifle to the right of center. For the serious newspaper, too, that is probably the desirable position. To enlist with the too-orthodox would be to tend toward prissiness and to risk losing touch with the popular tongue. To enlist with the too-liberal would be to invite the horrors of anarchy and to risk losing touch with the language of the literate.

For downright practical reasons, if none other, the too-liberal position is a poor one in the newspaper city room. How Scoop Smith writes on his own time when he is banging out the Novel That Will Live is his own affair. He can scrape his prose off a curbstone or wipe it off a television screen if he likes. But when he is writing for the newspaper he must fit himself into the newspaper's framework. For he is writing not primarily as Smith—actually, most of what he writes will not be graced with his name—but as a member of the staff of the *Hohunkus Harbinger*. His prose must be edited, as is everything that appears in the columns of the *Harbinger*. Suppose he fancies the construction "between you and I" and defends it on the ground that Shakespeare used it, as indeed he did in "The Merchant of Venice." Should the copy editor pass it? Can he, with a deadline crowding in upon him, retire to an alcove and pore over textbooks to ascertain whether Shakespeare truly used such a construction, and what the grammarians from Ben Jonson to Franklin P. Adams think about it? Obviously not. When dozens of editors and hundreds of reporters are preparing prose for a daily paper they must have standards to follow. The standards may, and should, be so flexible that no writer need ever completely sacrifice individuality of style or freshness of approach. But the individuality and the freshness must be exercised in accordance with certain restrictions that are well understood by the staff and can be readily and surely applied.

Whence come these restrictions, these standards? Not entirely from the Tories, those ultra-purists exemplified by Miss Thistlebottom, a fictitious and yet all-too-real schoolmarm who gets a going-over once or twice in the pages that follow. They are the ones who decree that you must never, never end a sentence with a preposition; that you must never, never split an infinitive (and then, misinterpreting their own dictum, go on to say that you must never allow an adverb to divide an auxiliary from its main verb, though the reverse is more often the truth); that you must never, never use "none" as a plural; that you must never, never fuse a participle (presumably they would have you write, "The eggs were shipped from the farm without one's being broken"); and that "between" must never, never be used when more than two elements are involved. Surely, no writer can be blamed for refusing to slip into such a strait jacket.

Nor do the standards come entirely from the radicals, who take the position that if the people say it, it is correct. For the long pull—say a century or so—this contention may be true. But it is not of much practical use for now, today. For one thing, who are the "people"? Does a majority of 51 per cent win? And does it still win if most educated people—including writers, who claim language as one of their tools—find themselves in the 49 per cent minority? And, anyhow, is good usage a matter of taking a poll?

For another thing, what do the radicals mean when they argue that the people "say" it? Usually they are talking about spoken language. Although this is something similar to written language, it is yet distinct from written language. Many of our experts on usage set out by paying lip service to the distinction, and then end by conveniently forgetting it. But the distinction cannot be forgotten. This scrivener never matriculated in the Write-Like-You-Talk School, and does not believe in it. Writing is and must be a more precise form of expression than extemporaneous speaking. In speaking, most persons cannot frame their thoughts, let alone their sentences, as carefully as in the more deliberate process of writing. The speaker may be forgiven if he becomes entangled in a hopeless sentence structure, but not so the writer. The speaker who observes that a listener is beginning to ruffle his brow in puzzlement can make hasty repairs with, "What I mean is . . ." But the writer has no such opportunity; either his written words are clear or they are not. The speaker can use intonation, facial expression and gesture to help where his language is lame, but written words lie quietly on the page.

Here is found the key to the desirable restrictions. If writing must be a precise form of communication, it should be treated like a precision instrument: It should be sharpened and it should not be used carelessly. A book of instructions for use of this device would suggest to the writer that he choose the exact word, the one that flies straight to the target, rather than the diffuse word that hits other things besides the target; that he place each word where it will do its job best; that he construct his sentences so that they are tidy and logical; that in general he observe the grammatical practices that over the long years have bestowed continuity and orderliness upon the language.

To be sure, the English language is a changing and growing thing. All its users have, of course, a perceptible or imperceptible effect upon it. But in changing and growing it needs no contrived help from chitchat columnists or advertising writers or comic-strip artists or television speakers. It will evolve nicely by itself. If anything, it requires protection from influences that try to push it too fast. There is need, not for those who would halt its progress altogether, but for those who can keep a gentle foot on the brake and a guiding hand on the steering wheel. Of such contemporary influences not too many come to mind, but in the forefront surely would be the school, and right beside it, one likes to think, would be the serious press.

T.M.B.

*New York, July, 1958*

# Words That Need Watching

The compilation that follows is a kind of heterogeneous check list of word uses that are undesirable in writing—particularly in newspaper writing. They range from outright errors to merely weary and wasteful word combinations.

Underlying the list is the assumption that the desired level of usage is what one terminology describes as standard English and another describes as a straddling of the border between formal and informal English. This criterion eliminates most slang terms and a good many colloquialisms, except when they are deliberately used to impart a particular flavor to a feature story or to express an idea for which no other terms are available. Thus, when a word is dismissed in the following vocabulary as a colloquialism, this means not that it is criminal but rather that it is socially undesirable in the serious-newspaper community.

No comment is necessary concerning barbarisms, improprieties and the like, but perhaps a word should be said here about wasteful locutions (and a few more are said in the chapter headed "Helpful Hints for Hatchet Men"). Some word groupings are as usual and inconspicuous as the buttons on the sleeves of a jacket, and just as unnecessary. "In order to," "for the purpose of," "at the present time"— they slip by because of their inconspicuousness. In any kind of writing they dilute the mixture. But in newspaper writing they have the additional fault of wasting precious space. Many will be found in the following list, although they are not specifically labeled. In *Winners & Sinners* locutions of this kind often appear under the heading, "Forget-'em Words," which also applies to many other individual words for which most writers should have little or no use. These words, too, appear in the list.

The quoted examples in this vocabulary are, of course, from The New York Times.

**ABOUT.** (1) If a figure is explicitly stated to be an estimate, or is implicitly presented as an approximation in the form of a round number, the word "about" is redundant. Yet it appears often. For example: "In Louisville his audience was estimated at about 4,500." "Wilmington turned out about 1,500 to 2,500 listeners." Delete "about" in both sentences.

(2) "The slashing blades wounded Mr. Henkins about the face, head, throat and left ear." Here "about" is police-blotter lingo. What's wrong with "on"? Or with saying, "The slashing blades wounded Mr. Henkins' face, head, throat and left ear"?

**ACCUSED.** *See* "alleged, accused, suspected."

**ADMITS.** This headline appeared over a story reporting that Henry Wallace had confirmed Mrs. Lattimore's testimony that she had written a pamphlet issued under his name: "Wallace Admits Mrs. Lattimore Wrote Asia Pamphlet." If you go by the dictionary, the word "admits" is defensible; however, to many readers it connotes a conceding only after prodding. So, handle with care.

**ADVANCE PLANNING.** "With a Little Advance Planning, Culinary Chores for Easter Can Be Simplified." Planning is the laying out of a future course; "advance" is therefore superfluous.

**AGGRAVATES.** " 'The Smuggler,' with Gilbert Roland in the role of a fisherman who aggravates a dictator . . ." "Autos crept at an aggravatingly slow pace." "Aggravate" means "to increase or make worse"; it should not be used to mean "irritate" or "exasperate."

**AHOLD.** "Somehow, apparently, Mr. Russell's assistants thought, the Seaboard Councils got ahold of about 3,000 of the sealed envelopes . . ." "Ahold" is dialectal.

**AIR.** "The Columbia Broadcasting System awarded the grant and will air Mr. Gibson's script on its 'Rogers' show Wednesday evening." Jargon. "Air" in the sense of "broadcast" is a colloquialism; it is also an unnecessary word.

**ALL-AROUND.** "The league's best all-around second baseman more often than not during the last decade, he . . ." Make it "all-round." When you examine the words you find that "around" refers to positions with respect to a center, whereas "round" has the meaning of full or complete, which is the meaning that is wanted in "all-round athlete."

**ALLEGED, ACCUSED, SUSPECTED.** How to designate persons who have tangled with the law involves not only the question of prejudgment, which is at best unfair and at worst libelous, but also the question of proper use of words. To be concrete, how about such phrases—particularly in headlines—as "accused spy," "suspected intruder," "alleged thief"? All are improper, if for differing reasons. A wrecked plane is an actual plane that has been wrecked; a trained soldier is an actual soldier who has been trained. But when you say "accused spy" you don't mean an actual spy who has been accused; you mean a person who has been accused as a spy. And in some analogous cases the meaning is not even that: If your headline says, "Lawyer Defends Accused Banker," you don't mean a person accused of being a banker. These uses are, therefore, not only inaccurate but possibly ambiguous. "Alleged thief" is not proper for another reason: you don't allege a person, but rather a crime or a condition. Nevertheless, the necessities of head writing and long usage have established "alleged" in a category similar to "supposed" or "presumed." So while the use of "alleged" may be sanctioned, the use of the ambiguous "accused" and "suspected" is best avoided.

**ALL RIGHT.** *See* "one word, two words."

**ALL TOGETHER, ALTOGETHER.** "Kazanski batted in five runs all together . . ." It's possible to bat in five runs altogether, but it's not possible to bat in five runs all together.

**ALLUSION.** The words "allusion" and "reference" are often confused. An allusion is an oblique, indirect mention, which does not name the thing specifically but leaves the task of identification to the reader or hearer. A reference is a direct naming or description of the thing. Hence, "allusion" is misused in this sentence: "Russia eventually may be willing to overlook the destruction of her legation (an allusion to the recent bombing of the Soviet legation in Israel) . . ." Nothing covert there; it's a reference, not an allusion.

**ANACHRONISM.** "For the humanitarian who . . . went to Poland for the American Relief Commission of the Rockefeller Institute . . . it is almost an anachronism that he is one of the most decorated men in the country for his combat service." An anachronism (root: *chronos*—time) is an error involving a misplacement of time, such as a movie scene showing John Hancock signing the Declaration of Independence with a Paper-Mate pen. What is meant here is a paradox or an anomaly.

**AND/OR.** "The law allows up to $25 fine and/or thirty days in jail." Leave that monstrosity to the lawyers. Say simply, "$25 fine or thirty days in jail or both."

**ANIMAL.** *See* "it."

**ANOTHER.** "The port alone directly employed 250,000, with another 150,000 indirectly employed." "New York's public schools will greet their 890,700 young boys and girls officially today . . . another 331,000 will attend the parochial schools." "Another" means "one more of the same kind." In these two examples, "another" would be correct only if in each sentence the second figure were the same as the first figure. Why not use "more"? *See also* "other."

**ANY AND ALL.** "Democratic strategists have made determined efforts to divorce their campaign from any and all national implications." Choose either member of this cliché.

**ANY WAY.** ". . . she did not have the impression from Dr. Howard McC. Snyder . . . that he regarded the illness in anyway as serious. "Any way" should be two words except when it means "in any case."

**AROUND.** *See* "all-around" *and* "center."

**AS THE CROW FLIES.** ". . . a highway from Karachi, Pakistan, to Ankara, Turkey, by way of Iran and Iraq, which is a distance of 2,300 miles as the crow flies." *Winners & Sinners* knows very little about crows, except how they taste, but does know that this once shiny figure of speech antedates aviation days and is mighty tarnished now. Why not "by air"?

**AS THE RESULT OF.** This is a phrase that usually is inaccurate. For example: "Two women died and five firemen were hurt yesterday morning as the result of a four-alarm fire." Obviously, in a four-alarm fire there was more than one result. What was meant was "*a* result of."

**AS WELL AS.** *See* "both."

**ASK.** *See* "request."

**ASSASSIN.** "The police said that when the shooting took place at 8:30 P.M., the intersection was crowded, and they had no reason to believe the would-be assassin was firing at Murphy." An assassin is a person who either kills or tries to kill treacherously. Thus, for all practical purposes there is no such thing as a "would-be assassin."

**ATTACKED.** "An autopsy showed the girl had been 'strangled manually,' but had not been attacked." This is a euphemistic absurdity. If there is some mid-Victorian hesitation about using the word "raped," why not at least say "sexually attacked"?

**AT THE PRESENT TIME.** This phrase can always be shortened to "at present" or "now." In the following example it could be omitted altogether: "At the present time the Administration is preparing a bill that would give the Atomic Energy Commission authority to sell this property." Again: "Arthur B. Homer, president of Bethlehem Steel Corporation, said today the steel industry 'cannot afford' to cut prices at the present time." Why not use "now"— one word instead of four?

**ATTORNEY.** A lawyer writes to hand up a three-count indictment, to wit:

(1) That the word "attorney" is often used when what is meant is "lawyer." For example: "The court named Bernard Trencher, an attorney, to hear the case and report his findings." An attorney is one designated by another to transact business for him, and need not be a lawyer. A lawyer is a practitioner of law, and that is the term that usually should be used.

(2) That "jurist" is used as a synonym for "judge." For example: "At 8:20 A.M. yesterday a note was sent to Judge Mullen. The jurist said that . . ." A jurist is merely one who is versed in the law. Therefore, although a judge is, or should be, a jurist, a jurist is not necessarily a judge.

(3) That newspapers often say that defendants "plead innocent" instead of "not guilty." For example: "Dave Beck . . . pleaded innocent today to a charge of grand larceny . . ." Designating this locution as an "absurdity," the letter writer makes the point that "if a man were let aver that he is innocent, he might be required to prove it, and it is fundamental that no man is required to prove his innocence." The locution arose, of course, from a desire to avoid a possible typographical error in which the "not" might be dropped. However, let's use the proper form, "not guilty," calling the printer's attention to the "not." The risk should not be very great.

A plea of not innocent is entered on all three counts.

**AUDIENCE.** "Fire Draws Audience." Strictly speaking, an audience is a group of hearers. The word is sometimes extended to other groups, but there is no justification for extension in this situation.

**AWHILE.** *See* "one word, two words."

**BALDING.** "At the age of 47, he is small, slight and balding." There is no such word as "balding." Why not "baldish"?

**BANDIT.** "It was the largest cash robbery of a bank in many years, and possibly the largest ever carried out in the United States by a lone bandit." The word "bandit," accurate enough though it is, has a flavor of heroism about it these days. Avoid any suggestion of glorifying outlaws.

**BASTION.** "Air Troops Smash Vietminh Bastion." Literally, a bastion is a structure jutting out from a main fortification; by extension it is a fortified outpost. It is not a base fifty miles behind the lines, as was the military establishment described in this story.

**BEAR.** *See* "bull."

**BECAUSE.** *See* "reason . . . because."

**BEFORE IN THE PAST.** "As never before in the past . . ." Redundant.

**BELOW.** "He stands on the terrace of his apartment on the twenty-fourth floor and watches the crashing girders as they fall from the Manufacturers Trust Company building to the ground below." Strike out "below"; that's where the ground usually is. *See also* "toward the ground."

**BI-.** The story said the House had passed a bill providing for payment of Army and Air Force members twice a month. The head spoke of "Measure for Bimonthly Checks." "Bimonthly" means every two months. Likewise, biweekly means every two weeks, although this word can be used (but in the interest of precision shouldn't be) to mean twice a week.

**BID IN.** "The [Lincoln] letter . . . was bid in at $1,100 by the Carnegie Book Shop of New York, acting as agent for the Friends of the Detroit Public Library." The phrase "bid in" has a particular technical meaning: to top the highest bid of a bona fide customer in the interest of the owner of the item. It does not mean merely to acquire through a bid.

**BISECT.** ". . . the modernization of the four roads bisecting the big park." "Bisect" means "cut in two," which is not what four roads do to the park. Make it "crossing."

**BLAME.** "Blame on" is a colloquialism, as in this head, "Lukewarm Church Blamed on Women," and in this line, ". . . they blame this . . . on the hazards of events overseas." Find substitutes—forms of "attribute to" or "lay to"; or change the construction—"blame for" or "put the blame on."

**BOAT.** Brooks Atkinson comes tacking down wind, footlights awash, to make the point that a "boat" is a small open vessel, usually propelled by oars, and that larger or seagoing craft are "ships" or "vessels." "I know professional seamen are very rigid about these terms," says Cap'n A'kinson, "and that applies to Conrad, from whom I first learned of these distinctions." In a story about the icebreaker Westwind it was said that she was going to "clear the way for captive boats." "Vessels" or "ships" would have been better.

**BOOST.** In its nontechnical senses, "boost" should be forgotten, along with "hike." "The United Steelworkers executive board is giving its top officers a healthy pay boost." Pure slang. (So, by the way, is "healthy" used in this way.) "The rate hikes provided these increases . . ." A hike is a tramp and a tramp is a bum and bum is the word for hike.

**BOTH . . . AS WELL AS.** ". . . for fear such an impression might produce ill will both in the United States as well as in Formosa and Seoul . . ." Either delete "both" or change "as well as" to "and."

**BRIDEGROOM.** *See* "groom."

**BRING.** The verb "to bring" denotes movement in the direction of the writer or speaker. Therefore the head, "U.S. Questions Crew of the Ship That Brought Arms to Guatemala," would be fine for *El Tiempo* of Guatemala but is incorrect for The Times of New York. Why not "carried" or "took"?

**BRING TO A HEAD.** "The matter was brought to a head last Monday when Arthur C. Ford . . ." When you stop to think of it, this is not only a cliché but a rather repulsive one: To bring to a head means to suppurate, or cause pus to form.

**BULL.** "General Nuwar is reported to feel that he has a bull by the horns and to have had second thoughts about the 'politification' of the Army." Wrong animal and wrong end of animal. The bull figures in the phrase "to take the bull by the horns." This is rather inadequately defined in Webster's as "to grapple with a difficulty"; actually it means "to face up to a difficulty and grapple with it." What is required in the quoted sentence is "has a bear by the tail," which means it is distasteful to hang on but dangerous to let go, with the added implication that you got into that predicament yourself. A similar phrase is "riding a tiger." Incidentally, if you let go of the bear or fall off the tiger, obviously you go from the frying pan into the fire.

**BURGERMEISTER.** "He says that the burgomeister invited him over to see the famous collection." It's either "burgermeister" (German) or "burgomaster" (English).

**BURGLARY.** The story of the robbery of a Times Square monetary exchange office described the deed as a "burglary." The story disclosed, however, that "neither the store nor the safe had been opened by break-through." This statement made the term "burglary" an incorrect description because the essence of burglary is a breaking and entering with the intent to commit a felony. No breaking, no burglary.

**BUYERS.** "Two New Gift Shops Bar Women Buyers." "Buyers" used in conjunction with "shops" is ambiguous; it suggests purchasing agents. What was meant was "patrons" or "customers."

**BY.** The word "by" is short, but that fact should not tempt a headline writer into misusing it, as in this headline: "Expert Plans to Catch Cobras by Bare Hands." The word should be "with." Another example: "TB Contracted Mainly by Infected Air, Researcher Says After Hospital Survey." It should be "through" or "from."

**BY MEANS OF.** "The spindle is rotated by means of a foot pedal." Generally, "by" will serve nicely for "by means of." (Incidentally, take that pleonastic foot off the pedal.)

**CABLEGRAM.** " 'For God's sake, keep Senator Nixon on the ticket,' said a cablegram signed by the master and officers of the American ship Sea Gallant off the Japanese coast." A cablegram is a message that travels by cable. Very unlikely that the Sea Gallant dragged a line all the way across the Pacific.

**CANNOT.** *See* "one word, two words."

**CASKET.** *See* "euphemisms."

**CELEBRANTS.** "Thousands of New Year's Eve Celebrants See Wild Drama of Speed, Gunfire, Capture." "Chief Police Inspector Stephen P. Kennedy . . . put the number of celebrants at 500,000." A celebrant is a person who presides over a religious rite. A person who makes whoopee, as they used to say, is a celebrator.

**CENTER.** "The strikers are at odds over their actual grievances, but these appeared to center around the contract's wage, guaranteed hours of work and vacation provisions." The verb "center" means "to be collected or gathered to a point." Therefore, "center on" or "center in," but not "center around." If you like the word "around," use "revolve," "cluster" or something of that sort to precede it.

**CHAIN REACTION.** "Jackie Gleason's unrehearsed fall set off a chain reaction of thousands of local and long distance telephone calls . . ." Chain reaction does not mean a great quantity; it means a process in which a cause produces an effect that in turn becomes a cause and so on.

**CHAIR.** "Bokhari of Pakistan Chairs U.N. Council." It's probably only a step from this kind of usage to saying that Leonard Bernstein podiums the Philharmonic orchestra, that Dr. Fosdick pulpits the congregation or, when Mr. Lodge takes the floor in the U.N., that Lodge floors the Assembly. Nouns do become verbs, but not overnight; they usually have to pass tests of necessity and serviceability, and slowly win acceptability.

**CHECK.** The phrase "check into" is one of those unnecessary slang phrases that grow like weeds in the garden of English. Take this example: "Sgt. 1/C Phil M. Bustos is kept busy checking into developments." Or this one: "He said he also had asked Mr. Carr to check into such rumors." In neither sentence is any preposition necessary. But if a writer feels he simply must have one, why not turn to "on," which has been a fairly respectable teammate for "check" for a long time?

**CHORD.** ". . . it requires only a pair of eyes to gaze at the sky, and vocal chords with which to utter a forecast." Vocal chords are possible, but they could not be produced with only a single pair of eyes present. Knock the "h" out of those chords.

**CITIZEN.** "Mr. Epstein became a British citizen in 1906." The British are "subjects," not "citizens."

**CLAIM.** ". . . Mr. Casper claimed that a college degree was a business necessity." The word "claim" should not be used as a synonym for "say," "assert" or "declare" except when there is at issue an assertion of a right, a title or the like.

**CLERGY.** *See* "rector" *and* "reverend."

**CLIENT.** ". . . during the trial of Dr. John Bodkin Adams for the murder of an aged client." Physicians have patients, not clients.

**COHORT.** "But before the students sheepishly returned to their dormitories, they had brought about the arrest of two of their cohorts . . ." A cohort is a band or company, not an individual.

**COINED TITLES.** "Governor" is a fine, legitimate title. "Convicted bookie" prefixed to Harry Gross is a coinage that is as phony as a plugged nickel. "Professor" is a valid title. "Communist leader" placed before Palmiro Togliatti is not. There is no excuse for arbitrarily fashioning titles out of mere descriptive phrases. Make it either "Harry Gross, convicted bookie" or "the convicted bookie, Harry Gross." Incidentally, if a legitimate title is a mouthful of four words or more—*e.g.*, "Minister of Posts and Communications"— it will make for smoother reading to place the title after the name rather than before it.

**COKE.** "Cleansing with soap and water is sufficient for spilled coke and soda pop." Coke is not only a fuel and a short name for cocaine, but also—as the Coca-Cola people keep reminding us at the drop of a Pepsi-Cola bottle—a registered nickname for Coca-Cola. As such it should be capitalized. Better yet, don't use it. *See also* "Teleprompter" *and* "Drunkometer."

**COLLISION.** (1) "Mr. Crotty was changing a flat tire when a second car smashed into his automobile . . . The collision ruptured the gasoline tank." When two things collide they strike or dash against each other, *i.e.*, both are in motion. No collision here; it was the "crash" or the "impact."

(2) "Two light planes were in collision over a suburban area of Lincoln today." The clumsy phrase "were in collision" in place of the simple "collided" apparently originated in the distant past in a half-understood caution. This caution presumably was that if you were to say that one plane or car "collided with" another you might be seeming to place the blame and thereby inviting a libel suit. From that point some editors jumped to the conclusion that "collided" was a dirty word, not to be used in any circumstances. A safe position but a ridiculous one.

**COMBINE.** ". . . President Eisenhower's order to negotiate a contract with a private power combine to supply power to the Tennessee Valley Authority." The noun "combine" not only is colloquial (except when it means a piece of farm machinery), but also most often carries with it the suggestion of something illegal or fraudulent.

**COMPANY.** *See* "firm."

**COMPARE.** "The purpose of the Executive Board can be compared with the function of the United States Bureau of the Budget . . ." When you liken one thing to another, make it "compared to"; when you examine two things to determine their differences and their likenesses, make it "compared with."

COMPLECTED. ". . . Señor Covarrubias was a plump, dark-complected man." "Complected" is branded in the dictionary as dialectal. Most likely it is a back formation, that is, a nonexistent word coined from an actual word that is erroneously supposed to be derived from it. If "connection" is derived from "connect," and "inflection" is derived from "inflect"—so the reasoning probably went—"complexion" must be derived from "complect." However, the root of "complexion" is the same as the root of "complex." "A dark-complexioned man" is better.

COMPRISE. "He also gave the names of the four books that comprised the body of Roman civil law." "Comprise" has the meaning of "contain, embrace, include, comprehend." Thus, the whole comprises the parts, but not vice versa. Also to be avoided is "comprised of." What is wanted in the example cited is "compose," "constitute" or "make up." *See also* "include."

CONCERN. "Mr. Duff is a member of a law concern in Washington, D.C." A concern is a business or manufacturing organization, not a professional one. Make it law firm or law office. *See also* "firm."

CONSPICUOUS BY THEIR ABSENCE. "Delicacies associated with the holidays were expected to be conspicuous by their absence in thousands of homes." This weary phrase is conspicuous by its presence.

CONSULS GENERAL. "Consul Generals Elect." It's consuls general.

CONTEMPORARY. *See* "modernistic."

CONTINUALLY. "When McSorley's finally closes its swinging doors, the oldest place in town that has reportedly been continually in the business will be Pete's Tavern . . ." The word here should be "continuously." "Continual" means over and over again, "continuous" means unbroken. Here's a mnemonic aid, compliments of *Winners & Sinners:* "Continuous" ends in *o u s,* which stands for *one uninterrupted sequence.*

**CONTRACTUAL.** "Mr. Gray said that Servel, in turn, paid Whirlpool $1,600,000 to assume its contractural obligations . . ." The word is "contractual."

**CORPORATION.** *See* "firm."

**COUNTRY.** *See* "Pronouns for countries," page 122.

**COURSE OF.** "The course of," when used to mean "during," can always be omitted. Here the words threw a paragraph into an extra line of precious space: "Both opinions were given in the course of a news conference about political developments relating to the state campaign next fall." "In," "at" or "during" would have sufficed.

**CRESCENDO.** "Soviet 'Hate America' propaganda has reached a new crescendo of violence and volume . . ." A crescendo is a rising or an increasing, not a loud point. "Peak" would have been better.

**CUSTOMERS.** *See* "buyers."

**DENTIFRICE.** "Dentists have discovered a 'new' dentrifice that cuts the rate of tooth decay among adults." The word is "dentifrice," the final syllable coming from the same root as "friction."

**DEPRECATORY.** "Zsa Zsa Gabor said, 'I'm short of the necessary adjectives.' Coward embraced her and made deprecatory noises." The word intended here is "depreciatory." A "deprecatory" noise would be a disapproving one. A "depreciatory" noise would be a belittling, disparaging one.

**DESERT.** *See* "Sahara Desert."

**DIAGNOSE.** "He was diagnosed as suffering from high blood pressure." You diagnose the condition, not the patient.

**DIFFERENT.** "Describing the bribery plot, the prosecutor said that two different men had approached Mr. Jones in his room at the Plymouth Hotel . . ." Naturally the two men were "different"; what was meant here, apparently, was that two men approached Jones on different occasions.

**DIG.** "Coast Oil Digging Urged to Cut Debt." Oil wells are usually drilled rather than dug.

**DILEMMA.** "The question is basically the common suburban dilemma: Should construction of apartments be allowed in former one-family areas?" A dilemma is a situation entailing a choice between two distasteful alternatives. There was no suggestion here of such alternatives. Use "problem" or "predicament."

**DIMENSIONS.** *See* "proportions."

**DIS-.** "Therefore Dulles almost became a bore upon the topic from the instant he disemplaned." "Emplane" means to go aboard a plane; "disemplane" would therefore mean to un-go aboard a plane. With a simple word like "deplane" available, why choose the awkward, complicated "disemplane"? The same suggestion could well be applied to "debark" rather than "disembark" and to "disfranchise" rather than "disenfranchise."

**DISCOVER.** "The material [Ameripol SN synthetic rubber] was discovered in 1954 by Goodrich-Gulf scientists." A thing that is discovered was already in existence but unknown. A synthetic, therefore, is not discovered but invented or developed.

**DISINTERESTED.** "They [alley cats at a cat show] appeared to be totally disinterested in social climbing." "Disinterested" means neutral, having no selfish interest. Here the word should be "uninterested."

**DISTINCT.** *See* "separate."

**DOMINICAN REPUBLIC.** Unfortunately, there is no short way of referring to the Dominican Republic for headline purposes. The following head is therefore incorrect: "Dominica Retorts to Labor Charges." Dominica is a small island in the Windward group, quite unconnected with the Dominican Republic.

**DONE.** "Ecuador Rail Line Done." "Done" in the sense of completed or finished is colloquial.

**DOWN.** *See* "up."

**DRUGS.** A story about allegations of marijuana sales in schools carried the head, "Jansen to Seek Inquiry on Drugs." A drug is anything used as a medicine. Most narcotics are drugs, but all drugs are by no means narcotics. The pharmacists object, with some justice, to this imprecise usage.

**DRUNK.** "The actor was convicted today of drunk driving." The adjective "drunk" is used predicatively, as in "the driver was drunk," but almost never attributively, that is, preceding the noun it modifies. Make it "drunken driving."

**DRUNKOMETER.** The Drunkometer should be capitalized. It's a commercial gadget and in competition with the Alcometer and the Intoximeter.

**-EE.** The suffix "ee" is properly applied to a noun in a passive sense to indicate the person or thing to which something is done. In recent years, however, there has arisen a tendency to use the suffix indiscriminately, and to use it even when there is already a perfectly good word to express the desired thought. "Trainees" is fine; they are persons to whom something is being done—they are being trained. "Refugees" seems to be an ancient enough malformation to be respectable; in addition, there is no other word to convey the idea. But even the excellent Webster people seem to be confused on some others. They sanction "escapee," yet label "standee" colloquial. Perhaps the best procedure is to stop coining needless words, particularly if they are malformations.

**EMOTE.** "Although Miss Booth appears to be mismated, she transcends the stereotyped situations by sensitive emoting and timing." The verb "emote," take it from the dictionary, is jocose. There is no slight suggestion of jocosity here.

**EMPHASIZE.** *See* "stress."

**ENORMITY.** "Impressed by the enormity of the job and the far-reaching scope of the military, Mr. Lovett knows . . ." "The enormity of the collection long ago discouraged the academy with its limited staff." Authorities on usage are virtually unanimous in reserving "enormity" for the idea of wickedness. "Enormousness" is the word for great size.

**ENTHUSE.** "The idea of new faces enthused Mr. Hope so much that he . . ." The verb "enthuse" is a back formation from "enthusiasm," and is classed as a colloquialism.

**EQUALLY AS.** "It is recalled that an almost parallel situation involving a man equally as determined as President Chiang . . ." Fowler* considers "equally as" to be "an illiterate tautology."

**EUPHEMISMS.** A story on the death of Vishinsky contained the word "mortician" once and the word "casket" four times. These were, of course, euphemisms for "undertaker" —itself an ancient euphemism—and for "coffin." Euphemisms are not fig leaves, intended to hide something; they are transparent veils, intended to soften grossness or starkness. When their purpose is to avoid vulgarity or arousing of disgust, they have a legitimate place in news writing. (Remember the tabloid head about the man transformed by surgery into a girl: "Doctors Say Christine Can't Date Yet"?) However, it must be recognized that from the minute the veil of a euphemism is manufactured it begins to wear thin. Consider the transition from "toilet" to "washroom" to "bathroom" to "lavatory" to "john" and so on, undoubtedly ad infinitum. The changing mores of the times make it necessary to go on producing new veils. When, however, the purpose of a euphemism is not to avoid vulgarity, but rather to skirt the fringes of emotion, it has no place in factual writing. In general, news writing hews to

---

* H. W. Fowler, *Modern English Usage* (London, Oxford University Press, 1952).

the facts and lets the emotions fall where they may. Therefore, when a man "joins the majority" or "passes away" we
say he dies, when the "mortician" arrives we call him an
undertaker and when the "casket" is displayed we designate
it a coffin.

**EX-.** At some time in the dim past some reputable editors evidently decided that the prefix "ex" must be attached only
to the principal noun of a phrase, never to its modifier.
Thus we get "Waldorf Ex-Headwaiter Admits '51 Tax
Evasion," or, still sillier, "Tax Ex-Official Held." Any day
now one may expect to read a headline about a "Bathing
Ex-Beauty"; if so, it will probably be written by a copy ex-
editor.

The reason for the decision of the old-time editors is
clear, if not cogent: If the prefix is attached to the modifier it might seem to qualify only that word rather than the
whole phrase. Fowler criticizes "the ex-Tory Solicitor-Gen-
eral" as meaning the man formerly was but no longer is a
Tory. But the trouble is not entirely the danger of mis-
understanding; it is also the illogicality of coupling the
"ex" to the part when the intention is to couple it to the
whole.

Obviously we have here a dilemma. In most writing the
dilemma can be ducked by using "former" instead of "ex,"
but not so in headlines or in quoted speech. Therefore *Winners & Sinners* wondered at one time whether a proper solution would not be the frank coinage of a word "ex" that
would require no hyphen. We then would say "Ex Tax
Official Held." Opinions were invited—and offered—from
lexicographers and other experts.

However, the world did not seem to be ripe for coinage
of the adjective "ex." At any rate, *W & S*, after teetering at
the tip of the springboard, decided to walk back to shore
despite many letters that said in effect, "G'wan, jump!" The
discussion made a ripple, however. Sufficient evidence ac-
cumulated to expose as a baseless superstition the notion
that "ex" may be hooked only to the principal noun of a
phrase. Subject to review in five years, the discussion was
thereupon closed by *W & S*.

**FACTS.** *See* "true."

**FALSELY FABRICATE.** "Mr. Abakumov was said to have falsely fabricated this case." A redundancy. Fabricate in its nontechnical sense means to invent or devise falsely.

**FARTHER.** The general preference is to restrict "farther" to ideas of physical distance and to use "further" for everything else. This, then, would be definitely improper: ". . . the Thor's production prototype was farther advanced than that of the Army." Fifty years hence copy editors probably won't have to worry about this distinction because it looks as if "farther" is going to be mowed down by the scythe of Old Further Time.

**FEWER.** *See* "less."

**FIGURATIVELY.** *See* "literally."

**FINALIZE:** "It was disclosed here today that Enrico Mattei was in Teheran two weeks ago to finalize negotiations with the Iranian Government." A supernumerary word with a gobbledygook ring. What's wrong with "complete" or "conclude"?

**FIRE.** "Thirteen were still on the U.N. payroll Dec. 17 but two were due to be fired yesterday." Colloquial.

**FIRM.** A "firm" is a partnership, which has no standing in law as an entity distinct from its members in the way that a corporation is a legal person. Thus it is improperly used in this head: "Nash, Hudson Merger Approved; Firm to Be 4th Biggest in Industry." In short, a corporation is not a firm. Also, "Judge Defers Action After Firm Bids for Cincinnati Paper." In this case it was the Portsmouth Steel Corporation. Use "corporation," "company" or "concern." *See also* "concern."

**FIXIN'S.** "A real Thanksgiving feast with turkey and all the fixin's was eaten . . ." "Tomorrow Americans will eat Thanksgiving turkey and the 'fixin's' . . ." Gee, Maw, does we-all have to eat them thar warmed-over clichés again this year?

**FLATLY.** "The United Nations General Assembly flatly rejected tonight . . ." "Communist delegates at Panmunjom flatly refused yesterday . . ." Almost always superfluous.

**FLAUNT.** ". . . Secretary Dulles . . . charged the South Korean Government with 'unilateral action' flaunting the authority of the United Nations Command . . ." "Flaunt" means to wave or to make a boastful display. "Flout," which the writer had in mind but couldn't quite reach, means to treat with contempt.

**FLOUT.** *See* "flaunt."

**FOLKS.** "Single folks topped the list, with 70.8 per cent having headaches . . ." "Folks" is colloquial. Even without the "s" it is considered archaic, or arch, or both, and therefore not suitable for general, straightforward writing.

**FORELADY.** "After receiving word from the forelady of the jury, Mrs. Rae Rattner . . ." In the first place, "forewoman" would be preferable to "forelady." But in the second place, "foreman" would be preferable to either. Our tendency is to avoid feminine forms—in writing, that is.

**FORTUITOUS.** "So Tobin wound up with the Lions, who already had an ace quarterback in Bobby Layne. Never was a more fortuitous deal made." "Fortuitous" means "happening by chance"; it does not mean fortunate.

**FOUNDER.** "Five persons were rescued from the schooner Amberjack, which foundered and apparently sank in heavy seas yesterday." You don't say a ship foundered and apparently sank; if the ship foundered it did sink because that's what to founder means—it has a built-in sink.

**FRANKENSTEIN.** "One would like to know what will happen when the politicians get through, and what would have happened had they not created a Frankenstein . . ." Frankenstein was the fictional physiology student who constructed the monster, not the monster itself. Therefore make it "Frankenstein('s) monster."

**FULSOME.** The story said that Sydney S. Baron was praised in glowing terms by Carmine De Sapio, and went on: "The publicist was also the recipient of less fulsome praise from Governor Harriman . . ." "Fulsome" does not mean full, but overfull and offensive because of insincerity.

**GAMBIT.** The word "gambit" does not denote merely an opening move or piece of strategy, as was intended in an editorial heading, "Moscow's Latest Gambit." In chess the word refers to an opening in which a piece is offered or sacrificed to obtain a strategic advantage. Derivatively it means a concession to get things started. There was no suggestion of a Moscow concession in the editorial.

**GENDARME.** Picture caption: "Paris gendarmes, grappling yesterday with . . ." Morris Gilbert, acting as *chef de protocol* to *Winners & Sinners*, observes that French cities have policemen, villages and other small communities have what we would call constables, and the rest of the countryside is policed by gendarmes, who are thus somewhat equivalent to our state police. Facetiously, Americans tend to refer to any French cop as a gendarme, but it's neither accurate nor, if truth be told, funny.

**GENDER.** "The South is beginning to experiment with a legal type of segregation, based on gender . . ." Gender pertains to grammatical distinctions, sex to physiological ones.

**GILD THE LILY.** "In fact, instead of gilding the lily . . . it lampblacks the stove." The oft-misworded literary reference is from Shakespeare's "King John" and goes as follows: "To gild refined gold, to paint the lily . . ."

Here's another confused literary reference: "He [Loesser] is not the first popular composer of our day to seek to spread himself. His grasp exceeds his reach." It's vice versa in the Browning poem "Andrea del Sarto": "Ah, but a man's reach should exceed his grasp, Or what's a heaven for?"

**GOT.** "He got into the union at the age of 15 and got married five years later." The first "got" is meaningful—it suggests more of an effort than "entered" or "joined"— but the second "got" is a gaucherie. Ambrose Bierce is not to be taken as the last word on words; still he has a point when he says in *Write It Right* that if "got married" is correct, "we should say, also, 'got dead' for died; one expression is as good as the other."

**GROOM.** "Sara Delano Roosevelt ... and Anthony di Bona-ventura ... were married yesterday afternoon in a small Italian church ... to which the groom and his family belong." Always make it "bridegroom," except for the man who makes his living caring for horses.

**HEAD.** *See* "bring to a head."

**HEAD UP.** *See* "up."

**HEALTHY.** *See* "boost."

**HITHERTO.** *Until now* is meant when the word "hitherto" is used. The following, referring to a building erected in 1862, is incorrect: "Mr. Stewart spent the hitherto unheard of sum of $2,750,000 to construct the six-story building." Make it "theretofore," or, still better, reword the sentence.

**HOPEFUL OPTIMISM.** "Peiping's confidence in closer Chinese-Japanese relations was based on more than hopeful optimism." Delete "hopeful."

**HURT.** "The department's 37,500 post offices do not hurt from want of business." This archaic-sounding use of "hurt" is described by the Oxford English Dictionary as "now only colloq."

**IF AND WHEN.** ". . . Senator McCarthy's design, which the Administration without doubt will strongly resist if and when active resistance becomes necessary." Try dropping "and when" out of this cliché, and see whether there is any difference.

**IMPLY.** *See* "infer."

**INCLUDE.** The paragraph began by saying that seven Giant players would return to New York from Pittsburgh, then continued: "The seven included Antonelli, Williams, Sal Maglie, John McCall, Grissom, Hoyt Wilhelm and Castleman." The word "include" usually suggests that the component items are not being mentioned in their entirety. If all items are being mentioned, as in the foregoing sentence, it would be better to say "were" or, if there is an irresistible urge for a fancy word, "comprised." *See also* "comprise."

**INDIVIDUAL.** "It is the impression of some individuals in the trade that earlier plans for a Weaver-Caesar operation have been virtually abandoned." "Individual" should not be used as a synonym for "person" except when the intention is to be jocular or contemptuous, or when the desire is to distinguish the one referred to from a class or a different category, as ". . . it was planning to award German corporations as well as individuals a part of the assets." *See also* "person."

**INFANTRY.** A short story about the Ninth Infantry Division carried the head, "9th Infantry Arriving." Military attachés of *Winners & Sinners* advise that in Army usage "9th Infantry" would mean 9th Infantry Regiment and nothing else. The proper way to denote an infantry division is to say "9th Division." Divisions other than infantry carry a qualifying designation, such as 2nd Armored Division, 11th Airborne Division, etc.

**INFER.** ". . . was I attempting to belittle two of the greatest American writers when I inferred that *Moby Dick* is overstuffed and that James . . . ?" To infer is to deduce; to imply (which is here the intended meaning) is to signify or to hint.

**IN ORDER.** "The United States, Britain and France have invited Yugoslavia to send a military mission to Washington in order to discuss defensive planning . . ." Delete "in order" unless you are being paid by the word.

**INTERNECINE.** A subhead concerning a pier union dispute in which there had been no killings said, "Internecine Struggle." "The Pentagon is experiencing one of the greatest internecine battles since . . ." "Internecine" comes from the

Latin root *necare* (to kill), and means deadly or character-ized by slaughter. It should not be confused with "intra-mural" or "intertribal."

**INTRIGUE.** "He has always been intrigued by big problems." Dictionary or no, this is a use that is best avoided on at least two grounds. First, it is an erroneous borrowing from French, in which the word means "puzzle"; second, "in-trigue" has become a kind of fuzzy, all-purpose word to ex-press meanings for which there are already perfectly good, precise words like "mystify," "enchant," "interest," "pique" and "excite."

**IT AND SHE.** (1) Is an animal a "he," a "she" or an "it"? Usage on The Times is to employ the personal pronoun if the animal has a name; otherwise to use "it." We don't al-ways call a spayed a spayed.

(2) "The German U-505 as she was carried . . . early yesterday to Chicago's Museum of Science and Industry, where it will be set up as a memorial." Defeated, disarmed and desexed. Make it "where she will be set up."

*See also* "Pronouns for countries," Chapter 3, "Syntax Sinners."

**JUDGE.** "The appointment of City Court Judge A. David Benjamin as . . ." It should be "Justice." Here's a mnemonic aid based on information supplied by Joseph C. Ingraham (and he'd better be right):

> In U.S. courts the *"judge"* holds sway,
> But at the top there's *"justice"*
> In each of nine Supreme Court seats.
> Don't wonder why—there just is.
>
> In State it's *"justice"* all the way,
> But note these four exceptions:
> Appeals and Claims and County courts
> And Court of General Sepsions.*

**JOINED TOGETHER.** "Two desolate isles off Staten Island are to be joined together . . ." Delete "together."

---

* Poetic License A2196.

**JURIST.** *See* "attorney."

**JUSTICE.** "Chief Justices of the Supreme Court of the United States are rarer in our history than Presidents." Not only rare, but nonexistent. The correct title of the presiding officer of the Supreme Court is "Chief Justice of the United States"; his colleagues are "Associate Justices of the Supreme Court of the United States." *See also* "judge."

**KIDNAP.** "Two Seized Here in Boston Kidnap." The noun is "kidnapping."

**KILOWATT.** "The accord also would allot to the Niagara Mohawk Power Corporation 445,000 kilowatt hours of power lost to that company when its Schoellkopf plant was two-thirds destroyed . . ." The measure of productive capacity, which is what is wanted here, is the kilowatt. The kilowatt hour, which is the amount of energy transferred or expended in one hour by one kilowatt of power, is used to measure production or consumption. The difference is akin to that between the capacity of a bucket and the amount of water that can be moved in it in a given period.

**KIN.** "Gouger's Kin Offers 'Amends' to Charity." Kin means relatives collectively, not—as was the fact in this story—an individual. When used correctly, "kin" is always plural.

**KIND OF.** "Kind of" or "sort of" implies a subdivision of a broad category. You don't have a subdivision of a particular thing. Therefore you don't write "kind of an apple" (a single piece of fruit), but you do write "kind of apple" (generic term). Likewise you don't—or rather shouldn't—write: "Paula was a little uncertain about what sort of a place the White House was." Paula shouldn't be sounding her "a."

**KNOT.** "The Wasp . . . is limping home at eight knots an hour." Knot is a unit of speed: a nautical mile an hour. Therefore never use "an hour" after "knot." By the way, don't disabled ships ever do anything but limp?

**LADY.** The social distinction between "lady" and "woman" has no place in the columns of a newspaper. "Lady" may be admissible as a humorous gimmick occasionally, but normally it has no more justification in a news story than the word "gentleman" in place of "man." Even the social distinction seems to be disappearing, if, indeed, it is not being reversed. A recent ad in the classified columns of The Times called for a "young lady to assist in high-class men's shop." And Porter G. Perrin's *Writer's Guide and Index to English*\* cites the woman looking for work who asked, "Are you the woman who wanted a lady to wash for her?" The word "lady" appeared twice in a story about a grandmotherly type who robbed a Los Angeles bank, and once in the otherwise fine head on the story: " 'Grandma' Strikes Again. Gray-Haired Lady Robs Third Coast Bank and Escapes." With the character already typed by the word "grandma," the word "lady" was unnecessary. Incidentally, after having said the woman was about 50 years old, the story referred to her as "the nice *old* lady." Lord only knows how many readers we lost then and there.

**LAST.** "The shooting was the last in a series of outbreaks that has stirred civic action to cut juvenile crime." "Last" has the connotation of final. Make it "latest."

**LATE.** ". . . Mrs. Franklin D. Roosevelt, widow of the late President." A redundant form. Say "widow of the President."

**LATTER.** "These issues are the Communist demand for inclusion of the Soviet Union as one of the 'neutral' nations . . . the enemy refusal to accept restrictions on airfield construction . . . and . . . repatriation of war prisoners. Staff negotiations on the latter point broke up last week . . ." "Latter" refers to the second of two things, not the third of three. In this example, why not say, "negotiations on the prisoners issue"? In any event, "latter" should almost be a forget-'em word, because it compels the reader to look back to the previous passage.

**LAW.** "Mr. Danaher has been in the law business in Washington and Hartford . . ." There's no business like law

---

\* Revised edition (Chicago, Scott, Foresman and Company, 1950).

business. The law is a profession. Would you say a doctor was in the medical business? *See also* "concern."

**LAWMEN.** "Mr. Cole said tonight he was discriminated against by North Carolina lawmen because he is white." What on earth are "lawmen" and what is the need for such a coinage?

**LAWYER.** *See* "attorney."

**LEAVE ALONE.** Obviously we cannot, even if we would, reform the English language. What we can do, however, is to make the best and most precise use of the tools at hand. One way to do this is to let each word express a meaning of its own, and not burden it with some additional meaning that is more exactly expressed by another word. For example, despite common usage (which the dictionary reflects), "leave alone" can have and should have a meaning different from "let alone." "Leave alone" can and should mean exclusively "cause to be in solitude," and "let alone" can and should mean exclusively "cause to be undisturbed." Common usage, however, has given "leave alone" both meanings, to the detriment of precise expression. Lest it be thought that the point is purely academic, observe the ambiguity of this sentence: "Something new was added when Durocher was seen to leave the third-base coaching line discreetly alone." What was meant here was not that Durocher walked away in solitude, but that he did not erase the white coaching line, as had been his custom. The phrase should have been "let alone." A "growing language" is a fine thing. But let its extreme advocates be very sure that when changes are accepted the language is really growing and not merely growing obscure.

**LESS.** "He could get even less games than did Hoad . . ." The general rule is to use "less" for amount and "fewer" for number.

**LILY.** *See* "gild the lily."

**LIT.** "Mr. Hall also lit into Mr. Stevenson . . ." Slang.

**LIT UP LIKE CHRISTMAS TREES.** ". . . Washington station WWDC, whose switchboard lit up like a Christmas tree as soon as the Senator went off the air." "But Wall Street had no way yesterday to keep a lid on investor demand. Telephone switchboards through the district were lit up like . . ." Complete the foregoing sentence in exactly two words. Mail your answer with two box tops to "Dead Letter Office. Care of Postmaster, N. Y."

**LITERALLY.** "But yesterday the United States Court of Appeals literally put the money in his pocket." If the court did that it would have made one of the news pictures of the year. As is almost always true, the writer meant "figuratively," not "literally."

**LIVID.** ". . . in the tradition of some previous Soviet opera films that have filled the old Stanley with howling music, livid color and static atmosphere." "Provoo's face became livid. He leaned forward, banged his fist on the witness box and shouted . . ." Livid means either black and blue or the color of lead. It does not mean vivid or red.

**LONGSHOREMAN.** *See* "stevedore."

**MASTERFUL.** The distinction in good current usage between "masterful" (imperious, domineering) and "masterly" (skillful, expert) is worth preserving. "Masterly" is never misused; "masterful" often is, as witness these examples: "In a masterful display of seamanship . . ." "By masterful cut and manipulation of material so that it stands away from the bust . . ." "Monteux Masterful at Stadium Again."

**MATINEE PERFORMANCE.** " 'King Solomon's Daughter' will receive a series of Sunday matinee performances . . ." Omit "performances"; a matinee is a daytime, especially an afternoon, performance.

**MAYORALTY.** ". . . last year's Democratic mayoralty primary." Why reach for the noun "mayoralty" to use as an adjective when the adjective "mayoral" is right at hand?

**MEANS.** *See* "by means of" *and* "ways and means."

**MENIAL.** "Menial" carries the connotation of something degrading. It is inappropriate to speak of "porters, janitors and other menial employees."

**MINION.** "This signal achievement gave Leo Durocher's suddenly inspired minions their sixth victory in a row." Used facetiously, the word is a cliché; used seriously it means either a loved one, or such derogatory things as a servile dependent, a fawning favorite or creature.

**MILITATE.** *See* "mitigate."

**MINISTER.** *See* "rector."

**MITIGATE.** "The fact that he is Roman Catholic mitigated unfairly against him . . ." "An official ruling then mitigates against eventual withdrawal of postal privileges." "Darkness, rather than stormy conditions, mitigated against spotting the tiny lifeboats." "Mitigate" means "moderate" or "soften." What the writers had in mind was "militate," which means "have effect, for or against."

**MODERNISTIC.** A caption said: "Some of the Churches That Point Up the Trend Toward Modernistic Design." Although you won't find it in the dictionary, the reference of "modernistic" is to a shortlived, exaggerated design style that flourished in the Twenties and Thirties. Louis Silverstein, promotion art director at The Times, tells *Winners & Sinners* that the word now has a derogatory connotation, implying "pseudo-modern" or "outdated modern." What was meant in the caption was "modern" or "contemporary."

**MORTGAGE BURNING.** A story about the 100th anniversary of St. John's in the Village spoke of "a mortgage-burning ceremony." A member of the bar informs *W & S* that to obtain discharge of a mortgage, the original mortgage must be filed; or, failing that, a special order, usually obtainable only after much legal huffing and puffing, must be filed. Actually, what the Village church burned was a copy of the mortgage release. In similar stories it might be well to point out what document was really destroyed, to alert prospective mortgage-burners to the peril of too literal a ceremony.

**MORTICIAN.** *See* "euphemisms."

**MOUNTAINS.** *See* "Sierra Mountains."

**NAB.** "Nab 447 Delinquent Drivers." Slang.

**NATION.** "U.N. Says Captives Will Resist Shift to Neutral Nation." Nation denotes the community or people rather than the territory of a country. What was meant here was a physical transfer to another land, not a mere transfer of jurisdiction.

**NAUSEOUS.** "As Hamner slid into the bag he was hit on the left elbow by Roy's throw. He went to third on the error, but became nauseous. Tom Micellota was sent in to run for him." He didn't become nauseous unless he turned other people's stomachs; what he became was nauseated.

**NAVY DEPARTMENT.** "Mr. Wilson took these suggestions under advisement and left the matter of Colonel Schwable's future assignment to the discretion of the Navy Department, which includes the Marine Corps." *Winners & Sinners* is reliably informed that it should have read "Department of the Navy." The Department of the Navy is composed of two co-equal services: the Navy Department (confusing, isn't it?) and the Marine Corps. In other and perhaps clearer words, the Navy Department is something different from the Department of the Navy.

**NEAR-RECORD.** "New York City registration, which ended last night, set a near-record." This is like saying, "The team scored three near-touchdowns." Just as nothing was "scored," so, in the registration, nothing was "set." A somewhat similar example is this head: "Near Riot Is Averted at Hudson." What actually took place was, perhaps, a near riot; what was averted was a full-fledged riot.

**NEE.** "Specifically, Jelke was convicted of inducing, enticing and procuring Pat Ward, nee Sandra Wisotsky . . ." Nee means born. You're born with only your family name; your given name is given afterward. It might have been written: "originally named Sandra Wisotsky."

**NERVE-RACKING.** "Emotionally exhausted from their nerve-wracking experiences of the day before, the customers sat in numbed immobility for most of yesterday's World Series game at Ebbets Field." "Nerve-racking" is the way we spell the trite word.

**NEW RECORD.** "By stroking five home runs in his trips to the plate Musial established a new major-league record . . ." "New" is superfluous with "record" except where a direct comparison is being made with a previous record.

**NOT TOO.** A certain critic of the drama submits the following as an example of one of his personal anathemas: "The Communist negotiators . . . were not too certain what it might prove to contain." Doesn't the writer mean "not certain"? asks the drama critic. He does. Literary understatement, known as litotes, has its uses: for purposes of humor, sarcasm or emphasis. When used for other reasons, it smacks of a cliché. To put it another way, it's not too good.

**NOW.** *See* "at the present time."

**OFFICER.** " 'But that story about an onion odor on his breath,' the officer said, 'that's hooey.' " Despite the dictionary, there is a feeling in these parts that "officer" for "policeman" has a provincial flavor, like "counselor" for "lawyer." But apart from that consideration, it is worthwhile to preserve the distinction between ordinary cops and officers, *i.e.*, those of higher grade. A story about a police lieutenant properly bore the head, "Police Officer's Trial Delayed."

**ONE AND THE SAME.** "The final proof that the mystery city and Morgantine were one and the same place was furnished by . . ." Try omitting "one and" and see whether it makes any difference.

**ONE OF THE.** "One of the purposes of the dinner was . . ." For economy's sake it could just as well be "one purpose" or "a purpose."

**ONE WORD, TWO WORDS.** (1) ". . . the story of Jimmy Piersall, a big league ball-player who, for awhile, was a mental case . . ." "Awhile" is an adverb. "While" is a noun, which often appears in the prepositional phrase "for a while" (three words). Therefore you say, "I slept awhile," or "I slept for a while," but not "I slept for awhile."

(2) "Statements made sometime ago by the Atomic Energy Commission . . ." "Sometime" means at a point of time, thus, "Statements were made sometime last month." In this instance, however, the "some" is intended to be an adjective modifying "time" (as if it were "some weeks ago") and therefore "some time" should be two words.

(3) "Tug, 25 Feet Underwater in Mud, Is Derricked Off Harbor Bottom." "Underwater" is an adjective and is correct only when it modifies a noun. What is required here is "under water."

(4) While the subject is under discussion, here are two more guides: "Cannot" is preferred to "can not" and "all right" is a must instead of "alright," which is not recognized in correct usage.

**ORAL.** *See* "verbal."

**OTHER.** "The pupil assignment bill was pictured by the Governor as providing the answer to the problem. The other four bills would . . ." Strictly speaking, "other" pertains to a thing distinct from a like thing already mentioned; for example, "one apple and the other apple," or, "four bills and the other four." But not, "one bill and the other four." Make it "one bill and the four others." *See also* "another."

**OVER.** "Figures released a week ago show that highway deaths are down 11 per cent in the state over the same period a year ago." If it's a reduction it's not "over," it's "under." Or you can make it "as against" or "compared with."

**OUT.** *See* "up."

**PARLIAMENTARIAN.** "Recent communications from Washington to the French Government . . . were offensive to French dignity, Premier Antoine Pinay told parliamentarians of his own Independent party today." "Last January Canada proposed the establishment of a consultative assembly composed of parliamentarians from all the Allied countries." A parliamentarian is an authority on the rules and usage of parliamentary assemblies. Members of parliaments may or may not be parliamentarians.

**PASS AWAY.** *See* "euphemisms."

**PASTOR.** *See* "rector."

**PERSON.** "Old drawings found in an attic here are adding laurels to a deceased artist whose prime job had been to make persons laugh." That usage would make several persons laugh, but the artist's job was to make people laugh. Use "people" for large masses; use "persons" for an exact or small number. *See also* "individual."

**PEOPLE.** *See* "person."

**PER.** "The Soviet shoe industry produced about three shoes for each person . . ." This is planned economy? Although it is usually advisable not to mix Latin and English, "per person" might have been better here to suggest a statistical rather than a literal meaning.

**PERSONAL FRIEND.** "Mr. Driggs had been a personal friend of the late Orville Wright . . ." Sovereigns may have nonpersonal friends, but not we commoners.

**PINCH HITTER.** As a synonym for "substitute" or "replacement" the phrase is a weary cliché. In addition, it usually is misused. In baseball, of course, a pinch hitter is a player sent to bat because his manager believes he will do a better job in the circumstances than the man he is replacing. A tenor hastily inserted in the cast to replace a singer who is indisposed is not a "pinch-hitting tenor." He is not expected to do even as good a job as the missing star, much less a better one. And never mind that "loosely" definition in the dictionary.

**PLAY.** Following is a letter received from Bronson Ragan, organist of the Church of the Holy Trinity in New York: "In the Times account of the Truman-Daniel wedding I noted that 'the organ played the Trumpet Voluntary by Henry Purcell.' In this connection I recall reading once of an English Bishop, who at a service announced, 'Let the organ play.' Whereupon the organist, the late distinguished William T. Best, retorted: 'Yes, let the damn thing play!' and stalked out of the organ loft." That, it should be remembered, is an organist speaking.

**PLEAD INNOCENT.** *See* "Attorney."

**PLENTY.** ". . . the Weather Bureau forecast 'earmuff weather' for New Year's Day—no rain or snow but plenty cold." Whether "plenty" is being used here as an adjective or an adverb, it is colloquial.

**PLURALS OF NAMES.** The head on a story about John R. Crews and his wife said: "The J. R. Crews' Wed 40 Years." Plurals of names ending in "s" are formed by adding "es"; therefore, the Joneses, the Crewses, etc.

**POINT.** "The report stressed the point that the salaries of the 43,000 teachers . . ." Delete "the point."

**PREDICATED.** "The shakedown racket, predicated on the Chinese-American's ties to his family still in Red China, is cutting deeply into . . ." In good usage "predicate" is not synonymous with "base" or "found." It means to assert, or affirm one thing of another.

**PREMISE.** "He was serving a sentence for breaking into a premise in an attempted robbery . . ." In logic alone can you have "a premise"; in legal matters the word is used only in the plural.

**PREPARATORY.** "As the former Far Eastern commander reviewed his service in the Orient preparatory to leaving for Paris . . ." The review in no sense prepared him for his departure; what the writer meant was simply "before."

**PRESENT.** *See* "at the present time."

**PRESENTLY.** "The *Times* series pointed out that all the presently suspended Monmouth employees deny . . ." "Presently" should be reserved for the meaning "forthwith" or "soon"; it should not be diluted to take in also "at present."

**PREVENTIVE.** "Preventative" appeared in a news story. The authorities agree that the form "preventive" is preferable.

**PRIEST.** *See* "rector."

**PROPORTIONS.** ". . . super-tankers, whose proportions exceed the present facilities of the canal." "Proportions" expresses merely a relationship, and except in the loosest usage has nothing to do with size. The right word here would be "dimensions" or "size."

**PROPOSITION.** "Vito Romano, a suspended patrolman, denied yesterday that he had propositioned two members of the . . ." There's no such verb.

**PROTAGONIST.** "The main protagonist of the play is one Nick Bellino . . ." There is only one protagonist in a play, not a main one.

**PROVEN.** "The effectiveness of the treatment was proven . . ." "Proven" is archaic. Use "proved."

**PUPIL.** "The decision of school boards in North Carolina's three largest cities to admit a limited number of Negro students to previously all-white elementary schools . . ." Those who attend elementary schools are pupils; those who attend higher institutions of learning (high schools may be included among these) are students.

**QUERY.** "U.S. Citizen Dies in Haitian Prison. Beaten During Police Query, Embassy Says." A query is a question, not a questioning. Use "inquiry."

**QUOTE.** "Johnson Denies Quote." "Dr. MacCraken correctly linked a famous quote with the character who said it . . ." "Quote" is jargon; use "quotation."

**RAVISHING.** "Elm Beetle Infestation Ravishing Thousands of Trees in Greenwich." Insex? Keep your mind on your work, buster. The word you want is "ravaging."

**REACH SHOULD EXCEED GRASP.** *See* "gild the lily."

**REASON . . . BECAUSE.** "He said the reason he had broken down was because his mother had died two days before the hearing . . ." "Reason" and "because" have the same connotation. Eliminate one or the other.

**RECTOR.** An alert Yankee, name of John Fenton, questions the clerical usage in this sentence: "The Rev. John Vanderveer Cooper Sr., pastor of Christ Protestant Episcopal Church . . ." Shouldn't it be "rector"? he asks. *Winners & Sinners* sought guidance from the local chaplain, George Dugan, religious editor, who advises that Protestant Episcopal clergymen in charge of parishes are always *rectors*. Methodists, Congregationalists and Unitarians prefer to be called *ministers*. Lutherans are *pastors* as a general rule. Baptists will settle for either *minister* or *pastor*. Roman Catholic parish clergy are always *pastors;* if there is more than one priest in the parish the top man is *pastor* and the others *priests* on the staff. Amen.

**REFERENCE.** *See* "allusion."

**REFUTE.** "Monaghan Refutes Views of Inspector." "Refute" means "to disprove"; its use puts us on Monaghan's side instead of in the center of the road, where—in any debatable matter—we belong. "Disputes" would be better.

**RELATIVELY.** "Relatively" should be used only when there is an expressed or clearly implied comparison. Improper: "United States military sources expressed shock that a plane carrying the President would have twenty-six persons aboard, a relatively heavy load." Relative to what? There is no typical plane or load.

**REMAINS.** "An army truck arrived to carry his remains to Kuala Kubu Bahru." "Remains" is an unsavory word when you stop to think about it. It might be applicable to a centuries-old archeological find that no longer retains the form of a body. In this story the corpse wasn't yet cold.

**REMAND BACK.** "However, the Appeals Court remanded the case back to the trial court . . ." Delete "back." Redundant. A similar redundancy is this one: "In sixteen ballots taken in the Assembly, Mr. Wellington Koo and Mr. Kuriyama see-sawed back and forth." Omit "back and forth."

**REPLICA.** A replica is a facsimile or quite close copy, with the additional meaning in fine arts (in which field it finds its proper use) of a copy made by the original artist and hence of equal value. Therefore the following caption is incorrect: "A replica of the original home of the society at the Clos de Vougeot in Burgundy was made in spun sugar by the hotel's pastry chef." There are so many words that convey the meaning usually intended ("model," "copy," "reproduction," "miniature") that "replica" should be forgotten except for its rare proper job.

**RESULT.** *See* "as the result of."

**REQUEST.** "The President has requested Congress for both these powers." The verb "request" is not idiomatically followed by "for." Although the verb "ask is so followed, the analogy is misleading. Make it either "has asked Congress for" or "has requested Congress to grant."

**REVEREND.** Placing this title before a surname with nothing in between is incorrect. "Rev. Turner Is Heard" is to be avoided. The title should be followed by the given name or by initials or, in a second reference, by "Dr." or "Mr." In the body of a story, of course, it is always preceded by "the." *See also* "rector."

**ROB.** "$9,200 Payroll Robbed." You can rob a paymaster or a bank, but not a payroll. "Rob" means to steal from. If you think of "rob" as standing for "*relieve of booty*" you'll never fall into the illiterate usage.

**ROCK 'N' ROLL.** An issue of the *AP Log* noted that in one day's Associated Press report this phrase had arrived in seven different versions. The Times has published a few, too. "In the interests of unanimity," said the *Log*, "we hereby prescribe as AP style: rock 'n' roll." It seems appropriate, if repulsive, so we'll string along, hoping the while that the whole business will roll down the drain before too long. So it's rock 'n' roll—no hyphens, no quotes. No peace.

**ROOFTOP.** ". . . every balcony and rooftop on the steep hills lining the streets was crowded with spectators." "Housetop" or just plain "roof," but not "rooftop."

**ROW.** "South Africa Row on Defense Grows." "Attlee Suffers Setback in Row With Rebel Leader." To begin with, "row" is colloquial. To end with, it overstates the situation most times because it means "a noisy quarrel or a brawl." The only thing to be said in its favor is that it counts three and a half headline units.

**RUSSIAN.** *See* "Soviet."

**SAFE.** *See* "vault."

**SAHARA DESERT.** "Press agents told the nation she was born in the Sahara Desert . . ." "Desert" is implicit in the word "Sahara"; therefore use "Sahara" by itself. *See also* "Sierra Mountains."

**SANDHOG.** "Three to six months ahead of schedule, sandhogs have holed through on the first link of the twenty-five-mile East Delaware Tunnel, which will insure New Yorkers against any future water shortages." The term "sandhogs" is restricted to laborers who work under pneumatic pressure; it does not apply to ordinary tunnel diggers.

**SAVE.** "Those who were nurses earned an average of $66 a week, more than those in any other profession save chemists, mathematicians and statisticians." Did you ever use "save" in conversation or a letter to a friend? Leave it to the poets and the fancy Dans.

**SCARCELY.** "Governor Stevenson drove through the city in a motor cavalcade this evening but without causing scarcely a ripple." The word "scarcely" (like "hardly") is equivalent to a negative; avoid doubling up on it.

**SELF-CONFESSED.** "Here in New York the self-confessed slayer of Eileen Fahey . . ." The idea of "self" is implicit in "confessed." Say "confessed slayer."

**SENIOR CITIZENS.** "Senior Citizens Get Advice on Fashions." Let's leave the euphemism to those who feel a need for it. There are plain words to say the same thing; *e.g.*, in descending order of harshness, "the aged," "the old," "the elderly" and "oldsters," the last of which is somehow missing from Webster's although it appears in the Oxford. *See also* "euphemisms."

**SEPARATE.** "Dr. Teller . . . offered thirteen separate suggestions . . ." Does "separate" contribute anything to the meaning? "They stressed that forty-eight separate and distinct projects were involved . . ." Strike out either adjective (or both, for that matter) and see whether there is any difference.

**SERVICE.** ". . . the West Shore line, which services both states." The word "service" is overburdened enough these days without compelling it to work overtime to replace the sturdy word "serve."

**SEX.** *See* "gender."

**SHAMBLES.** "The place [dormitory of the New Jersey State Prison Farm] was a shambles." A shamble was originally a bench, then a bench for displaying meats, then by extension an abattoir. Figuratively, the plural means a scene of slaughter, not merely a wrecked or littered place.

**SHIP.** *See* "boat."

**SHIPPER.** A head on a story referring to steamship owners and operators contained the phrase, "Shippers Assailed." People who own ships and who move cargo on piers are not shippers: shippers are people who send goods, by any means of conveyance.

**SHOW.** "Mr. McLeod failed to show for questioning . . ." Purely colloquial. Why not "appear"?

**SHUT.** *See* "up."

**SIERRA MOUNTAINS.** ". . . F.B.I. agents . . . arrested two long-missing Communist party leaders in a hide-out in the Sierra Mountains . . ." "Sierra" means mountains; therefore to say "Sierra Mountains" is redundant. *See also* "Sahara Desert."

**SIMPLE REASON.** "Shipping sources said here yesterday that they welcomed the lower air rates, agreed upon Monday in Cannes, France, for the simple reason that heightened interest in travel to Europe . . . was bound to benefit all means of transportation . . ." First, the phrase takes five words to say what can be said in one word—"because." Second, it sometimes seems to suggest a superior attitude toward the reader: "The reason is simple; why didn't you think of it yourself, you dope?"

**SITE.** "Kremlin Offers U.S. 10-Story Site for Its New Embassy in Moscow." A site is a place or location. You can't have a ten-story site any more than you can have a ten-story plot of ground.

**SKIRT AROUND.** "The tanker, the 1,900-ton Pianetta, was expected to skirt around submerged obstacles . . ." Delete "around."

**SMALL IN SIZE.** "Although small in size, the Somersworth had a distinguished war record." There might be some point in the phrase if the sentence read: "Although small in size, the ship was large in glory." But as it stands, "in size" is wastefully redundant.

**SOME.** "Some," when used before a figure, means "approximately" or "more or less." Therefore, this usage is ridiculous: "Some 35,683 attended the races at Aqueduct."

And this one is redundant: "President Eisenhower has made a happy gesture in gathering at the White House some thirty-odd leading figures in the sports world . . ." *See also* "about."

**SOMETIMES.** *See* "one word, two words."

**SORT OF.** *See* "kind of."

**SOVIET.** "Soviet" denotes a Russian governing body, not a Russian person. Hence, "Soviets' U.S. Trip Stirs Up Worries," as the headline for a story about four diplomats, is erroneous.

**SPELL OUT.** "Spell out" is a tired old work horse that deserves a rest. Certainly there is no need to force it into this redundant harness: "Although the Government officials refused to spell out details behind the indictments . . ."

**SPIRAL.** "Prospects for ending the sixty-five-year ban on the sale of precolored oleomargarine in this state spiraled today . . ." A spiral, like many another twist, has no sense of direction.

**STERN DUTCH UNCLE.** "The state's Motor Vehicle Commissioner delivered a stern Dutch uncle talk yesterday to fourteen persistent violators of the traffic laws." A Dutch uncle is one who reproves with great severity; hence, his talk is always "stern."

**STEVEDORE.** To most readers (and the dictionary) "stevedores" and "longshoremen" are virtually indistinguishable. In waterfront usage, however, stevedores are employers.

**STICK UP FOR.** "President Tito had never ceased to insist that he would stick up for his independence." A juvenile colloquialism that has no place in a serious story.

**STRANGLED TO DEATH.** "Rubinstein was found strangled to death on Jan. 27, 1955 . . ." Delete "to death." That's what "strangled" means.

**STREAMLINED.** "A streamlined program of teacher training designed to attract persons into the profession was outlined yesterday . . ." The word is usually a meaningless jazzer-upper. Unless the plan was to cut down wind resistance in training teachers, what was intended here was "new," "novel," "improved," "more efficient" or some other more precise substitute for the fuzzy "streamlined."

**STRESS.** Sometimes the bare definition of a word in the dictionary does not quite catch the overtones the word may carry in actual use. For example, the verb "stress" is defined as meaning "to place emphasis on," yet it means more than that when used as in this headline: "Soviet Deceitful, Dulles Stresses." The reader tends to supply the idea that what is being stressed is "the fact that." The same thing takes place with the word "emphasize": "Marion B. Folsom . . . emphasized that the program was designed to strengthen and stimulate state and local programs, and not to supplant them." To avoid seeming to use loaded words, it is better to employ ordinary verbs of saying, or verbs that suggest allegation. In that way the writer will not appear to be straying from the narrow path of objectivity.

**SUBJECT.** *See* "citizen."

**SUCCEED.** "The textile industry . . . succeeded today in making the first major breach in the Administration's stand . . ." Substitute "made" for "succeeded in making" and make your writing tighter.

**SUSPECTED.** *See* "alleged, accused, suspected."

**SWAP.** "The next step is to complete the final arrangements for the swapping of war prisoners." Colloquial.

**TARGET.** "The Wage Board, it was learned, has set Thursday as the target for completing its recommendations . . ." Comments Clifford J. Laube: "I think reporters never far get who overplay the trick word 'target.'"

**TELEPROMPTER.** "Teleprompter" is the registered designation of a device used by television speakers. There are other similar gadgets. "Talkathon" is the trade-marked name of a marathon audience-participation radio program. Do not use either as a generic term. *See also* "Coke" *and* "Drunkometer."

**TITLES.** *See* "coined titles."

**TOPSY.** "In the absence of such reorganization, the city's court structure as a whole has just 'growed,' like Topsy . . ." "Like Topsy, that Government-held surplus of farm commodities 'just keeps growin'.'" Once and for all, Topsy's exact words, punctuated variously depending on the authority you consult, were: "I 'spect I grow'd." No "just," no "jes'," no "growin'," no nuffin'. Anyway, Topsy, Queen of the Clichés, should drop dead.

**TOTAL.** "A total of" is excusable when used to avoid starting a sentence with a numeral; in almost all other situations it should be deleted.

**TOWARD THE GROUND.** "The helicopter was about 500 feet over the field when trouble developed, and it began to sink toward the ground." Delete "toward the ground." *See also* "below."

**TOW-HEADED.** Nothing wrong with the word, but it makes imps out of printers. *E.g.*, "Two bright, two-headed youngsters in overalls put away man-sized portions of scrambled eggs." Use "blond," "flaxen-haired"—anything.

**TRANSPIRE.** "The treaty looked to the appointment of a governor for the territory, but this never transpired." The nontechnical meaning of "transpire" is "to be emitted as a vapor, hence, to leak out or become known"; it should not be used as a fancy synonym for "happen" or "take place."

**TRIGGER.** "High official sources here think the impending arming of West Germany may have triggered the fall of Soviet Premier Georgi M. Malenkov . . ." "The drift away from support of the pacts in France triggered by the defeat of Premier Pierre Mendes-France . . ." "Trigger," a word apparently brought into fashion by the hydrogen bomb (triggered by an A-bomb), threatens to be one of the most overworked words of the generation. Perhaps this paragraph will trigger a return to such solid words as "cause," "produce" and "begin."

**TRIO.** "The trio was honored for the part they played in the hazardous transfer by lifeboat of two injured crew members . . ." Let's leave aside, but not overlook, the discrepancy in number between "the trio was" and "the part they played." Let's focus rather on the word "trio." It means a set of three, or three individuals with at least some kind of loose organization. It does not mean any old three individuals. If there had been two persons in this story, would the writer have said "the duo"?

**TRUCULENT.** "President Syngman Rhee . . . continued yesterday to manifest a truculent, unbending attitude toward the armistice agreement that was nearing completion at Panmunjom." If truculent meant what the writer probably thought it did—aggressively defiant or something of the sort—it would be a loaded word that had no business in the story anyway. However, it happens to mean "marked by savage or barbarous ferocity, cruel."

**TRUE FACTS.** "No matter what the true facts of the situation are, the Arab world seems . . ." Delete "true"; there are no such things as false facts.

**TRY.** As a noun, "try" is colloquial, as in the head, "Actress in Suicide Try."

**TRY AND.** ". . . Mr. Smart decided to try and get Ernest Hemingway to write for the publication . . ." "Try and get" for "try to get" is a colloquialism that is best avoided.

**TYPE.** The noun "type" has in recent years been teaming up with other words to emerge in the guise of an adjective, as in "V-type engine." But the metamorphosis is not complete and probably never will be. Although "V-type engine" has a perfectly proper sound, "high-type man" remains a vulgarism. Between these two extremes there are gradations that are not so easily labeled; for instance, "a series of character-type comedies" or "a New Deal-type candidate." Since the usage seems to have originated with technicians, this origin may offer us a clue to the propriety or impropriety of the usage. Perhaps it may be said that the "type" compounds should be used as adjectives only when the reference is technical or at least highly specific ("O-type blood," "cantilever-type bridge"), and that at all other times "type" should remain a noun ("high type of man," "comedies of the character type"). That guide should hold for the next half century anyway.

**UNDERWATER.** *See* "one word, two words."

**UNINTERESTED.** *See* "disinterested."

**UNKNOWN.** "It is understood that the Shah and Queen Soraya will be in Rome only a few days . . . after which they will continue their journey toward an unknown destination." What was intended here is "undisclosed" or "unascertained" rather than "unknown"; surely the Shah knew his destination, unless he was traveling under sealed orders. Similarly, an unclaimed body should be that of an "unidentified man" rather than that of an "unknown man." A small point, perhaps, but attention to minutiae is of the essence of precision.

**UNPRECEDENTED.** Here's an exhibit that shows why you should forget "unprecedented." "The Cardinals plan to go ahead with the day-and-night double-header against two different rivals, believed to be unprecedented in the major leagues." The very next day: "Meeting two different rivals on the same day had not been done in the National League since 1883." "Unprecedented" is a favorite word of the "gee-whiz" school of newspapering, press agentry and advertising. *See also* "Mania for uniqueness," Chapter 2, "Storytelling."

**UP, DOWN AND OUT.** (1) ". . . Frank D. Doyle is just leaving on a three-month leave of absence to head up the press relations for the Mayor's campaign for re-election."

Of what use is the "up" aside from completing a contemporary cliché?

(2) "400 Blouse Shops to Be Shut Down." Instead of padding the head with the word "down," why not try to get more information into it?

(3) "A new police procedure to speed up the transmission of stolen-car alarms to the men out on patrol . . ." Delete "up" and "out."

**VAULT.** There is a common tendency to use the word "vault" imprecisely, especially in robbery stories. For example: "The vaults are to the right of the lobby. One is inside the other. The outer one is 2 feet by 4 feet, the other a foot square." A vault is a permanent part of a building and is a room that is, generally, a space big enough to walk into. The things referred to in the foregoing example were undoubtedly safes.

**VERBAL.** ". . . many promises will be made by candidates to the voters of the nation. They will be verbal promises, however. The Canadian election law prohibits candidates from putting anything in writing." It is true that dictionaries sanction the use of "verbal" to denote both spoken and written communication. "Oral," however, can apply to spoken language only. Confronted with a choice between a word that can mean two things and another that can mean only one, are we not making better use of the tools of language if we select the precise word?

**VERITABLE.** "At one point in recent years he had to worry over more than 700 horses, not counting the veritable menagerie of less domesticated beasts." Those beasts were indeed a menagerie. What does "veritable" add to the thought? Nine times out of ten it is an unnecessary word.

**-WARD.** "Two programs . . . for diverting surplus waters of two northern California rivers hundreds of miles to the southward . . ." "The fountain would have to be moved a little to the westward . . ." The suffix "-ward" denotes "direction to" or "motion toward." Therefore, the words "to the" create a redundancy and should be omitted.

**WARN.** "Warning that the United States is preparing a new world war directed against the Soviet Union, Nikita S. Khrushchev . . . has called on the Moscow party organization . . ." To warn is to give advance notice of an impending unpleasantness, and the word "warn" suggests acceptance of the reality of the impending event. To be completely fair, "warn" should not be used when what is involved may be a charge, or merely somebody's pipe dream. "Saying" would be a good neutral word.

**WAYS AND MEANS.** Except as the name of a governmental committee, that phrase is two-thirds excess baggage, like "if and when." Yet it crops up: "At the close of its afternoon session the American League did reveal that it was giving serious consideration to ways and means of speeding games." Pick one or the other. Incidentally, tight editing would have made the sentence read as follows: "After its afternoon session the American League did reveal that it was considering ways of speeding games." *See also* "by means of."

**WHETHER OR NOT.** Usually the "or not" is a space waster; *e.g.*, "Whether the terrorist statement was true or not was not known." When, however, the intention is to give equal stress to the alternative, the "or not" is necessary: "The game will be played whether it is fair or not."

**WHENCE.** "And prior to that the youngster had last pitched in 1950 for Dallas, from whence the Braves purchased him . . ." "Mr. Praeger, as orderly and meticulous as Vienna (from whence he came), continued . . ." The word "whence" has a built-in "from." Therefore, despite the fact that "from whence" has occasionally been used by good writers, it is tautological and is best avoided.

**WHIR.** ". . . when the TV cameras began to whir this morning he made himself the central figure . . ." TV cameras don't whir, grind or roll; they just look at you red-eyed.

**WIDOW.** *See* "late."

**WINDFALL.** "This was a windfall for the French Premier and an unexpected acquisition." Which is what a windfall is.

**-WISE.** "Saleswise, the new candies are doing very well." Slapping the suffix "-wise" onto words promiscuously and needlessly is, at the moment, a fad. Help stamp it out.

**WOMAN.** *See* "lady."

**WORSE.** "He observed that if worse came to worse, and France did not finally ratify the treaty arrangement . . ." Idiom sometimes has a way of flying in the face of logic. Admittedly "worst comes to worst" is not logical; nevertheless it happens to be the idiom and has been so at least since the days of Thomas Middleton (1570-1627).

**ZOOM.** "Melville zoomed down the incline in 2:15:2, a full second ahead of Tommy Burns of Middlebury." "Zoom," an aviation term, concerns only upward motion.

# Storytelling

In writing the purpose is to communicate. In news writing the purpose is to communicate rapidly—and this also means easily. The excerpts from *Winners & Sinners* assembled in this chapter are intended to provide pointers on how the purpose of news writing can best be accomplished.

At the outset the news writer has to ask himself what it is he is writing about, what the news really means. Unless he answers this question properly he may find himself writing about a man drawing horsehair over catgut instead of about Isaac Stern playing a Bartók concerto. Inevitably, the essence of the news will provide the lead, or opening, of the story. That, then, is the first concern of what follows.

The next concern is with the manner of making the news easily understood—by interpretation, by simple explanation and definition, by answering every question that might arise in the reader's mind, by reaching for the concrete instead of being satisfied with the abstract, by introducing touches of color to make the story vibrant and by relating the news to human beings. This last consideration cannot be emphasized too often or too strongly. As *Winners & Sinners* observed on one occasion:

"All news, whether it be political, economic or sociological, does not exist in the abstract, but springs from the day-to-day lives of people, and one function of journalism must be to bend it back to the level whence it sprang. Eternally basic is how people live."

After considering matters that mainly concern content, this chapter then turns to form: the kind of sentence and the kind of paragraph that best smooth the reader's path. Finally comes a miscellany of writing faults.

Specimens of both winners and sinners appear throughout

the chapter. The sinners are, of course, anonymous; the names of the winners are parenthesized.

## WHAT DOES IT MEAN?

That is the question a reporter must ask himself when writing a lead for a story dealing with involved legal, legislative, political or technical matters. When he does not, what sometimes happens is a sentence like this: "The influential Committee for Economic Development issued a report today that may provide valuable ammunition to opponents of President Eisenhower's request for cancellation of automatic tax reductions scheduled for April 1."

Here's how a reader's thought processes would probably operate on that sentence: "Let's see now. 'Tax reductions.' Ah, that's good. But wait. 'Cancellation of tax reductions.' That's bad. No it isn't either; they're talking about 'opponents' of cancellation of tax reductions, and the ammunition is on their side, so . . . that means . . . hell, give me a copy of the *Staats-Zeitung*."

When the copy editor tries to write a head for the story he cannot fool around with all these ins and outs; he must draw away from the story to discover its significance. Then he writes: "Report Urges April 1 Tax Drop If . . ." What he does is to ask himself, "What does it mean?" That is what the reporter should do, too.

The failure of a reporter, entangled in legal mumbo jumbo, to ask himself "What does it mean?" resulted in the lead reproduced below at the left. Notice how the rewritten version at the right distills the essence of the story.

A prisoner serving a life sentence for a murder won a writ of habeas corpus yesterday in the United States Court of Appeals. The court held that he had been "unconstitutionally victimized by officialdom." (First edition)

A prisoner serving a life sentence for murder will get a new trial because of mistreatment by the New York police. (Final edition)

It is not sufficient, when writing for United States readers, to say, "The Minister of the Army, Arturo Ossorio Arana, has removed Maj. Gen. Francisco Jose Zerda as Commander in Chief of the Argentine Army." Surely the overt action is symptomatic of something. That something, whatever it is, would make a better lead for readers unfamiliar with the situation.

*-w&s-*

Following is an example in which the reporter went straight to the heart of the matter. The superficial news was the signing by the President of a Congressional resolution increasing the loan guarantee authority of the Federal Housing Administration for home improvement purposes. The reporter avoided the temptation to make this surface information his lead. Instead, he placed it in his second paragraph and, taking a long look, came up with this lead: "The White House gave the go-ahead signal today to hundreds of thousands of home owners who want to add a new room for the new baby, re-roof the house or add an extra bathroom." (Anthony Leviero)

*-w&s-*

The lead should be brief and lucid, but it should also seize upon the ultimate meaning of the story. This may require cutting through the underbrush of surface developments to discover what lies underneath. It may dictate deferring some of the particularization until later in the story. Here is an example of a lead that, while short enough, is so intent on trees that it sees no forest:

"The Supreme Court refused today to hear an appeal from lower court decisions holding the Louisiana Fair Trade Law and the McGuire Act, a Federal statute, constitutional."

What is the Louisiana Fair Trade Law? What is the McGuire Act? Even if you knew, these would be mere underbrush. The crucial question is: What is the meaning of what the court did? Another reporter asked himself this question and wrote the following lead: "The long legal battle over the constitutionality of 'fair trade' ended today when the Supreme Court refused to consider the issue. From now on manufacturers and wholesalers can fix the retail prices of their branded and trade-marked goods . . . and enforce these prices through the courts."

Achieving a lead like this requires distilling and redistilling the content of the story until you have the clear liquid of real meaning.

*-w&s-*

As each lead comes up, the writer and the editor must ask: Is this the essential meaning of the story? Is there anything in this sentence that can be omitted and placed elsewhere in the story? Is the sentence as direct as it can be? Here is an example of a lead that was adequate to begin with (left), but was susceptible of improvement (right):

The New York, New Haven and Hartford Railroad is willing to freeze commutation rates at existing levels pending the working out of a plan to peg them into the sliding scale of national cost-of-living statistics. (First edition)

Pegging commutation rates to the cost of living is being considered by the New York, New Haven and Hartford Railroad. (Final edition)

## DIRECT LEADS

One thing that militates against simple, direct leads is the inclusion of an unnecessary source or attribution, usually put there because of the notion that a time element must appear in the first sentence. For example:

"The Atomic Energy Commission announced plans tonight for another series of tests for atomic and probably hydrogen weapons at the Government's Pacific proving grounds." Why not say directly: "Another series of tests . . . is planned . . ."

Again: "A gift of $1,000,000 in securities by John D. Rockefeller Jr. toward revitalizing Harvard University's Divinity School was announced today by Dr. Nathan M. Pusey, president of the University." Why clutter the lead with the announcement by Dr. Pusey? The news is that the gift was made.

Of course, if the lead is a controversial or moot statement, some form of attribution is mandatory. It is not a good idea to have the first paragraph say, "State and county medical societies, because of their political composition, are furnishing the most serious hindrance to prepaid medical services and group practice," and then leave to the second paragraph the statement, "This opinion was given by . . ."

In general, however, the lead should be examined to discover elements that can be deferred in the interests of brevity and directness.

Some leads are so cluttered with names and long titles in the first few lines that they virtually dare the reader to smash his way into the stories. Here is one: "The New York branch of the National Association for the Advancement of Colored People asked Herbert Brownell Jr., Attorney General, yesterday to . . ." And another: "George V. Allen, Assistant Secretary of State for Near Eastern, South Asian and African Affairs, said tonight that Israel's request for permission to buy United States arms was still under consideration." In this second example Allen need not be included in the lead at all.

Here are three more examples of similarly cluttered leads (left) with suggested changes (right) to make them briefer and more direct:

H. C. Hansen, Premier of Denmark, has told Marshal Nikolai A. Bulganin, Soviet Premier, that Denmark is determined to remain in the North Atlantic Treaty Organization.

Denmark has told the Soviet Union that she is determined to remain in the North Atlantic Treaty Organization.

Lord Mills, Minister of Power, said today that a plan had been worked out between British and French electricity authorities for the exchange of electricity by submarine cable.

A plan has been worked out between British and French electricity authorities for the exchange of electricity by submarine cable.

For the first time since the American film industry adopted a self-regulatory morals code governing the making of motion pictures in 1930, that document has been "streamlined" and revised. (First edition)

The film industry has revised and relaxed its code of morals and taboos for the first time since the code was adopted in 1930. (Final edition)

Notice also in the last example that the final edition lead, though shorter, contains an additional item of information—in that important word "relaxed."

*-w&s-*

Still another illustration of the tendency to jam too much into sentences, especially lead sentences: "The United States delegation, with the authorization of President Eisenhower, announced today that the Atomic Energy Commission had allocated 220 pounds of fissionable material for use by other countries under the United States' atoms-for-peace program." For purposes of the lead, all that is necessary is, "The United States has allocated 220 pounds, etc." The intervening facts are merely mechanics.

*-w&s-*

Excess baggage is carried in this one: "Dr. Robert Cushman Murphy, ornithologist associated with the American Museum of Natural History for thirty-five years, has retired as the museum's Lamont Curator of Birds, it was announced yesterday." Why unnecessarily lengthen the lead with that final phrase?

*-w&s-*

On the other hand, a reporter—in a commendable effort to write a crisp, attractive lead—occasionally comes up with a superfluous one, almost as if he had written his story and then tacked an extra sentence atop it. Here is an example: "The English teachers of this state are up in arms." The second sentence, as edited, made a newsier lead: "The English teachers of this state complain that they have become the jacks-of-all-trades of the teaching profession." Short, striking leads are, of course, desirable, but be sure they really say something.

*-w&s-*

An additional danger lurks in the desire for a simple lead. In the magazine *Editor & Publisher,* Roy H. Copperud made a good point about leads that compel the reader to match up references. In this game a generalized term in the opening paragraph must be matched with a later particularized reference. For example:

"An economist said today that a long-range foreign economic aid program offers advantages that may 'more than offset' the tax burden to this country.

"H. Christian Sonne, Chairman of the Board of Trustees of the National Planning Association, recommended a five-year program of economic development assistance abroad . . ."

The reader, you see, has to figure out that Sonne is the "economist" referred to in the opening paragraph—not an insuperable obstacle, to be sure, yet a low hurdle that interrupts his stride. The reason for the generalized term in the first paragraph is, of course, a good one: to avoid cluttering the opening with cumbersome names and identifications. What is needed is simply a phrase tying the second reference to the first. Notice how much smoother this example is:

"New York's 'mad bomber' became the center of a bitter legal dispute yesterday between a prominent criminal lawyer and a prominent judge.

"The lawyer, James D. C. Murray, charged that the judge, John A. Mullen . . ." (Jack Roth)

Solicitude for the reader is always desirable.

*-w&s-*

A corollary to the foregoing item: In an effort to simplify a lead the reporter will often properly omit an encumbering identification—for example, ". . . Lessing Rosenwald declared today." Then, however, a subsequent paragraph refers merely to "the chairman of the board" or "the former chairman of the board of Sears, Roebuck," leaving the reader a little unsure whether this is Mr. Rosenwald or someone else. Why not clinch matters by saying in the subsequent reference, "Mr. Rosenwald, the chairman of the board, etc."?

-w&s-

Watch out for the double-barreled or I-don't-know-which-I-like-better lead. It assumes three forms: (a) two big mouthfuls connected by "and"; (b) a long sentence beginning with "as" or "while" or "although"; (c) the participial attack. Any one of these three may on occasion be acceptable, but usually they stymie crisp, simple writing.

Here is an example of (c):

"Holding that traditional prison punishment is a futile means of dealing with the increase of crime in the United States, a United States criminological psychiatrist said here today that crime could best be reduced by the prompt detection and treatment of anti-social tendencies in early childhood and adolescence." (First edition)

Since the reporter clearly couldn't make up his mind which of these two ideas was the better, and since the two together are too much for a reader to swallow at one gulp, the copy editor had to step in. He reduced the lead to one simple statement:

"A United States criminological psychiatrist said here today that traditional prison punishment was a futile means of dealing with the increase of crime in the United States." (Final edition)

A second paragraph then took up the other idea. Surely this version makes matters easier for the reader.

-w&s-

Remember those puzzles in which you had to find the hidden pony? Usually the pony was concealed, upside down, in an arabesque formed by bushes or the leaves of a tree. Once you found it you could hardly believe it had been there all along. There was a challenge in discovering it. Some stories present the same kind of challenge; the information is there but the reader may have to go to some pains to dig it out. For example:

"The United States Air Force has been invited informally

to send two or three senior officers to Moscow for Soviet Aviation Day, June 24 . . .

"The formal invitation, addressed to the Air Force Chief of Staff, Gen. Nathan F. Twining, has not yet been delivered. But the informal bid was enough to start the White House and the Pentagon talking about a possible visit by the Joint Chiefs of Staff, if they should be invited by the Soviet Government."

That final sentence would puzzle a hasty reader. "I thought it said up there they *were* invited," he might say to himself. Then he would notice, if he hadn't switched by this time to another column or another newspaper, that a different group was being referred to in the final sentence. Why not save him this extra trouble and bring the pony out of the foliage by making it, ". . . talking about another possible visit—one by the Joint Chiefs, etc."?

By the way, did somebody say that readers shouldn't be hasty? Perhaps they shouldn't be. But, brother, every newspaper reader is a hasty reader, and we might as well reckon with that fact.

## INVITING LEADS

To take the good with the bad, here are some items from *Winners & Sinners'* department of "Inviting Leads":

"After a week of tears, April bowed out yesterday in a glow of golden laughter." (Farnsworth Fowle)

*-w&s-*

"A man who bills himself as the World's Most Popular Astrologer received an unfavorable reading yesterday in Manhattan Supreme Court." (Layhmond Robinson)

*-w&s-*

"Ever wonder what the doctor does before the patient arrives? A two-day exhibit of hobbies that opened yesterday at New York Medical College, Flower and Fifth Avenue Hospitals, gives a fairly good idea." (Emma Harrison)

*-w&s-*

This one is a good simple lead on a complicated story: "A violent explosion, touched off by arsonists, shattered a nine-story downtown loft building at 9:45 o'clock last night and caused a fierce five-alarm fire. Two men were killed in the blast. One of the victims was believed to have been one of the four criminals who set the blaze; and the other, one of four detectives who had been trailing the suspects." (Robert Alden)

-w&s-

"The lead tenor in a prison quartet led the bass and baritone to freedom last September, but the Federal Bureau of Investigation has arranged for a return engagement at the Kentucky State Reformatory in La Grange." (Edward Ranzal)

-w&s-

"For the first time in five days a Floridian could walk abroad today without the risk of having his hand gripped by a potential President of the United States." (Russell Baker)

-w&s-

"The American Museum of Natural History has a new exhibit of contemporary anthropology—a collection of zip-guns, slingshots, knives and billies taken from young Homo un-sapiens whose habitat is New York." (Ira Henry Freeman)

-w&s-

"Chinchillas, one of the few rodents that can make a woman shriek with pleasure, attended a mass meeting in New York last week." (Nan Robertson)

-w&s-

"Britain is discovering that there are almost as many difficulties in laying down the white man's burden as there were in assuming it." (Thomas F. Brady)

-w&s-

"The Transit Authority took to the skies yesterday in an effort to find a solution for the earthbound problem of bus bunching." (Stanley Levey)

*-w&s-*

"A British bank has challenged the widely held belief that when the United States sneezes economically the rest of the world gets pneumonia." (Thomas P. Ronan)

## INTERPRETATION AND THE ABUSE THEREOF

Locating the border line between three-dimensional reporting and editorializing poses a problem for both writers and editors. Often a deadpan recital of a surface happening, though accurate and objective, will be inadequate, if not downright misleading.

For example, a bald statement of Mike Quill's abandonment of his free-ride plan for the New York City Transit System would not have said nearly as much about either the union leader or his action as was contained in this supplementary sentence: "The quixotic Mr. Quill, who holds the undisputed national championship for threatening strikes and other pressure moves that never come to pass, announced that the union was scuttling its 'Operation Santa Claus' before it saved riders on eight privately owned bus lines their first dime." (Abe Raskin)

Perhaps that paragraph goes a little far, but it is surely headed the right way. Three-dimensional reporting is becoming more and more desirable as the news grows more complex and the reader's time to explore it and grasp it lessens. Two cautions, however, go out to the reporter. First, be sure that your knowledge of the subject is complete, so that you know all the answers; second, be sure that you can distinguish between objective appraisal and subjective opinion.

*-w&s-*

Interpretation that smacked of editorializing came up in a story about the purging of books in libraries by the United States Information Service in Germany. It contained this paragraph:

"These and other recent developments in Germany have done much to undo the Herculean efforts of United States occupation forces in the post-war years to present American democracy to the German people as a magnet to draw them away from totalitarian attitudes."

This thought probably belongs in the story, but it is controversial and, as presented, would be difficult for the reporter to substantiate. Undoubtedly it was expressed to the reporter by someone in a position to know. Why not, then, attribute it?

*-w&s-*

Characterization, too, can border on opinion, and should be excluded from the news columns. A paragraph about the President's news conference contained this sentence: "The ambiguity of his replies sent some men away convinced that the major policy change was indeed in prospect, but the White House later took pains to explain that this was not the case." Strike out the words "the ambiguity of" and you retain the same meaning without the editorial flavor.

*-w&s-*

*Footnote on characterization:* The press agencies recognize only three types of women: beautiful, pretty and attractive. This classification is similar to the grading of olives, under which colossal means fair size, mammoth means medium and large means pretty damn small. Unhappily, the agencies feel obliged always to slap one of the adjectives on a woman. Thus: "George Edward Grammer, 35-year-old father of three children, was convicted today of deliberately killing his wife and trying to make her death look like an accident so that he could marry a pretty New York secretary." Now, one man's dish is another man's pot; beauty, prettiness and attractiveness are subjective judgments. Why not drop them and stick to objective reporting?

*-w&s-*

Loaded phrases must be avoided, too. Here are two that betray a point of view: (1) "They are supporters of the Baath, or 'Arab Resurrection' party, which is spreading *like a weed* through the Arab world." (2) "The report, *unfortunately for the United States,* indicates that the Russians have attained quality in education, as well as quantity."

Finally, there are, of course, loaded words—words that seem to express opinions rather than simple facts. Two examples: (1) "Three Democrats from Tennessee, who conceivably could be competitors for high office in 1956, share a lot of the credit for the long, unrelenting fight against the Eisenhower Administration's effort to wed public and private power facilities in the T.V.A. area." Would the Republicans concede that the three Democrats were deserving of "credit"? (2) "It was his second attempt to flee Soviet tyranny." "Tyranny" involves a judgment; it is an editorial writer's word, not a reporter's word.

## DISTORTIONS AND INJUSTICES

A letter to The Times from the editor in chief of *America* Magazine, the Rev. Robert C. Hartnett, complains about the coverage of two of his speeches. His letter points up a principle that should be brought to the attention of reporters and editors: When the lead of a story reporting a speech is built on a topic other than the speaker's main theme, that theme should be summarized somewhere in the story.

What perturbed Father Hartnett was that the leads of both stories were based on remarks he had made about Senator McCarthy, while in one story his main topic was compressed into a single paragraph and in the other was omitted altogether. Both reporters had included brief summaries of the speaker's principal topic, but in one instance the summary was perhaps too brief because of the space restrictions and in the other it was lost in a rewriting for the purpose of compression.

For some time a memo, now yellowing with age, has been on a Times bulletin board. Signed by Frank S. Adams as city editor, it says: "In all stories that deal at considerable length with one speech let us try to include one paragraph that will give the theme of the address." Delete the words "at considerable length" if you like, but keep the principle in mind.

*-w&s-*

When a speaker or writer makes a fuzzy statement, care

should be taken to determine what he actually meant before
paraphrasing the statement. This is especially important when
the subject is a sensitive one. For instance, J. B. Matthews,
former staff director of the McCarthy subcommittee, wrote a
controversial sentence in *The American Mercury,* and it was
subsequently paraphrased in The Times in varying versions.
Here is the record:

Original sentence: "The largest single group supporting the
Communist apparatus in the United States today is composed
of Protestant clergymen."

Version A: "Mr. Matthews provoked a storm by his article
. . . calling the Protestant clergy 'the largest single group supporting the Communist apparatus in the United States.'"

Version B: ". . . a statement by J. B. Matthews . . . that
Protestant clergymen formed the largest American group supporting Communism . . ."

Version A and, to some extent, Version B seem to suggest
that the Protestant clergy as a whole supports Communism.
This was not asserted in the original, nor was it intended, as is
evidenced by this further sentence from the Matthews article:
"It hardly needs to be said that the vast majority of American
Protestant clergymen are loyal to the free institutions of this
country . . ." The only preventive for errors like this is care
and clear thinking.

*-w&s-*

In the 1930's New York had, briefly, a Mayor named John
P. O'Brien. Whatever his other merits, he was not gifted with
gracious use of the language of Shakespeare, Milton and
Robert Moses. When he repeatedly tried to attribute his
political gaucheries to misquotation by the press, the reporters
at first took it, then decided to gang up on him. Everything
he said was taken down in shorthand and his quotations were
printed verbatim in the papers. His Honor quickly hollered
uncle.

The point is that unless there is a special reason to do so,
we should not print unedited the grammatical slips of spon-
taneous speech, which even an educated person might make.
One special reason to print such slips would be in situations
like O'Brien's; others would be provided by testimony in
court, a Presidential news conference, a document, a pre-

pared speech or a purposeful effort to reproduce dialect or a manner of speech.

However, Dr. Dodds, the president of Princeton, should not be quoted as saying that he was "impatient at seeing law schools, medical schools, business schools come down here and persuade young men to enter those professions whom we thought would be good teachers." We need not rearrange a badly constructed sentence for him. But we should assume that a college president, when his mind is on the subject, knows the difference between "who" and "whom." (Although, now that this subject has come up, there is a recent president of Columbia whose syntax often falls a trifle short of perfection. But it didn't seem to affect his standing in the Electoral College.)

And, as long as we have mentioned reporting of dialect: A story said that Miss America 1957 arrived here accompanied by luggage, her mother and a Southern accent. A few paragraphs later this appeared: " 'Ah used to love to play jungle, swingin' on wisteria vines,' she said. 'Ah played baseball an' rode ponies an' once Ah broke mah left arm fallin' out of a tree.' " Let's avoid writing in dialect. Not only is there the pitfall of reproducing it inaccurately unless one's ear is exceptionally alert, but also there is usually the danger (although it is not present in this example) of suggesting class, social or racial snobbery.

*Also:* There is such a thing as false condescension—like patting a midget on the head in the belief he is a small boy. A form of it is the following: "The crunch of peanut shells in 'croocial' moments at Ebbets Field may lack some of its old rhythm this season." Is "croocial" a specialized Brooklynese pronunciation of "crucial"? The answer is no. It is the normal pronunciation of the word, just as the phony dialectic renditions "sez" and "kum" are the normal pronunciations of "says" and "come." In none of these do the odd spellings or quotation marks make sense. Something else again would be the traditional, if imaginary, Brooklynese, "a poil from an erster," or the more exact Brooklynese, "a pay-ul fum uh erster."

## EXPLAIN, EXPLAIN, EXPLAIN

To grow and be vital a newspaper must attract the young as well as the mature. Does it makes sense, then, to produce a paper that is incomprehensible to youth? All of which is by way of repeating that specialized situations and technical terms must be explained in ABC language; that expertness on the part of the reader must not be assumed.

Take this story, for example: "The Federal Reserve Board today reduced margin requirements on stock market transactions from 75 per cent to 50 per cent, effective when the stock exchanges resume on Tuesday after the Washington's Birthday holiday." Why should it have been left to a paragraph 400 words later to explain the meaning of "margin requirements"? The newspaper's need for young readers should dispose of any impulse to remark, "Anyone who doesn't know what margins are has no business reading The Times." But if not, the question should then be posed, "Are readers of the *Wall Street Journal* less knowing than readers of The Times?" This was the *Journal's* lead on the same story: "The Federal Reserve Board lowered margin requirements on stock purchases and short sales from 75% to 50% effective at once. The move means buyers of stocks now have to put up only 50 cents for each $1 of stock bought, whereas before the board's action they had to put up 75 cents. The broker extends credit for the difference between what the customer puts up and the price of the stock."

When you work on a newspaper you must keep the school kids in mind constantly. You'll need them to pay your salary by and by.

*-w&s-*

Explanation by analogy is one of the best ways of making something seem familiar. A fine example of this kind of elucidation was the comparison of the relationship of the Vanguard engine's thrust and the rocket in flight to that of a circus seal and the ball it balances: "If the ball tends to roll off the seal's nose to the left, the seal moves its nose farther to the left, putting itself in a position to thrust the ball back to the right." (Milton Bracker) Then came a paragraph describing how the Vanguard's engine operates similarly.

Another example clarified the workings of a fusion bomb: "The process is analogous to the lighting of a cigarette in a high wind when one has only one match. It is not enough to light the match—one must be able to shield it against the wind long enough for the cigarette to be lighted." (William L. Laurence)

*-w&s-*

A simile often does the trick: "Here at Gonen . . . the boundary is halfway up a ridge of rocky hills . . . Living and working here is like cleaning the steps of the New York Public Library every day, while a man with a gun and a grudge against you watches from the upper floor of a Fifth Avenue building." (Scth S. King)

*-w&s-*

How to make statistics meaningful is demonstrated in this graphic passage: "The new altitude record—almost twenty-four miles—exceeds the old record by 36,000 feet. How much of a jump that is can be appreciated by recalling that 36,000 feet is an average altitude for those almost-invisible jet fighters that often make their presence known by their vapor trails overhead." (Richard Witkin)

## UNANSWERED QUESTIONS

Suppose you had been out of the country for several months or were an ordinary forgetful reader, and read a story about "the Lanza parole case" without further explanation. You'd be a little irritated, wouldn't you? Or suppose you came upon an extensive feature about gasoline tax refunds for boat owners, and the story never even hinted why they were entitled to such refunds. Or suppose you were not too knowing about financial matters and you read that "the Administration had sought an open-end, long-range spending permission," and no explanation of "open end" was offered. Or suppose the story said that "the film co-stars Hal March." You'd be curious about who the other star was, wouldn't you?

Eternally we must be vigilant to spot the questions every story raises and to answer them, every one. Unanswered questions are primarily the responsibility of the reporter—but ultimately, like almost everything else, the responsibility of the copy editor. There is a crossword puzzle every day on The

New York Times book page; let there be no other puzzles anywhere in the paper.

*-w&s-*

Small items of information that many readers find interesting are sometimes annoyingly omitted from news stories.
Here is a little round-up of some that should be included:
1. The denomination to which a religious leader belongs.
2. In a sketch or close-up, the place of birth of the subject.
3. When a foreign notable makes a speech in this country, the
language in which he speaks. 4. Names of lawyers in important litigation. 5. Names of architects when new buildings are
going up.

*-w&s-*

A while back, a dispatch related that the Orthodox prelate
of Cyprus had blamed the British for bomb outrages on the
island. The dispatch did not tell in what form the statement
had been made—in a speech, a statement, an interview, a
conference with reporters (foreign or domestic), an article in
the press or a conversation with his charwoman. In many parts
of the world, including this country, such information helps
in assessing the news. And it takes only a brief phrase to fur-
nish it.

*-w&s-*

A story about the induction of Supreme Court Justice Vin-
cent A. Lupiano said that his 84-year-old father, acting as
elevator operator, greeted him with, "Buon giorno, figlio felice
auguri." Translation, please.

*-w&s-*

"Moss Hart is being treated for a dislocated neck and
shoulder at Harkness Pavilion," said a one-paragraph story.
How did he get it—golf, falling downstairs, reaching for
royalties?

*-w&s-*

A story about the French cantonal elections said that Georges Bonnet had scored a notable victory and added that under a Government rule he had been declared ineligible for re-election. Nowhere did the story tell why he had been declared ineligible. The correspondent would reply, no doubt, that he had explained this once before. He had, too—exactly one week before at the end of an inside-page story. But suppose Susie had wrapped her lunch in that copy of the paper before Papa got a chance to read it?

*-w&s-*

"It was a surprise to see Fullmer 'heel' Robinson in the fourth." "Fullmer was warned for 'heeling' Robinson in close." Both of these sentences appeared on the same page. Want to know what heeling is? Then buy the *New York Daily News:* ". . . pushing his gloves in Robinson's face."

*-w&s-*

A story about Mohamed V on a visit in the West used the term "quarter horse" in head, picture caption and story, all without further explanation. Eight students at a near-by journalism school were asked to write down what they thought it meant. Only one knew. The other answers ranged from, "A riding horse kept close to the rider's quarters," to, "In my childhood I used to take pony rides for a dime; considering inflation and the fact that a horse is bigger than a pony, I don't think a quarter is unreasonable." The definition is in the dictionary, but few readers tote dictionaries around with them. And few of our readers live out on the range, where these horses of unusual endurance under the saddle, able to gallop at high speeds for about a *quarter* of a mile, are bred.

*-w&s-*

One dispatch said Miss Autherine Lucy had testified "with deliberation and occasional flashes of dry wit," but the reader was not vouchsafed a single example of same. Another dispatch said that "the Prime Minister was subjected to a storm of vituperation and abuse" and a "wave of ridicule and criticism," but again there was no documentation. If you whet the reader's appetite with statements like these, it would be well to throw him at least a crumb of "such as."

-*w&s*-

In telling about the President's veto of the Rivers and Harbors bill, a story spoke three times of public bills and private bills without explaining the difference between them. Moreover, in summarizing vetoes of legislation passed by Congress, it said merely: "Fourteen were pocket vetoes. No bill became law without his signature." Of course, if you just graduated from high school—and especially if you got an A in your civics course—you probably know all about pocket vetoes and under what circumstances bills become laws without the President's signature. The rest of us, however, will have to turn to Article I, Section 7, Paragraph 2 of the Constitution.

-*w&s*-

A picture and story in the Real Estate Section described a new office building at 260 Madison Avenue without disclosing at what street that might be. Naturally, it's a simple matter for a New York reader to find out for himself. All he needs to do is go to his savings bank, obtain one of those "Guide to Street Numbers" cards, then take the number 260, cancel the last digit, divide by 2 (provided July does not contain an "r"), let the light of a full moon fall over his left shoulder and add the key figure 26.* Or he could go to the Public Library and look it up on a city real estate map. But wouldn't it be better for the newspaper to do the work for him? Wouldn't it be a good idea to follow the rule of locating an avenue address by reference to the nearest street?

-*w&s*-

Omission of information can be annoying. For example: "Known as 80 Park Avenue, the proposed building will contain suites of two to five rooms . . . S. R. Firestone said rentals would start at about $138 for two rooms, $158 for two and

---

* Does not run on Sundays.

one-half rooms, $217 for three rooms, $225 for three and one-half rooms, $234 for four rooms and $334 for four and one-half rooms." Aunt Minnie was interested in those five-room apartments.

-w&s-

The purpose of translating foreign terms, such as those referring to measurements, currency and the like, into American terms is, of course, to help the reader. The following passage from a story about the Pripet Marshes does not do this: "The project involves the drainage of about 40,000 square kilometers (a kilometer is nearly five-eighths of a mile) . . ."

First of all, when the original statement is one of area, why supply a translation key that is a linear measure? Second, after the editor finds the proper translation key (in this example, that a square kilometer equals 0.386 square miles) why not work out the multiplication for the reader and tell him the area is equal to about 15,400 square miles? Third, the editor should ask himself whether the original foreign term is necessary at all; that is, whether the statement should not be set forth in American terms to begin with. There are times when this should not be done—for example, when it is desirable to retain the terms of an official document, when a comparison with a previous official plan is pertinent or when a translation of currency units would be misleading.

But in many other stories—and the Pripet Marshes story is one in point—nothing is achieved by using the terms "square kilometers," "hectares" and "centners." In fact, a height of absurdity was touched when the story said that the plan would increase the Soviet grain harvest "by millions of poods (a pood equals 36.113 pounds)." Correspondents and editors alike should keep the poor reader in mind constantly.

-w&s-

It sometimes happens that a story inadvertently raises an unanswered question. Here is an example: "Recent action by the Administration to speed reporting of changes in industrial working hours has emphasized the importance of this business index." Even an alert reader would probably come up sharply at the end of that sentence with the question, "*What* business index?" and then have to go over the sentence a second time to identify it. This kind of writing is common enough to warrant a special word of warning. A reader should never be compelled to re-read a sentence to extract its meaning. For the sake of clarity, take nothing for granted. When you introduce something to a reader give it a real introduction: name it and describe it.

## ANSWERED QUESTIONS

To show how questions can be answered in a news story without wasting space, a few examples are appended:

In a London story that turned largely on the term "convertibility," a brief but illuminating paragraph began: "Convertibility in this sense means the ability to exchange the pound freely for any other currency, particularly the United States dollar, which is the money most in demand in the world today." (Clifton Daniel)

-*w&s*-

"The Chancellor said the Government was not satisfied with the way in which Britain's balance of payments—the difference between import costs and export receipts—and gold and dollar reserves were moving." (Frank Bailinson)

-*w&s*-

"She was born with talent, including absolute pitch (the ability to name any note or combination of notes, upon hearing them.)" (Harold C. Schonberg)

-*w&s*-

The story was about LIFO. Don't know what LIFO is? All right: "LIFO (Last In-First Out) is a method of valuing inventories. It works in favor of the taxpayer in periods of rising prices. It assumes that goods sold by a business were the last items it added to its inventory, and prices them accordingly. If the goods actually were bought earlier at cheaper prices, that profit is eliminated for income tax purposes." (Carl Spielvogel)

-*w&s*-

A story about the increase in margins said that the requirements applied to short sales as well as to stock purchases, then immediately added this clear explanation: "A short seller borrows the stock he wishes to sell and replaces it later with stock purchased at what he hopes will be a lower price." (John D. Morris)

*-w&s-*

"Ambehaving, the second choice, threw a stifle as he left the gate." Want to know what that means? Okay: "Stifle trouble for a horse is like knee trouble for a man. A man with a 'trick knee' is in trouble when it pops out of place; a horse with a thrown stifle is in the same kind of trouble." (James Roach)

*-w&s-*

## CONCRETE VS. ABSTRACT

Expressing the general in terms of the particular is an almost infallible way of making an economic or political story more understandable and more interesting. If it is a story about a British bank rate increase, the usual way of presenting one angle might be:

"The further tightening of the credit squeeze is likely to lead to unemployment as industries dependent on credit find money supplies dwindling."

Admittedly that is fairly clear. But how about this version:

"Higher interest rates and dwindling money supplies may bring unemployment. Let's say ABC Widgits Ltd. has been expanding with the aid of bank loans. Now it may not be able to borrow as much as before and may thus have to curtail operations and lay off widgit makers."

This approach is not possible in all economic stories. There was one about aid to India in which it was not possible. But the story began thus:

"On the desk of the Finance Minister of India is a slim yellow folder. It is a carefully worked out report that his Government hopes it will never have to use, but fears it will.

"T. T. Krishnamachari, the businessman-politician who sits

behind the desk, picked up the folder today and weighed it gently.

"'I have been working on this for three months,' he said. 'It's the final word to my colleagues on what this country will be able to do and will not be able to do if we do not get more foreign assistance.'" (A. M. Rosenthal)

That is, of course, a gimmick lead. Still, who, having been thus invited into the story, would not read on? A reporter cannot go wrong if he somehow finds a way of relating his story to concrete things, to human beings.

-*w&s*-

A clear dispatch on the status of the pound sterling was made even clearer by an extended passage that got down to cases by saying, "Suppose you are an American importer of British automobiles . . ." (Edwin L. Dale Jr.) That approach is always helpful.*

-*w&s*-

A report about the Pakistani coalition government might have been a dull and abstract political piece, but it was brought to life because it was deftly based on a description of the National Assembly, meeting during the strain of a fasting season. (A. M. Rosenthal) Recommended reading.*

-*w&s*-

If one picture is worth ten thousand words, one concrete illustration in a complicated story is worth at least five hundred. A story about American efforts to bolster Japan's trade mentioned "a triangular pattern of concessions." Then came a paragraph giving a specific example involving Japanese silks, Belgian pottery and American films. The example made the story understandable in a flash. (Dana Schmidt)

## DABS OF COLOR

Sometimes all that is needed—or possible—to bring an abstract story down to earth is a descriptive sentence or a mere

---

* This dispatch appears in full in the Appendix.

phrase. Such a one as, "Senator Langer, chewing his cus-
tomary cellophane-wrapped cigar, said . . ." (Russell Baker)

Here are a few more examples:

"As he talked, Mr. Ben-Gurion was transformed from a
rather tired man, suffering from influenza, sitting in a blue
bathrobe in a hotel room, to one of his nation's greatest
visionaries." (Harry Gilroy)

*-w&s-*

"Few of the 2,000 industrialists who had heard the address
were still in the ballroom when Mr. Meany, his teeth clench-
ing a cigar, and Mr. Sligh, a tall, lean furniture manufacturer,
confronted each other. The room was loud with the bustle of
waiters . . ." (Homer Bigart)

*-w&s-*

"Nervously, Señor Maza twisted a yellow pencil in his
hands. Dag Hammarskjold . . . sat impassive at his right, his
chin propped on his hand." (Lindesay Parrott)

*-w&s-*

". . . Mr. Khrushchev read from a prepared text rather than
making his usual unrehearsed statement. The silver-rimmed
glasses that he uses for reading gave him an unusual profes-
sorial look." (William J. Jorden)

*-w&s-*

". . . Senator Everett M. Dirksen, the Illinois Republican
and orator, looking Byronically disheveled . . ." (Russell
Baker)

*-w&s-*

"One of the most frequent occurrences in the House is the
ringing of bells whenever the order of the Chamber is disturbed. A Radical Deputy set off noisy bells tonight by charg-
ing that the Government would next try to establish a Peron-
ista church." (Edward A. Morrow)

*-w&s-*

In what might otherwise have been a drab diplomatic story, the following sentences gleamed: "This [the Pacific Union Club] is a vast, heavy, square brownstone house set in a raised formal green yard on Nob Hill. It not only survived the San Francisco earthquake but is so massive and heavy that it looks as though it might very well have started it." (James Reston)

*-w&s-*

Speaking of color, an offbeat story began this way:

"The local Sons of Liberty will be stirred to learn that Paul Revere, silverſmith, arrived yeſterday by horſeback from Boſton with the lateſt intelligence about a tea party there that has occaſioned much excitement among Patriots and Confiderable Diſcomfiture to the Governor." (Murray Illson)

The writing style, as can be seen, was appropriate to the typographical gimmick: use of the old-style "*ſ*," for which the "f" is the closest modern approximation. Too bad the effort was lavished on a publicity stunt; still, the effort was a noble one. But admittedly this sort of thing can be done only once in the average newspaperman's lifetime.

*-w&s-*

Just as a baseball fan likes to read about a game even though he's seen it, so, it may be presumed, a TV viewer welcomes touches of description and perhaps objective commentary about a program he has observed. Such touches are even more welcome to a reader who has not seen the program. Moreover, they lend color to a story that might otherwise read like a dull rewrite of a transcript. Brief phrases or sentences will do the trick. Examples: "The jaunty-looking New York lawyer appeared fairly at ease during his broadcast. Asked what he would do if Mr. Truman declined to take disciplinary action, Mr. Morris smiled and said slowly . . ." (Emanuel Perlmutter)

Incidentally, the reporter should remember that TV imposes a harsh test on his accuracy. If he writes that the candidate wore a striped tie, there may be a million people who saw plainly that the tie was polka-dotted. Readers are looking over the reporter's shoulder as never before.

*-w&s-*

Affairs attended by the public also impose a test on the reporter. Necessarily, stories about evening events like dinners often are written in advance from hand-out texts. But coverage of the event itself must not be allowed to degenerate into a mere routine telephone check to see whether the speeches were delivered as scheduled or, if the event was attended by the reporter (as it should be), to a mere "Okay" call to the office regardless of what happened.

Not infrequently a speaker whose advance text looked dull catches fire in the presence of his audience, or he interpolates a ringing thought or omits a salient point. Or, as in the case of Dean Pound before a Brooklyn Bar Association meeting, casts away his prepared manuscript. "His eyes were 'somewhat beclouded' by a cold and he was not sure he could read it. Then for a full hour he delivered the address in substance, including citations and dates." (Peter Kihss) Readers are entitled to convincing evidence like this that the reporter actually covered the story, and if they happen to have been participants in the event themselves they are quick to notice the absence of such evidence. It is all the worse for the paper if the guests are knowledgeable community leaders, as they are likely to be if the event is a dinner of any importance.

-*w&s*-

To conclude this section on "Dabs of Color," following is a selection of winners in the "Bright Passages" category:

"The skyscrapers' tops, almost lost in the upper storm, were dreamy looking structures, seen through the blowing snow curtain. Bridges and steeples wore lovely winter lace." (Meyer Berger)*

"When Mr. Molotov finished speaking, the Russians applauded vigorously. And when he returned to his seat they went conspicuously into the 'Gee, boss, you were great!' bit." (Gladwin Hill)

"Even while their masters sleep, instruments hum and click in the laboratories here . . . This subtle symphony of electronic sounds symbolizes the mechanized probings typical of the International Geophysical Year." (Walter Sullivan)

"The spectators had seen a stylish Yorkshire terrier twinkle-

---

* This story appears in the Appendix.

toe before them, a bundle of animation in a small package. They had thrilled to the gaiety of an Afghan, long hair flouncing in a self-made breeze. They had admired the even strides of an English springer spaniel. They had seen a compact, sparkling Sealyham terrier patter down the aisle on short legs. Mostly, though, they appeared to like the deep, rolling gait of the phlegmatic bulldog and the smooth-flowing, powerful strides of the clean-limbed boxer." (John Rendel)

"Not even in Paris do drivers play wrinkle-fender with more abandon than in Warsaw, and the pedestrians there tease the drivers like bullfighters in a ring." (James Reston)

"The Swedish vessel's bow had been crumpled back between thirty and fifty feet; she stood as if foreshortened by a dull and clumsy ax, wielded by a giant. The Andrea Doria looked tired but serene." (Milton Bracker)

"Pat O'Brien's voice rose and fell like a dog cart making its way over the hills and vales of Donegal." (Gilbert Millstein)

And in a story about a defense alert: "On Fifth Avenue the traffic signals continued to flash their red-green, red-green, but futilely. It was like a telephone ringing in an empty room." (Philip Benjamin)

## HOW PEOPLE LIVE

The following is from a letter by a great man: "Of political correspondents I can find enough, but I can persuade nobody to believe that the small facts which they see passing daily under their eyes are precious to me at this distance . . . Continue then to give me facts, little facts, such as you think everyone imagines beneath notice . . ." Thus did Thomas Jefferson, writing from Paris, anticipate *Winners & Sinners* by about 170 years. It was not this, of course, that made him a great man—not this alone, that is.

Under the headings "How People Live" and "Innocents Abroad," *W & S* has repeatedly noted with approval stories reporting small facts of everyday life in foreign lands. But it is not always necessary to devote an entire piece to this type of intelligence. Sometimes merely a brief passage will do the job: "Cheers in the Commons are not to be confused with the full-throated roars of football stadiums. They consist of a constant repetition of the words 'hear, hear.'" (Drew Middleton) Frequently the insertion in dry political or economic stories of what *W & S* has referred to as dabs of color will accomplish the purpose: "In the corrugated iron barracks where the delegates began gathering in this Central Indian city it was impossible to find a politician who had any doubts that the party would keep control of Parliament . . ." (A. M. Rosenthal)

An innocent abroad should explain to innocents at home. When the Egyptian Government decided to take over a playland for the rich in the heart of Cairo, Albion Ross brought the situation home to New Yorkers this way: "The situation is much the same as if Central Park in New York were a private club."

Unfortunately, many news stories are almost pure abstractions. They seem to originate and to exist in interplanetary space. Wherever possible—and admittedly it is not always possible—they should be related to the lives of individuals, or at least placed in a tangible setting peopled by flesh-and-blood beings.

*-w&s-*

As "innocents abroad," foreign correspondents can and should interpret more than merely the political doings of the countries in which they are stationed. Drew Middleton excellently exploited an opportunity in a dispatch beginning, "The British are going off the beer." Taking off from a simple economic fact about the decline in beer sales, his story touched on social customs, everyday lingo, installment buying, the influence of television and the teen-age problem. It all added up to an illuminating view of present-day Britain and Britons.

In the category of "How People Live" were dispatches on Madrid's *serenos* (Benjamin Welles), on grumbling by the Poles (Sydney Gruson) and on shopping in Prague (Elie Abel).*

## ONE IDEA TO A SENTENCE

This is a dissertation on the short, simple sentence. For the research information and many of the conclusions presented

---

* These dispatches appear in full in the Appendix.

here, *Winners & Sinners* is indebted to the American Press Institute and James H. Couey Jr., former Sunday editor of the *Birmingham News*.

Let's begin before the beginning. Readers these days have less and less time for their newspapers. The competition for their nonworking time grows constantly. Television, of course, is the latest competitor and a strong one. As Mr. Couey puts it, newspapers have not lost readers to TV, they have lost only time.

What conclusions should the press draw from this? Well, first, that newspapers should resist further inroads into the time devoted to them by making themselves more attractive and more indispensable. Second—and this is the angle that concerns us—that newspapers should find ways of getting information across to readers more easily, more quickly. The way to do this is to frame stories so that everything is immediately clear. The reader must never have to go back and re-read a sentence to grasp its meaning. He must be enabled to comprehend at once.

How can this be done? A few years ago a researcher applied himself to the problem. He noticed that one daily columnist-commentator had the reputation of being more understandable than his competitors. He examined the man's writings to find out why. He found that the only major factor that appeared consistently was a shorter average sentence. By "sentence" he meant the number of words between two periods. He did not mean the number between the first word and a semicolon, or between the first word and an "and" or between the first word and a "who" or a "which." He was talking only about the number of words from point to point. Let's leave aside for the moment whether the diagnosis was completely accurate. But there is no doubt that it was a significant finding. The question was whether it would stand up under testing.

Tests were made and were continued. The procedure was to submit a news story to a group of college students—not to newspapermen nor even to journalism students, who might have specialized interests, but to ordinary English majors. The students were allowed to read the story only once, but without time limit. Then they were asked a few questions about it to test the information they had derived. Next, a rewritten version of the story with reduced average sentence length was submitted to a different group of students and the same questions were asked.

Here is an actual story from a trade journal that was tested:

> Total word count in this story   271
> Total number of sentences          5
> Average words per sentence        54

American London Shrinkers Corp. has spent a year and a half experimenting and compiling data on the shrinking and finishing of man-made fibers used in combination with woolen and worsted yarns and is now equipped to handle all types of blends, it is made known by Theodore Trilling, president.

The trend toward blends in suiting and coating woolens and worsteds brought with it the need for a variety of alterations in the shrinking and sponging operation, Mr. Trilling adds, pointing out, for example, that the Orlon content in a fabric turned yellow, the rayon and acetate content tended to moire and the 15 to 20 per cent of nylon now often used to give added strength tended to shine.

No new machinery is involved, just alterations in the processing, such as a change in the action or the weight of the apron of the leader, but it took a lot of trial and error observations, testing to make sure that further shrinkage would not take place, and tabulation of the data before the "we are now in a position" statement could be made, it was added.

Special reports of the tests and their results have been passed along to the mills and selling agents of these blends, and in some cases they have served as a guide in the correction and improvement of these fabrics, Mr. Trilling states.

He adds that his firm has been offering its 100 per cent woolen and worsted finishing and shrinking service to the industry for the past 55 years and that with the alterations to handle blends now completed, an important step has been made.

|                                              | CORRECT |
| QUESTIONS ASKED STUDENTS                     | ANSWERS |
| -------------------------------------------- | ------- |
| Who is making the statement?                 | 26%     |
| What firm is doing the work?                 | 18%     |
| How long were experiments under way?         | 30%     |
| What kinds of materials are involved?        | 11%     |
| What, briefly, is the story about?           | 9%      |

The really significant question is the final one. This is the one, it was decided, that tests reader comprehension. To be rated "correct" an answer did not need to be elaborate. Almost any relevant one- or two-word reply was so rated.

Following is the shorter-sentence version of the same story:

| Total word count in this story | 265     |
| Total number of sentences      | 21      |
| Average words per sentence     | 12 plus |

American London Shrinkers Corp. has come to the end of an 18-month search.

One year and a half ago that firm set out to find a safe way to shrink, sponge and handle blended materials without damage. Much experimentation was required. Many volumes of data were gathered. The trial and error method was given a thorough test.

And now—success.

Theodore Trilling, president of American London Shrinkers, has announced that the problem has been solved.

Exactly what was the problem?

The trend toward blends in suiting and coating woolens and worsteds created the necessity for developing some alterations in shrinking and sponging operation.

Mr. Trilling mentioned the "change color" problem. He pointed out that the Orlon content tended to moire. The 15 to 20 per cent of nylon, used to give strength, tended to shine. These "color changes" do not occur in the new process.

No new machinery is needed, Mr. Trilling said. He made clear that only alterations in the processing are necessary. He referred to alterations such as a change in action, the weight of the apron or the leader.

The firm's president emphasized that many tests were

required to make sure no further shrinking would occur.

Reports of the tests and results have been passed on to the mills and selling agents of these blends, Mr. Trilling said. In some cases the new information has served as a guide in the correction and improvement of fabrics, he added.

This is an important step in the industry, according to Mr. Trilling.

| QUESTIONS ASKED STUDENTS | CORRECT ANSWERS |
|---|---|
| Who is making the statement? | 68% |
| What firm is doing the work? | 55% |
| How long were experiments under way? | 71% |
| What kinds of materials are involved? | 29% |
| What, briefly, is the story about? | 64% |

Let it be said at once that neither story would win a Pulitzer prize. Yet, note the 64 per cent comprehension of the second version as against the 9 per cent of the original.

When the objection was raised that the story was a technical one and that people in the trade would do better with it, the story was shown to executives and other workers in a mill town. Sure enough, their comprehension of the original piece was higher than that of the students. But—and this is an important but—the rewritten version raised the percentages of correct answers proportionately as much as it had in the case of the students.

Other stories—nontechnical ones—were tested. It should be emphasized that these were not isolated tests. They were performed repeatedly over a period of four or more years. Always they produced what appears to be a correlation between average sentence length and comprehensibility.

Let's return now to the suggestion introduced earlier in this dissertation concerning the accuracy of the diagnosis. You will notice that in the second version of the test story there are some relatively long sentences. But the average sentence length is cut by such sentences as, "And now—success." This circumstance raises the question whether average sentence length is actually the key to comprehensibility. W & S thinks not; it thinks that sentence length is less than the answer, yet considerably more than a coincidence. If you will examine the revised version of the story you will find that almost without exception there is just one idea to a sentence. That is the common denominator. That, it is believed in this corner, is the key to comprehensibility. Confining a sentence to a single thought will usually reduce the number of words. That is why the relation of word count to comprehensibility is more than a coincidence. But the basic factor is, "one idea, one sentence."

W & S once said: "Now don't go and take this as a rule or a formula, but generally it speeds reading if there is only one idea to a sentence." The aversion to rules and formulas still holds. Perhaps it accounts for this critical inspection of the "average words per sentence" finding. The inherent idea that reporters should count the words in their sentences, even though that is not explicitly advised, is as distasteful as the thought of their counting the number of affixes, syllables, personal references or anything else.

Even the one-idea-to-a-sentence advice should not, to repeat, be taken as a rule or a formula. For one thing, there are instances in which two or more thoughts are as inseparable as Siamese twins. To take an extreme example, it would be nonsense to write: "The American flag is red. It is also white. It is blue, too." For another thing, it should be remembered that the relaxed reader who picks up The Times Magazine is a different man from the coffee-gulping, subway-riding reader of the daily paper.

The argument is sometimes advanced, "What difference does the length of the sentence make so long as it is clear?" But clarity is not the sole criterion; the important thing is ease of comprehension. And small blocks of meaning are more easily comprehended than large ones. After all, a quart of gin is perfectly clear, but you wouldn't try to drink it all in one draught.

For the reporter or correspondent intent, as he should be, on delivering the news to the reader pronto, W & S can think of no better maxim than its original one: "Generally, it speeds reading if there is only one idea to a sentence."

*-w&s-*

On the next page is a Model T sentence containing several ideas. Doesn't a sprinkling of periods, as in the version at the right, make it easier to digest?

| | |
|---|---|
| The Egyptian revolutionary leader, long an advocate of better relations with the West, who risked his political future in signing a compromise agreement on control of the Suez Canal zone, in an interview expressed bitterness and disillusion over the results of his dealing with the West. | The Egyptian revolutionary leader has long been an advocate of better relations with the West. He risked his political future in signing a compromise agreement on control of the Suez Canal zone. But in an interview he expressed bitterness and disillusion over the results of his dealings with the West. |

-*w&s*-

Take a look at the following admittedly clear but double-barreled sentence:

"It is argued that the Senate Judiciary Committee's bill not only would invalidate unilaterally a series of solemn agreements on assets with the wartime allies of the United States, but also would give the West German Government and the industrialists a powerful instrument with which to force such small countries as the Netherlands to surrender German assets in lieu of reparations."

The sentence can easily be broken in two. Can there be any doubt that it would be more easily grasped? To be sure, the double-barreled sentence cannot be flatly ruled out. Sometimes the thoughts are too closely related, as in: "It was not only hot, but also humid." But in general, "one thought, one sentence" is a pretty good news-writing rule.

-*w&s*-

Another Model T sentence: "Dr. Samuel H. Sheppard, young, good-looking, prosperous osteopath, whose hobbies are water-skiing and sports cars, is accused of ferociously beating his wife, Marilyn, to death in her bed in their suburban, $31,000 home on the shore of Lake Erie early in the morning of July 4." As one reader remarked, shouldn't the sentence have also told what kind of oil burner was to be found in the cellar?

-*w&s*-

Here's what may result when a press service disregards the precept of one idea to a sentence and when one of our copy editors does nothing about it: "A special grand jury, called to investigate Gov. Leroy Collins' reason for recommending commutation of Walter Lee Irvin's death sentence, today heard the editor of a weekly newspaper tell of two bombings of her home." Let's try it again—slowly this time. On second thought, let's not bother.

*-w&s-*

Too much is crammed into this lead: "A hero and heroine of Hurricane Diane, which swept the East with destructive floods last August, were among eleven men, a housewife and a teen-aged boy and girl cited today for outstanding acts of bravery by the Carnegie Hero Fund Commission." What, by the way, is "a teen-aged boy and girl"? What, for that matter, is "a hero and heroine"? And what, it might be added, is a copy editor?

*-w&s-*

Sports writers in particular seem addicted to the overloaded sentence. The following mid-Victorian lead contains four or more ideas; surely one would be preferable: "Scoring four times before its own goal line was crossed, Princeton downed Harvard, 35-20, as 34,000 chilled fans watched at Palmer Stadium today in the opener of the Big Three round robin."

*-w&s-*

Another example: "Junior Gilliam hit two home runs off Allie Reynolds, who gave up all the Brooklyn runs in the first four innings, and Billy Cox hit another one off the Chief as the Brooks won their fourth straight game and their twenty-first of the spring—all against major clubs." Writers must watch out for that little word "as." When you start to write it, ask yourself whether it wouldn't be a better idea to punch the period key on your typewriter instead.

*-w&s-*

In breaking up a sentence that contains more than one idea it is not always sufficient merely to insert a period. Take this sentence, for example: "Prime Minister Eden gave way tonight to Opposition goading and disclosed that his Government would take the Suez dispute to the United Nations Security Council rather than use force." The copy editor recognized that these two ideas would be better as two sentences, but all he did was put a period after "goading." He should have recognized that the second idea was the news of the story, and that the two thoughts should have been reversed.

*-w&s-*

A dissent to the one-idea-to-a-sentence principle is expressed in a recent book by Charles H. Brown, *Informing the People.**  The author terms the principle "a pernicious development" because "the rule [N.B.: it has never been a 'rule' in The Times office] implies that every idea is of equal importance and this simply is not so." Let it be said at once that there is no such implication because no one would contend that all sentences are of equal importance. The author illustrates his point with this example: "The new directive was disclosed yesterday. It was issued under the signature of the chairman of the board. It stated that bids must be obtained on all purchases of more than $250."

The author then suggests a rewording that he feels would be clearer: "The new directive, disclosed yesterday, was issued under the signature of the chairman of the board. It stated that bids, etc."

It may be conceded at once that the rewording is smoother, if not "clearer." However, the example he has chosen is an absurdly literal interpretation of the one-idea-to-a-sentence principle. In it, there is no more reason to regard "disclosed yesterday" as a separate idea calling for a separate sentence than there is to regard "new" as a separate idea.

The author of the book concedes that the principle has its utility in discouraging marathon leads, and he adds: "It also may be true, as one editor has written, that one-idea-one-sentence writing speeds reading, but it does not necessarily

* Henry Holt and Company, Incorporated, New York, 1957.

follow that it assists comprehension." But what is the distinction between reading and comprehension? If by speed of reading he means merely the rate at which the little black symbols are registered visually, then nothing would affect it except changes in the type or in the reader's glasses. Apart from this limited physical sense, speed of reading must include comprehension if it means anything at all. So when the author concedes that one-idea-to-a-sentence speeds reading, does he not concede the whole case?

## SHORT PARAGRAPHS

Among the ways in which a massive paper can be made more inviting and easier to read is to shorten paragraphs. It is not desirable to go to the Brisbanian extreme of making each sentence a paragraph unto itself (although for the lead sentence this is a pretty good idea). At the same time it should be remembered that a paragraph that is a good size anywhere else becomes elongated and clumsy in the narrow newspaper column. And it cannot be denied that short paragraphs are easier to grasp quickly, that they provide welcome white space in our all-too-solid columns and that they minimize the chance of a reader's losing his place in the large areas of small type.

You won't catch *Winners & Sinners* laying down any limits for paragraph length. Formulas like that are silly. And much depends on the degree of intimacy between the thoughts that are being expressed. What *W & S* will say is that when it comes to paragraphs a bread box is better proportioned than a filing cabinet.

## TROVE OF TROUBLES

Under this heading appears a miscellany of representative writing (and thinking) defects that crop up in news copy. They are mostly attributable to the carelessness that sometimes accompanies the haste imposed on the reporter.

*Ambiguity.* (1) "The decision to strike followed rejection of a proposal by the Publishers Association of New York City that all issues be referred to arbitration." Did the association reject the proposal or make it?

(2) "However, except so far as foreign policy is concerned,

things have not yet developed to a point where Syria is irre-
vocably lost to the East." Who would be losing and who
gaining?

-*w&s*-

*Gobbledygook.* "Improved financial support and less oner-
ous work loads . . ." Translation (by Clifton Daniel): "Higher
pay and less work . . ."

-*w&s*-

*Jargon.* "During the last few years, however, critics have
pointed out a growing inability to handle the demanding
tessitura of the Wagnerian roles." Know what "tessitura"
means? Neither does the average reader of the general news
columns, where the word appeared.

-*w&s*-

*Jet-propelled dictator.* "Overhead new Sabre jets, given to
Spain by the United States, whistled low over the trees . . .
General Franco himself could be seen on the reviewing stand
following the fighters as they swept out of sight."

-*w&s*-

*Height of qualification.* "Inspector O'Brien, 60 years old,
is said to be married to a close relative of Mayor Impellitteri's
wife." Sounds as if the paper were mongering rumors.

-*w&s*-

*Stoking the Hot-Stove League fires.* "By a coincidence, the
right-handed pitcher who wears uniform No. 17 was the
Brooks' seventeenth signer." Gad, it seems almost incredible!

-*w&s*-

*Irrelevant and incompetent.* (1) "Chief Magistrate John M.
Murtagh withheld a jail sentence on Reig because the latter,
who weighs 300 pounds, came into court voluntarily." (2) "As

the candidate reaffirmed his aim of establishing the principles of equality stated in the Declaration of Independence, one guest remarked: 'Aren't his eyes pretty?' "

-w&s-

*Yrs. of 15th inst. recvd.* ". . . Mr. Gaither said that he was already in receipt of the musical's book . . ." There's no business like show business but business English has no business in the news columns.

-w&s-

*Good trick.* ". . . the Brooks put three of their safeties back to back . . ."

-w&s-

*How long is a piece of string?* "The only disquieting element in the portrait was a fabulous double necklace of ropes of pearls hung with a baroque pearl pendant the size of a rock." How big is a rock?

-w&s-

*Hearts-and-flowers writing.* "The spiritual beauty of Christmas became an eternal reality today for Mike Korcheck, 24-year-old star shortstop of the Brooklyn Dodgers' farm team at Fort Worth, Texas." Translation: Mike Korcheck died.

-w&s-

*Baa.* " 'I guess you can call me the family black sheep,' he said, looking sheepish."

-w&s-

*Eh?* "But the black moths were at a disadvantage in past years. Their natural habitat, the tree trunk, camouflaged them if they were black and white . . ."

-w&s-

*Unfortunate juxtapositions.* (1) A dispatch about an article Sir Winston Churchill wrote in 1931 speculating on the potential horsepower of the hydrogen atom ended with the sentence, "At the time, Sir Winston was out of power . . ." (2) A story about the Old North Church Steeple Fund said a $10,000 gift had put the fund "over the top."

-*w&s*-

*Double meaning.* "Mist, frozen by near-zero temperatures, coats trees and walks around Niagara Falls . . ." Like the fog, perhaps, it comes on little cat feet.

-*w&s*-

*Shortcut.* Using a single word to apply to two other words in a sentence so that it has in one use a literal meaning and in the other a metaphorical meaning is the rhetorical figure known as a syllepsis. It is a very ticklish figure to use in serious writing because it so often borders on the ludicrous. Here is a borderline case of the kind that is best avoided. "The tank fired, and the bridge and many hopes sank."

-*w&s*-

*Flophouse to fame, round trip.* "The bronze plaque awards are named after the fictional Horatio Alger of rags-to-riches success stories." Toddlers on the staff are advised (a) that Horatio Alger was not fictional, but real as anything, and (b) that if you don't know, don't guess—check it.

-*w&s*-

*Nice catch.* "A 43-year-old Brooklyn woman who jumped from a window of her flaming apartment yesterday morning was saved by a passing motorist who caught her in his arms."

-*w&s*-

*Bum sports.* "Triple plays can occur in international trade as well as on the gridiron." Let's see now . . . Johnny Lattner catches a forward pass, steps on second and throws into the corner pocket. Yep, that would do it.

-*w&s*-

*Not a must.* "Under the law the Wage Stabilization Board must approve any award recommended by an arbitrator." This kind of erroneous statement is common enough to warrant a footnote in anybody's book. What the writer meant, of course, was that the board "must pass upon" or "must approve any award . . . before it can become final."

-*w&s*-

*Wabbit does pratfall.* "Peter Cottontail must have hippity hopped down the bunny trail for record candy deliveries as the eternal promise of Easter renewal was marred by overcast skies." Microcosm, merchandising, macrocosm and meteorology all in one tasteless sentence.

-*w&s*-

*Born is a formula.* A *Reader's Digest* editor, Marc Rose, sent a Times editor a copy of an obit page with the following underlined: "Born in Des Moines, Iowa, Mr. Tuttle joined Phillip Ruxton in the business of making printing ink . . .", "Born in Frankfort, Ky., he was graduated from Centre College . . .", "Born in Kenosha, Miss Dibble studied at the School of Civics and Philanthropy in Chicago . . .", "Born in Brooklyn, N.Y., Mr. Friedman had been a trustee of the Hebrew Teachers College . . .", and eight more of the same. Commented Mr. Rose: "Born in Waukegan, Ill., I get damn sick of the non sequiturs."

-*w&s*-

*Ex post facto construction.* Watch out for what might be termed the "ex post facto construction," typified by this fictitious example: "The dead man grabbed the policeman's arm." Here are two actual sinners: (1) "Mrs. Cox was passing the wrecked store, Storktime, at 393 Bridge Street . . . when the truck . . . swerved from its course, hit a parked car and headed for the store." The store was wrecked, of course, only when the truck hit it. (2) ". . . John declared the general personally had 'persuaded' the dead soldier to re-enlist in the Army eight months ago." A dead soldier wouldn't be much good to any army.

*-w&s-*

*Long name.* "She gave her name as Miss Vivian Ether, a Western Union operator residing at 101 Lafayette Avenue." Make it "she identified herself as" or "she said she was."

*-w&s-*

*Lost articles.* Once upon a time (this is just a guess) an editor looked over his paper as it came fresh from the press and noted to his horror that every story on page 1 began with the word "the." He acted decisively. He ordered that thereafter no story was to begin with "the." Some of his disciples went out into the wide world. They carried the rule with them. Indeed, they went him one better and decided that no sentence must begin with "the." The identity of the editor was lost in the mists of history (lucky fellow), but his malady lingers on. Witness: "Cause of the disturbance was the proposed wedding between . . ." "Outcome of some of the conventions can be gauged in advance . . ." "Reason, he said, was to 'avoid inflationary trends' . . ." All you need do is think how you would write the sentence if it were inverted so that the de-articled noun did not come first. Would you then omit the word "the"? That should help end this latter-day abomination. Remember what the Bible says: "If I forget 'the,' O Jerusalem, let my right hand forget her cunning."

Omitting the article "the" before the word "police" has also for some mysterious reason become a usage peculiar to the press. Thus a reporter will write, "Mr. Kleme told police that . . . ," although he wouldn't dream of saying it that way in conversation. It is true that in certain contexts the article may be omitted. It is proper to write, "Police are necessary in a big city," just as it is proper to write, "State and church are kept separate under our concept of government." But outside that sphere of extreme generality it is not idiomatic to drop the article. The word "police" should be thought of as parallel to the word "army." In the same way as you say "the army" or "soldiers" you should say "the police" or "policemen."

*-w&s-*

*Mania for uniqueness.* "Two hundred and sixty-nine veterans of the Colombian battalion in Korea, the only Latin-American army unit in history to fight overseas, arrived here tonight . . ." Except in baseball, where everything is a statistic ("first left-handed shortstop with blond hair to field a ball on two hops on a Tuesday"), an expression of uniqueness should be a red flag. As to the Colombian battalion, a Brazilian official was quick to point out that a Brazilian force fought in Italy years earlier in World War II.

*-w&s-*

*Superlatives are the worst things.* A story about a watchmaker who flew his single-engine Beechcraft Bonanza from Hawaii to San Francisco in 1957 said: "Mr. Gluckman became the first man to make the 2,300-mile trip either way, or both ways, in a small plane." However, note this news item dated March 9, 1949: "A new world record for non-stop distance flight in a light private airplane was set today when Capt. William P. Odom landed his single-engine Beechcraft Bonanza here [Teterboro, N. J.] at 12:05 P.M. to end a 5,300-mile hop that started yesterday exactly thirty-six hours earlier in Honolulu."

*-w&s-*

*He (Jones) hit him (Smith).* Explaining a pronoun by parenthesizing a name after it is occasionally unavoidable in quoted matter, but in our own writing (which, of course, is so much better than that of the people we quote) it should very rarely be necessary.

An example: "Mr. Lane said that he was forwarding to United States Attorney General James P. McGranery a transcript of the testimony given before the commission on Friday by his (Lane's) administrative assistant." It is almost as if the sentence were addressed to two different readers—A, a stuffy soul, who cannot brook repetition of the name "Lane" and for whose benefit the pronoun "his" is used, and B, who would not understand to which person the "his" referred and for whose enlightenment the parenthesis is surreptitiously inserted in the hope that A won't notice it. Why not ignore A and simply say "Mr. Lane's"?

Here is another example, which goes to the absurd extreme of inserting three parentheses in a single sentence: "Corporal Brown testified that when Provoo enlisted his (Brown's) services in behalf of the Japanese, he got Provoo to agree that he (Provoo) would not ask him (Brown) to commit any traitorous act." The first parenthesis is rendered superfluous by the plain meaning of the words; the second and third could be eliminated by a simple reconstruction to make the sentence read, ". . . he got Provoo to agree not to ask him . . ." With that change all the pronouns in the sentence would refer to the same antecedent, all would be tidy and the parenthetical stumbling blocks would be removed.

In a way, the use of identifying parentheses is a confession of inability to construct a clear sentence.

*-w&s-*

*Partial quotations.* Introducing a partial quotation that causes an abrupt switch in the same sentence from third person to first person is by no means incorrect. But it often is clumsy. For instance: "He said, however, that there was no need to do so because he had already 'expressed myself fully' . . ." Another example: ". . . Dr. Jonas E. Salk, who developed the vaccine, preferred to remain in 'my role as an investigator.'" In sentences like these the quoted matter should be carefully examined to determine whether a quotation is indeed necessary; if it is, the writer should select only the significant words. In the first example it hardly seems necessary to quote the rather ordinary phrase. In the second, the "my" could be eliminated from the quoted matter. There is nothing wrong with either sentence except a lack of grace.

Another example: "He [Mr. Truman] smilingly conceded that he 'feels more kindly toward newspaper men now that one is about to become a member of his family.'" Obviously the word he used wasn't "feels" unless he said: "Mo'nin' y'all. Ah feels more kindly toward newspaper men, etc." The solu-

tion, of course, is to begin the quotation with the word "more."
Likewise, "his" should be "my."

-w&s-

Here are a few specimens of "writing by ear" intended to
demonstrate that sonic writing is not necessarily sound writing:

*The Compleat Malaprop.* An item about a fishing almanac
began: "The Brown-Forman Distillers Corporation of Louisville has definitely established the often-rumored connection
between its product and the gentle art of Isaac Newton."
What's so gentle about being conked with an apple?

*Of cats and kings.* " 'Even a cat can look at a king,' as Dick
Whittacker said." First of all, it's "Dick Whittington," and
second, he didn't say it.

*Bridge, anyone?* "To breach the gap between crowded institutions for the aged and the rising age population . . ."

*Japanese accent?* "He was tearing in, rickety-split, when he
saw he couldn't make the catch." The word is "lickety-split."

## CRAZY MIXED-UP METAPHORS

"Yet the President has backed him to the hilt every time
the chips were down."

"While Moscow is thus stoking up the 'cold war,' however,
Peiping is playing it pianissimo." Depends on whether you
like your "cold war" hot or sweet.

"Television spectrum handicappers noted that ratings may
have had some bearing on the matter. 'Arthur Godfrey and
His Friends,' which is fully sponsored, has felt the cutting
edge of 'Disneyland' . . ."

"The root problems . . . can be brought into pretty clear
perspective by subjecting the angry torrent of words to the
dissecting knife and exposing what lies beneath."

## MONOLOGOPHOBIA AND SYNONYMOMANIA

A monologophobe (don't try to look it up) is a guy who
would rather walk naked in front of Saks Fifth Avenue than
be caught using the same word more than once in three lines
of type. What he suffers from is synonymomania (don't look
that one up, either), which is a compulsion to distract and,

if possible, puzzle the reader by calling a spade successively a garden implement and an earth-turning tool.

The affliction besets sports writers especially. For instance: "Sugar Ray flattened Bobo in twelve *rounds* in 1950, out-pointed him in fifteen *sessions* in 1952 and knocked him out in two *heats* last Dec. 9." Not content with the legitimate variables of the sentence—the manner of the outcome in each fight and the length of time it took—the writer tries to make what should be a constant also look like a variable. Thus, the reader is left to wonder whether a session or a heat is some-thing different from a round and if not, what the hell?

Avoidance of monotony caused by repetition of a really noticeable word is desirable. But mechanical substitution of synonyms may make matters worse.

"Elegant variation" is the term applied by Fowler to this practice of mechanically inserting synonyms to avoid repeti-tion of words. Often this practice is merely a poor remedy; sometimes it is worse than the disease. In the latter category is the use of synonyms that fall strangely on the ear or eye, as in the following headline: "Heavy Snowfall Surprises City, Snarls Traffic. Biggest *Descent* of Season Causes Serious De-lays . . ." A pronoun will frequently prove a good cure. The foregoing head might have read, "Biggest of the Season, *It* Causes Serious Delays . . ."

*-w&s-*

Following is an example in which the use of a synonym was merely a poor remedy: "Somewhere among the thousands of skillful amateur wrestlers across the nation are sixteen outstanding grapplers who will win a place on the American team . . ." The use of "grapplers" suggests that perhaps they are something different from wrestlers. Why not use "ones," or use nothing at all after "sixteen"?

*-w&s-*

A cliché that undoubtedly had its origin in an unreason-ing fear of repetition is illustrated by the following passage: "It will be the third time in as many years that the dockers here will have had a chance to vote . . ." What's wrong with the more direct and more precise form, "third time in three years"?

Now, on the other hand, a little touch of monologophobia to avoid redundancy might have helped the framer of this sentence: "M. Gomulka's *decision* to join with the Polish 'liberals' could be *decisive* in *deciding* the fierce factional struggle . . ."

*-w&s-*

More monologophobia: "A Review on Gold. An Analysis on Why Yellow Metal Plays Its Part This Year." Notice how the clumsy phrase "yellow metal" conspicuously betrays the writer's fear of repeating a word. By the way, those two uses of "on" make one wonder whatever became of the word "of."

*-w&s-*

Still more: Want to know what charcoal is? It's "the ancient black substance."

*-w&s-*

Tom Rover almost never said anything; he usually averred, asseverated, smiled, chuckled, grinned (plain or mischievously), groaned, expostulated, ejaculated, declared or asserted. Tom apparently has made his impress on journalism, where synonymomania is a common affliction. The simple verb *say* never seems to be good for more than one inning; then writers or editors feel they must rush in all kinds of bush league relief pitchers. *Say* means to express. Here's what some of the others mean: *assert* is to express strongly or positively, *aver* is to express with confidence, *declare* is to express explicitly, particularly in a formal or public way. It is well to discriminate among these shades of meaning and not to assume that the words are completely interchangeable.

By the way, *add* is another of those relief pitchers; it is thrown in even when the second statement in no way amplifies or is even connected with the first. For instance: "He declared [ugh] the 'small business man is being squeezed' by the Republican Administration. Housewives, he added, are concerned about rising prices." Continued, yes; added, no.

# Syntax Sinners

Syntax concerns the manner of putting words together properly. The minimum objective is conveyance of meaning. But beyond that are objectives of precision, grace, logic, clarity and conformity with the traditions of the language.

A man could take a broad plank, nail four uprights to it and have himself a table. It would serve. He could eat off it, play stud poker on it and drink his friends under it. But unless he lived in a hovel he would not consider it a suitable piece of furniture for his house. One minimum principle of cabinet-making is that the legs of a table should be of equal length, but in addition there are other valid principles to which the cabinet-maker subscribes.

So, too, in language mere expression of understandable words is not sufficient. "Me good girl" is completely understandable. But no linguistic craftsman, nor even a person slightly educated in English, would settle for it. Proper syntax is not an esoteric art, but it calls for sturdier construction and more polish than pidgin English.

Over the years, the errors of syntax culled by *Winners & Sinners* from copy produced by professional writers seem to fall mainly into two categories. The first comprises slips of the most elementary kind—unattached modifiers, for example, or disagreement between subject and verb, or misuse of "whom." Study of these solecisms suggests that they result not from ignorance, but rather from haste or an understandable concentration on content that diverts attention from form. The remedy is obvious: care and a re-reading of what has been written.

The second category of errors embraces the more subtle syntactical points that are not discussed, or anyway not discussed in much detail, in the common run of grammar books.

They are perhaps too specialized for the nonprofessional writer—the intricacies of sequence of tenses, for instance, seem to constitute a problem that is almost peculiar to the newspaper profession. Yet anyone for whom writing is a major interest is bound to find himself face to face with these points at one time or another.

The listing that follows encompasses both these categories and, of course, much besides. Inasmuch as the examples are from actual news stories, it is obvious that these are errors that are really made, at least occasionally, rather than imaginary isolated ones fabricated to demonstrate a point. And if they are errors that are really made, it follows that they are the kinds that require attention.

**A, AN.** (1) *Shorthand.* A common piece of what might be described as journalistic shorthand is illustrated by these sentences: "A volcano erupting under the sea . . . has thrust its crater and cone an estimated 250 feet above the surface of the water." "The French have an estimated 40,000 troops and police on hand to maintain order." When you consider that the article "an" denotes singular number, the absurdity of these phrases becomes apparent. They are a telescoping of grammatically sound phrases ("an estimated height of . . ."; "an estimated total of . . .") into grammatically unsound ones. Let's restore the soundness. The price of two extra words is a small one to pay to achieve good English.

This is a similar common usage: ". . . a record 1,200-000 automobiles on highways in and near the city were predicted . . ." You can't say "a automobiles." The passage quoted is shorthand for "a record total of 1,200,000 automobiles," and that is the way it should be written.

(2) *"A" or "an" before consonant sounds.* "General Eisenhower found out today he could not indicate even passing interest in an historic picture . . ." "Mr. Byrnes . . . termed its 1954 decision against segregated public schools an 'usurpation of power.' " The preference these days is for "a historic." "A" is used before words beginning with sounded consonants or with vowels that have the value of consonants. Therefore: "a usurpation," "a utopia," "a European," "a uniform," as well as "a historic."

(3) *"A" or "an" before initials.* ". . . Churchill, speak-

ing at a M.I.T. Convocation . . ." The writer was obviously thinking of the sound of the words "Massachusetts Institute of Technology," not of the pronunciation of the abbreviation "M.I.T.," when he used the article "a." But people say "M.I.T.," just like that, so the article would have to be "an." And what people say is, in this situation, the test. For instance, you would not (at least, should not) write "an N.Y. Central spokesman" because people don't read or say "N.Y." as an abbreviation; they instantly translate it into "New York."

**ACTIVE VOICE.** *See* "switching voices."

**ADJECTIVE PILE-UP.** Under the illusion that they are saving space, writers sometimes pile up compounded adjectives before nouns. The offenses range from a fairly innocuous construction like "some as-yet-unidentified Tammany friend" to a more serious pile-up like "the presently used S-55 float-equipped craft." But no space was saved by the writer of either of these examples. Examination will show that the cumbersome qualifiers could have been placed after the nouns with as much economy and with greater smoothness. The two phrasings call to mind the Fowler in-another-context-cited example of German usage, "The since 1914 owing to the world-war befallen destruction of capital." This sort of thing, as Mr. Fowler points out, is grammatically sound in German, but indefensible in English.

**ADVERB PLACEMENT.** Some writers and editors, blinded by the split-infinitive obsession, seem determined not to split anything except hairs. Thus, they will not permit an adverb to divide elements of a compound verb. The truth is that more often than not the proper and natural place for an adverb is between parts of a compound verb. Example: "A broad reorganization of the Immigration and Naturalization Service virtually has been completed." Here the proper place for "virtually" is ahead of "completed." When the adverb and the verb constitute the equivalent of an adjective and noun ("virtual completion"), they should appear together.

Here are some more misplacements:

"The city almost will certainly be governed by a coalition . . ." Clearly the "almost" qualifies "certainly," and should be placed right before it.

". . . Mr. Harriman said he was considering seriously asking the Legislature to delay or abandon the inspection plan." The "seriously" is so badly placed that it actually perverts the meaning. It belongs ahead of "considering."

"In the past, eleven plans for removing troops gradually have been drawn up by the United Nations." Just what is meant here? Gradual removal of troops or gradual drawing up of plans? Obviously the construction should be: "for gradually removing."

"If the period of the truce were used by the enemy to build up bases . . . the Allied advantage largely would disappear." It should read, "would largely disappear."

ADVERBS. ". . . it was noted that mathematics was one of the poorest taught subjects on the elementary and secondary levels . . ." What is needed to modify "taught" is a "how" word, and a "how" word is an adverb, not an adjective. Therefore: "most poorly taught."

"He indicated the Giants also wanted Rip Repulski, an outfielder, but not bad enough to offer the kind of exchange the Cardinals want." Badly.


AMONG. *See* "between."


AS. *See* "like."


BETWEEN. (1) *Between and among.* In elementary school Miss Thistlebottom probably told you to use "between" for two things, and "among" for more than two. Which is a good rule for schoolchildren, who need rules. But, like all rules, it has exceptions. "Among," to be sure, always applies to more than two things, but the relationship it expresses is usually a rather loose one. When three or more things are brought into a relationship severally and reciprocally, "between" is proper. In the following passage "between" would be better than "among": "Apart from discussions among Washington, Paris and London on the prospective conference . . ." The idea of *two* is inherent etymologically in the word "between," but so is it inherent in the discussions here referred to: The meetings were being held by Washington and Paris, by Paris and London, by London and Washington. So, also, a treaty *between* nine powers would be completely proper and exact.

(2) *Between each, every.* "His nose ran and he sneezed between nearly every shot during the first round of golf he ever played in Scotland." Margaret Nicholson, writing about "between" in her new adaptation of Fowler,* says: "It must not be followed by a single expression in which a distributive such as 'each' or 'every' is supposed to represent a plural. Not 'A pitcher who tried to gain time by blowing his nose between every ball'; this must be corrected," says she, "to 'after every ball, between the balls, or between every ball and the next.' "

**BOTH.** The proper placement of *"both . . . and"* is identical in principle with the proper placement of "not only . . . but also." (*See also* "not only.") Whatever appears after the first member of these teams must be exactly paralleled grammatically by what appears after the second member— a noun in the first position must be matched by a noun in the second position, a verb must be matched by a verb, a prepositional phrase must be matched by a prepositional phrase. An example of a misplaced "both": ". . . even the men in the class had to admit that both from the viewpoint of economics and history, the age-old restrictions are disappearing." This may be corrected in one of two ways: first, by putting the "both" ahead of "economics" (this would provide a noun after "both" and another noun after "and"); second, by making it "both of economics and of history" (this would provide a prepositional phrase after each member of the team). In this example, as in so many others, correct grammar produces greater clarity and certainly greater orderliness.

**COLLECTIVES.** Whether to treat collective nouns as singular or plural is a continuing source of perplexity. The British seem to resolve their doubts in favor of the plural; the Americans seem to resolve theirs in favor of the singular. Both should resolve them in favor of logic.

* *Dictionary of American-English Usage* (New York, Oxford University Press, 1957).

If the idea of oneness predominates, treat the noun as a singular. ("The number of accidents is larger this year"— because "number" is thought of as "total.")

If the idea of more-than-oneness predominates, treat the noun as a plural. ("A great number of accidents are preventable"—because "number" is equivalent to "many.") It does not seem sensible to say, "The couple was married"; marriage is the joining of two persons, not something that is done to an already existing unit. Nor does it seem logical to say, "The couple was arrested in separate apartments."

Likewise, when "majority" means simply "most of," it would be preferable to treat it as a plural rather than write: ". . . the French people . . . have repeatedly shown that a majority of them is in favor of the Defense Community . . ."

Professor R. W. Pence of the Department of English, DePauw University, favored *Winners & Sinners* with a simple rule concerning "number": "Preceded by 'the,' 'number' is singular; preceded by 'a,' 'number' is plural."

It is also possible to lay down a collateral rule—one that is violated in this head: "Negro Couple Clings to Their Home." Rule: Once you have made your choice, stay with it.

**COUNTRIES.** *See* "pronouns."

**DANGLING PARTICIPLES.** *See* "unattached modifiers."

**DATA.** The use of "data" as if it were a singular noun is a common solecism; *e.g.,* "London Psychiatrist Asserts Data Is Lacking to Prove Soviet Superiority"; "Greenglass Data Is Old, Rogge Says." Data is plural . . . er . . . data are plural; anyway, you get the idea. But here is an incomprehensible variation, so cockeyed as to be a collector's item: "It is quite possible that the O.O.R. has reasons to believe these satellites exist, but is withholding its findings until more datum is uncovered."

**DIFFERENT.** "He also said 'different witnesses' than those who testified before the original grand jury would be called . . ." The misuse of "than" after "different" apparently follows the analogy of "other," but it should be remembered that "different" is different from "other." "Different than" is variously described by the authorities as "colloquial" and "incorrect."

**DOUBLE DUTY.** "Double duty" is a phrase that may be applied to constructions in which a single word is made to serve two purposes. Example: "The Army, which now regards organic aviation as integral as the rifle and bayonet . . ." Notice that the first "as" is bigamously wedded both to "regards" and to the second "as." Another example: Winston Churchill in *Triumph and Tragedy* . . . raises a question as to what extent these powerful pressures affected Mr. Truman." The "to" looks backward to "as" and forward to "what extent." Making one word thus do double duty is somewhat like hanging a picture on the wall to hide a crack. But not exactly like it, because the writers of such constructions don't know there is a crack, or else are not aware that it is a picture they are hanging.

A final example: "Many products are developed . . . after odor sniffers have come up with the right answers as to what use an aroma can be put." One of *Winners & Sinners'* outside contributors (bless 'em all) complained that readers had been cheated out of another "to," and added: "I want my other 'to.' I hope I am not wrong in asking you, whom I have decided to address this letter, which you may or may not reply, to, to, to."

Another kind of double duty is illustrated by this bifocal sentence. "Kwame Nkrumah, born in the mud-hut village of Nkroful in 1909, is pronounced as if it were spelled Quameh En-kroo-mah . . ." First Nkrumah is treated as a person ("born . . . in 1909"), then, when the sentence proceeds, as a name ("pronounced as if . . ."). Untidy writing.

**DUE TO.** The use of "due to" in the sense of "because of" when it modifies a whole thought instead of merely a noun is common but colloquial. An example of the misuse is this sentence: "Plans for adjournment next Saturday already had been abandoned due to the legislative tie-up." If you keep in mind that "due" is an adjective and therefore must modify a noun, its proper use becomes easy. Here are two simple sentences illustrating the wrongs and rights of the matter. Wrong: "He fell due to the icy sidewalk." Right: "His fall was due to the icy sidewalk." Which goes to show, perhaps, how one slip can be wrong and another right.

**EACH.** "Each" is, of course, a singular. When it is the subject of a sentence it takes a singular verb. "Each of the defendants is subject to a sentence of five years in prison." When it is merely an adjective in apposition with a plural subject, however, the plural subject remains in control and the verb is plural. Thus, this sentence is incorrect: "Mr. Siemer, who is 23 years old, and his wife, who is 22, each is subject to sentences of five years in prison . . ." It should be "are subject to."

So much for the number of the verb. The number of a later noun depends on whether the "each" comes before or after the verb. If it comes before the verb, the noun remains in the plural: "They each are subject to sentences of five years." If it comes after the verb, the noun becomes singular: "They are subject each to a sentence of five years."

Placing "each" before or after the verb depends in turn on how much stress you want to put on the separateness and distributiveness of the elements. When you want to hit the separateness hard, you place the "each" after the verb.

**EACH OTHER.** "He said Washington's action had been particularly damaging to the delicate relations between India and Pakistan at a time when the two countries had been developing a more friendly approach to one another . . ." Whatever may be said (and much has been) for and against restricting "each other" to two, there is logic on the side of not using "one another" for two, but restricting it to three or more. When only two parties are involved you are not thinking of "another"—any old "other"—but of *the* "other." Therefore "each other" is the proper phrase for two.

**EITHER . . . OR.** When two singular nouns are joined by "either . . . or" or "neither . . . nor," there is no trouble in deciding the number of the verb; it must be singular. But when one of the nouns is singular and the other plural, there apparently is difficulty. Witness: "Neither the tall, spare fisherman nor his friends denies that Mr. and Mrs. Morgan could rent their cottages for a better price . . ."

This usage is incorrect. There are three possible approaches to the problem. The first is to change the construction; *e.g.,* "It is not denied by either the fisherman or his friends . . ." The second is to seek out a verb that is neutral as to number; *e.g.,* "Neither the fisherman nor his friends would deny . . ." But if neither of these escape hatches is open, then the verb should take the number of the noun that is nearer to it, thus: "Neither the fisherman nor his friends deny . . ."

Another neither-nor trouble is exemplified here: "Neither he nor Mr. Taylor amplified their remarks." Make it "his remarks."

**ELLIPSIS.** Ellipsis permits the omission of a word in part of a sentence if it can be supplied, or understood, from a neighboring part of the sentence. The word to be supplied must, however, be in the same form (number, gender, tense) as in the construction from which it is understood. Therefore, these are incorrect: (1) "A large quantity of arms and ammunition was seized and about 150 suspects freed." Make it "150 suspects were freed." (2) "Irwin made a great leaping catch . . . for the final out of the seventh when the bases were filled and Wilhelm pitching." Make it "was pitching." (3) "The bonus would apply to all officers and enlisted men who have or will serve under fire . . ." Make it: "who have served or will serve . . ."

**ENUMERATION.** A normal enumeration or series follows the pattern "1, 2 and 3." An abnormal or incomplete or, as Mr. Fowler dubs it, bastard enumeration would be "1, 2 and A." Hence, a normal series would be, "He likes reading books, listening to music and seeing plays," whereas an abnormal series would be, "He likes reading books, listening to music and he doesn't go out much."

It's surprising how common this solecism is. Look at these: "The home side struggled along with weak pitching, anemic fielding and what hitting they did lacked authority." "The seniors, wearing chemises, rolled-down stockings and revealing rouged knees, performed . . ." "The owners pay fines, protest that rehabilitation of the old dwellings would be prohibitively costly and the situation remains unchanged in most cases." "The production models will have a speed of sixty-five miles an hour, a range of 150 miles and carry 300 pounds."

The error arises mostly, no doubt, from carelessness. But another factor is that some writers would rather kick their grandmothers than be caught repeating a word—in these examples the word "and," which should be inserted between the first and second items in the series. Such writers probably order coffee and doughnuts for breakfast, along with a portion of ham, eggs.

**EVERYONE.** *See* "pronouns."

**FATALLY.** *See* "incomparables."

**FUSED PARTICIPLES.** Although there are at least two schools of thought on the fused participle (the Fowler school and the Onions-Jespersen school),* it is best to avoid the construction as clumsy, smacking of illiteracy and grammatically unparsable. Here is a legitimate participle: "I saw him running down the street." What was seen was "him," and what he was doing was "running." Now for a fused participle: "I disapprove him running for office." What is disapproved is not "him," but his act of "running." The word "him" is thus left without any grammatical construction. The words "him running" afford a vague "sense fusion," but provide grammatical confusion.

There is evidence that writers who may never have heard of the fused participle instinctively shrink from it in its more obvious forms; *e.g.*, "It is pertinent for this corner . . . to speculate upon the possibility of *Mr. Chaplin being barred* from the United States—the possibility of *his being excluded* from making any more films in Hollywood." The possessive should, of course, have been used in both cases, but whereas "Mr. Chaplin being barred" apparently didn't sound wrong to the writer, he couldn't bring himself to write "him being excluded."

The corrective for the fused participle is often (but not

---

* Dr. C. T. Onions in *An Advanced English Syntax* and Professor Otto Jespersen in a paper, "Some Disputed Points in English Grammar," as discussed in *Usage and Abusage*, by Eric Partridge (New York, Harper and Brothers, 1942).

always) the use of the possessive before the gerund—*e.g.,* "his being." Frequently, however, an entirely different construction is advisable. For instance, "There is no chance of any of them going hungry," could be changed to, "There is no chance that any of them will go hungry."

It may be acknowledged that there are rare times when it is best to swallow hard and accept the fused participle as the best idiomatic way of expressing the idea. The example in the previous paragraph could be one of them, and another might be, "The town was captured without a man being wounded."

The fused participle is common, as this group shows: (1) "The Socialist union involved threatened to call for a general strike in the event of the *demands* not *being* met." Make it, "in the event [better yet, *if*] the demands were not met." (2) "There is no fear of the *Cabinet being* endangered before the National Assembly votes upon the Paris-London accords." Make it "Cabinet's" or "that the Cabinet will be endangered." (3) "The court ruled that the information passed to the Reds resulted in various *East Germans being* denounced by the Communists . . ." Would you say, "resulted in them being denounced"? Make "East Germans" possessive or write, "resulted in the denunciation of East Germans." (4) "This latest measure is one of several steps taken by Secretary Wilson to prevent the *ceiling* on expenditures *being broken* again next year." Since a possessive is impossible in this sentence, the simplest remedy is to insert "from" before "being broken."

**HOWEVER.** When the word "however" is properly placed in a sentence it throws contrasting emphasis on what precedes it. But sometimes it is difficult to find just the right place for it. A story about a speech by Secretary Dulles quoted him as speaking of the framers of the United States Constitution, then went on: "Delegates at the 1945 San Francisco organizational conference of the United Nations, of whom he was one, however, were ignorant of the atomic bomb . . ." The contrast intended here is between the framers of the Constitution and the San Francisco delegates. But the present construction erroneously throws the contrasting emphasis on "of whom he was one." The "however" could be placed after "United Nations," although it is usually better not to delay for so long its appearance in the sentence. Alternatively it could stand at the head of the sentence, thus establishing the contrast between the ideas of the two sentences. Incidentally, if your elementary school teacher told you never to begin a sentence with "however," forget it. The governing factor is simply this: Which ideas are to be contrasted? May Mrs. Phillips of P.S. 10 forgive us.

**INCOMPARABLES.** "Perhaps one of the most unique of Austrian exports is . . ." A thing that is unique is one and only; no comparative or superlative can be attached to it.

Here are two other terms that fall into the same category: "the more permanent curses of our age," and "nothing is more fatally dangerous to the G.O.P. . . ."

**INCOMPLETE ALTERNATIVE COMPARISON.** This term is exemplified by the following sentence: "Many families and single lodgers are resettling in other slums, as bad or worse than those marked for obliteration in the current slum-clearance programs." "Worse" is completed by "than," but how about "as bad"? It stands there in frustrated isolation. It cries for completion. One way to correct this, and a rather formal way, is to make it, "as bad as or worse than." Another and perhaps more graceful way is to complete the "as bad" immediately with an "as," going right on to the word "those," and tack on the "or worse" at the end of the sentence. One way or another, the construction should be tidied up.

**LAID, LAY.** "As reported by Miskolc officials, women laid down in the roadway to halt the movement of Soviet tanks." Down isn't laid; it comes off a duck.

"Erskine unfurled a wild pitch and Thompson scored the run that was to lay like a lead weight on the Dodgers the rest of the way." Lie.

"It [Peiping] laid low in Indochina and Formosa while the Korean fighting continued." If a writer is going to use the colloquial "lie low," let him at least employ the correct past tense: "lay."

**LIKE.** (1) A copy editor asked *Winners & Sinners* for guidance on those trick words "like" and "as." A few ideas are here advanced gingerly. The use of "like" as a conjunction introducing a clause that contains a verb is colloquial, if not illiterate, as in, "He painted like he had been an artist all his life." When "like" is not followed by a verb, however, its use is usually proper; *e.g.*, "He ran like a deer."

(2) At the other extreme is the writer who obviously was frightened by the word "like" in infancy: "A crowd of young adults raced up and down a Bronx street yesterday carrying marbles in spoons, jumping in potato sacks and generally behaving as children." You might expect that good grammar would demand this use of "as," but it doesn't. Moreover it sounds as hell.

(3) Another common error occurs in this type of sentence: "Like ancient Athens, democracy flourishes in the United States." Here the error is not so much one of grammar as of reasoning; it consists in comparing unlike things— in this instance, "Athens" and "democracy." For further enlightenment (or should the word "further" be deleted?) see Fowler's *Modern English Usage*.

**MAJORITY.** *See* "collectives."

**NAMES.** *See* "plurals."

**NEITHER . . . NOR.** *See* "either . . . or."


**NONE.** Miss Thistlebottom undoubtedly told you in grammar school that "none" always takes a singular verb. Although she was incorrect (the authorities agree almost without exception that "none" is more commonly a plural), she probably knew what she was doing, for the authorities are reticent about precisely when to consider "none" a singular and when a plural. It would be possible to set forth guides about the usage of "none," but to do so on The Times would open the news columns to a confusion of subjective judgments and the newspaper's incoming mail to a flood of vituperation from Miss Thistlebottom's colleagues and former pupils.

So a good, if not courageous, newspaper guide is to string along with "none" as a singular, with this exception: When the "none" cannot refer to a single, individual thing, make the verb plural. For instance: "The negotiations have been going on for two months, but none have succeeded." You couldn't possibly be thinking of a single "negotiation." Likewise: ". . . France has maintained the principle that none of her forces is [make it "are"] permanently committed to European defense . . ." There is no conception here of a single "force." An added suggestion: When the singular verb seems to be indicated but sounds prissy, why not change the "none" to "no one" or "not one"? For example: "Five persons were in the car, but no one [or "not one"] was hurt."

**NOT ONLY.** The misplacement of "not only" is one of the commonest writing faults. Examples: "Mr. Koota said Jackson not only knew Ruggiero . . . but also Anthony Anastasia . . ." "The battle in that part of the world . . . is not only costing France $1,000,000,000 a year, but it is killing more officers each year than France is turning out of her military academy." Correct placement of the "not only" is simply a matter of maintaining a proper parallelism; more specifically of making sure that the part of speech that follows the "not only" is paralleled by the one that follows the "but" (preferably, "but also"). In the first example the "not only" is followed by a verb, "knew," and the "but" by a noun, "Anastasia." Correct it by placing the "not only" after the "knew." In the second example the "not only" is followed by a verb, "costing," and the "but" by a pronoun, "it." This one can be corrected by merely deleting the words "it is" after the "but" (and preferably inserting "also" in their place). What it all boils down to, really, is tidy thinking. *See also* "both."

**NUMBER.** After years of lint picking, *Winners & Sinners* is in a position to say that the grammatical error that crops up most often in news writing is disagreement in number between subject and verb. This sort of thing: "More independence and initiative in agricultural planning was given today to the farmers . . ." Or this sort: ". . . the Egyptian version of Mr. Jernegan's remarks were published . . ." Or this: "Neither Carmine G. De Sapio . . . nor Richard H. Balch . . . are being invited." Avoiding this kind of error should be as easy and automatic as adding 1 and 1. It requires no more than glancing back to see what the true subject of the verb is.

Consider the novice golfer about to tee off. He grips his club and concentrates his gaze upon the ball. As he is about to swing, an ant scrambling up a blade of grass a few inches away catches his eye. He swings and—swoosh!—flubs his stroke. This is the kind of thing that causes the disagreement-in-number solecism. Watch a few more duffers: (1) "Finally, since *a demand* [the ball—keep your eye on it] for freedom and liberty [the ant—forget it] were [swoosh!] at the root of the several revolutions recalled in these pages . . ." (2) "*Part* of the present confusion and furor within the Pentagon over research and development spending *stem* [swoosh!] in large part from the fact the . . ." (3) "So much *water and oil has* [swoosh!] been drawn from underground areas in California that . . ." These hooks and slices do not arise from grammatical ignorance—the writers and editors certainly know that a singular subject takes a singular verb and that a plural subject takes a plural verb. They arise rather from distraction caused by something irrelevant; the real subject is lost sight of amid a tangle of other words.

*Error induced by "one."* "Captain Carlsen is one of ten Isbrandtsen shipmasters who flies his own flag." This is a common mistake. It should be "who fly their own flags," as becomes evident if you turn the sentence around: "Of ten Isbrandtsen shipmasters who fly their own flags, Carlsen is one."

*Error caused by inversion.* "Recommended is the establishment of a new state agency to provide pre-marital and post-marital counseling, a state-wide uniform civil marriage ceremony and mandatory conciliation . . ." Recommended also are not inverting the sentence like that.

*Error with copulative verb.* "Recommendations to the governments concerned is the fifth item of the truce agenda drawn up last July." In the case of a copulative verb linking nouns of equal value, the first one should be regarded as the subject and the verb should be governed accordingly. Therefore in the sentence cited make it "are."

*See also* "collectives."

**ONE ANOTHER.** *See* "each other."

**ONE OR TWO.** ". . . there was always one or two English-speaking Russians present . . ." It is true that when nouns of unlike number are linked by "either . . . or" or "neither . . . nor," the verb takes the number of the noun that is the nearer to it. In the sentence cited, however, we have not two independent nouns, but rather a phrase, "one or two," which means "a few." Therefore the verb should be plural. *See also* "either . . . or."

**ONLY.** "$35,000 Bond Thief Only Nets Paper." Proper positioning of "only" requires no more than asking yourself, "What does it actually modify?" In this headline it obviously modifies "paper," not "nets," and therefore should adjoin the word "paper." An interesting exercise for developing "only" awareness was cited in the publication *World Study*, distributed by G. & C. Merriam Company, as follows: "Eight different meanings result from placing 'only' in the eight possible positions in this sentence: 'I hit him in the eye yesterday.'"

**OVERREFINEMENT.** There is such a thing, in writing and in other fields, as overrefinement. Sometimes it results in outright crudity, as in the pose of the social climber who raises her teacup with her little finger stuck daintily out in the air. And as in this sentence: "Also in sort of mild pursuit were several depositors whose curiosities had been piqued by the turn of events." You can almost hear the writer (or editor) saying that if the depositors possess individual shirts, they surely must possess individual curiosities. Logically this is so; idiomatically it is not. It is difficult to frame a watertight rule; nevertheless it may be said that the noun remains in the singular when it applies to more than one person, *but* (a) represents a quality possessed in common, (b) is an abstraction, or (c) is a figurative word. Hence: "The fliers plunged to their death"; "The men earned their living"; "The three were held prisoner" (abstract) or "as prisoners" (concrete), and "Their curiosity was piqued."

Other kinds of overrefinement are shown in the following three examples:

"Williams worked longer than anyone yesterday, but today the Texan took things easily." The idiom here is "take it easy."

"For the first time the items on which the index is based include television sets, pajamas, fully fashioned nylon hosiery . . ." The adjective is "full-fashioned," meaning knitted to follow the shape of the leg.

"This is where a little money comes in handily." The idiom is "comes in handy."

## PARENTHETICAL PHRASES.

Failure to recognize a parenthetical phrase often produces a sentence that goes awry. The error is illustrated by this sentence, created for the occasion: "In 1776 President Truman said that the American people were a sturdy folk." Obviously, in 1776 Mr. Truman wasn't saying anything. The error consists in not noticing that "President Truman said" is a parenthetical phrase and that it should be set off by commas, with the "that" deleted.

Here are two actual sentences from a single story: "On Feb. 15 Mr. Hogan said that Fox, Ganz and Berner went to the apartment . . ." "In a nearby restaurant Mr. Hogan said that the detectives found the marijuana." A third example contains the same error, though it is not quite so obvious: "Right after the Oregon vote is counted, most of the leaders feel that their task would be greatly simplified were the general on the scene in the United States."

It should also be noted that the verb of the parenthetical phrase, since it is merely part of an interpolation, does not govern the other verbs of the sentence. The following example demonstrates the point: "While Mr. Truman was serving as chairman of the Senate Committee Investigating War Contracts, Mr. Cooper said that he had been loaned to the committee by the Washington Police Department . . ."

What this sentence literally says is that Mr. Cooper made his statement at the time Mr. Truman was chairman of the committee. But this, of course, was not the writer's intention. He erred by failing to recognize that "Mr. Cooper said" is parenthetical. Those words should be enclosed in commas, the word "that" should be deleted and the following verb, which is not governed by "said" but is in the same time level as "while Mr. Truman was serving," should be changed to "was loaned" (better yet, "was lent").

Here is a different kind of poor parenthesizing: ". . . the Prime Minister is elected, not as a United States President is by a nationwide vote, but is chosen by the party that wins a majority in the House of Commons." Lift out the parenthetical clause enclosed in commas and you find that the sentence has run off the rails and piled up in wreckage. Correct it by placing the "not" ahead of "elected" and eliminating the comma, or by deleting the words "is chosen."

**PARTICIPLES AS ADJECTIVES.** Participles are often used as adjectives (the *growing* plant, the *burned* child). But perfect participles (those ending in *ed, d, t, en* or *n*) cannot be indiscriminately employed as adjectives. It is proper to speak of the "wrecked plane," but improper to speak of the "crashed plane." Sounds like a puzzler, doesn't it? The answer seems to be that only transitive verbs are normally used this way. A plane that has been wrecked (transitive verb) is a wrecked plane, but a plane that has crashed (intransitive verb) is not a crashed plane. If you smoke you are not a smoked man, but if you smoke a herring it is a smoked fish. There are some exceptions to this principle, and the only way to account for them is on the basis of idiom arising from long usage. For example, "escaped convict" and "escaped prisoner" are well established, though "escaped Russian" is not. "Confessed spy" is another one that has made the grade. "Crashed plane" undoubtedly will make it in time, but has not done so yet.

**PARTICIPLES, DANGLING.** *See* "unattached modifiers."

**PARTICIPLES, FUSED.** *See* "fused participle."

**PREPOSITION AT END.** When Miss Thistlebottom taught you not to so much as whisper between the parts of an infinitive, she probably also told you that no writer would end a sentence with a preposition if he knew what he was about. We need not go the whole way with Miss Thistlebottom's rules—many of which were designed more for easy teaching than for better writing—to recognize that a sentence ending with a preposition is sometimes clumsy, often weak. For instance: ". . . he felt it offered the best opportunity to do fundamental research in chemistry, which was what he had taken his Doctor of Philosophy degree in." The end of a sentence is a conspicuous point and therefore can be a strong point. The end of the sentence just cited is like the last sputter of an engine going dead.

**PRONOUNS.** Pronouns and their reference words (antecedents or principals, if you like) often cause trouble. The mistakes (italicized) fall into three categories. First, wrong reference word: "She was one of ten chicks Mr. and Mrs. Sherry purchased in 1937 when *they* were six weeks old." Keep in mind that pronouns have an affinity for the nearest noun. Second, imagined (but not actual) reference word: "Patterson Will Remembers 5 Men Who Rescued *Him* From Foe in '18." Changing it to "Patterson's"—that is, making it a person rather than an adjective—would solve this one. Third, no reference word at all: "Dr. Barnes expressed his views before executives of city councils of churches. *It* was one of a number of meetings of . . ."

As a side issue, an editor questioned this sentence: "In the loftiest cathedrals of the land and in tiny parish churches, *their* very stones steeped in British history, preachers and prelates . . . paid their final tributes today to King George VI." "Doesn't the pronoun erroneously refer to preachers and prelates?" this editor asked. Nope. The blessed Mr. Fowler says: "The pronoun should seldom precede its principal." To which *Winners & Sinners* adds that it seldom does. Maybe that's why the principal is called an antecedent.

Ambiguity concerning the intended antecedent of a pronoun is a frequent cause of unclear writing. Example: "Secretary of State Dulles told Foreign Secretary Anthony Eden today that he had a 'bad habit'—doodling." Who has the bad habit? Unfortunately, the previously cited maxim that a pronoun has an affinity for the nearest noun does not always govern. If, for instance, you change the word "told" to "confessed to," it becomes instantly clear that Dulles has the bad habit, not Eden, despite the fact that "Eden" is closer to "he" than is "Dulles." The point is that clarity in the use of pronouns is not a mere matter of geographical position but rather one of meaning and context. Sometimes geographical proximity does suffice to make the meaning clear, but frequently a change of words or a different construction is necessary. It is the job of the careful writer to spot ambiguities and, having spotted them, to decide which of the remedies to apply.

Following are some examples of pronoun confusion:

"As a magistrate, he stirred some interest by holding invalid the arrest of persons for merely sleeping in the subway. The police still do it, however." Do what?

"A carelessly playful lion . . . failed to look before he leaped at the circus in Madison Square Garden last night, knocking down his trainer instead of jumping over his head . . ." The use of "his" to apply to two different reference words almost makes nonsense out of the sentence. Incidentally, this difficulty would have been avoided had the writer followed Times usage of employing "it" unless the animal has a name. (*See also* "It and She," Chapter 1, "Words That Need Watching.")

"Among the questions that stumped aspirants was one asking him to select the grammatically correct sentences among the following . . ." Never mind those following sentences, buddy; let's work on this one and change the "him" to "them."

*Pronoun after "everyone."* The pronoun to be used after the word "everyone" apparently troubles even our most careful writers, as witness: "Give everyone credit for having the courage of their convictions." This might get by in colloquial speech but it is not sanctioned in good writing. The possibilities available, then, are either to use "his or her" or to use simply "his." The first alternative is stilted and is to be shunned except when the issue of sex is present and pointed, as in: "The pool is open to both men and women but everyone must pay for his or her towel." Commonly, however, the word to be used is "his," as the nearest approach in this imperfect language of ours to a neutral personal pronoun. Therefore: "Give everyone credit for having the courage of his convictions." The women are willing to take the cash and let the credit go.

*Pronouns for countries.* The problem arises in a sentence like this: "Mexico was not invited despite *its* status as . . ." The style on The Times is to use the feminine pronoun in referring to a country except when the name includes a common noun. Thus. "France will state *her* position," "Russia massed *her* troops." But: "The Soviet Union declared *it* would attend," "The United States drafted *its* note."

However, there have to be exceptions:

"Guatemala, he said, was so small that a soldier could march across her in one day." The feminine pronoun should not be used when the reference is to the country as a physical, geographical domain rather than an abstract entity.

"M. Mendes-France agreed that France was 'the sick man of Europe,' but he denied she was decadent." Although the rule is to consider nations to be feminine, it is also the rule not to be absurd. Substitute "the nation" or "the country" for "she" in a sentence such as this.

**SEQUENCE OF TENSES.** In discussing sequence of tenses, the conventional books on grammar and syntax lead you a little way into the forest, point out a few trails you probably would have no difficulty in discerning for yourself, and then abandon you. For most users of English this is sufficient. For the newspaper writer, however, it is not enough, because journalism is, for the most part, recording the past—and not exclusively the immediate past, but successive layers or planes of past time. Hence the proper alignment of tenses is a continuing problem and a constant challenge. Let's explore the forest.

(1) In the present tense the sequence presents no problem: "He says he is hungry." Turning it into the past tense, you get, as the *normal sequence:* "He said he was hungry."

(2) To this normal past-tense sequence there are exceptions. When the subject matter of the dependent clause concerns something that is habitual, or permanently true, the present tense is retained. The *exceptional sequence* (or, as Fowler terms it, the vivid sequence) is used in such sentences as these: "The child did not know that dogs bite." "The teacher told the class that the earth revolves around the sun."

(3) A simple past event is recorded in the past tense: "The police *reported* the accident." An event prior to a simple past event is recorded in the past perfect tense: "The police reported that a car *had swerved* off the road." Still earlier events are also recorded in the past perfect tense:

"The police reported that a car had swerved off the road after its steering gear *had broken*."

This is about as far as most syntax books take you. Now let us unclasp our Boy Scout knives and proceed.

(4) The purpose of using the past perfect tense, of course, is to indicate the priority of events. If the subordinate clause includes a time element that itself indicates the priority, the past perfect becomes unnecessary, even redundant. Proper usage would be: "A close friend reported Jones *said* [not "had said"] *last week* that he would be elected."

(5) When the "he said" phrase appears anywhere but at the beginning of the sentence, the verbs in the other clauses are not affected by it; they remain in the same tense as in the original direct quotation. (The "he said" phrase does not govern the sentence; it is a mere parenthetical interpolation.) Hence this sentence is proper: "Jones is sure, he said, that he will be elected." *See also* "parenthetical phrases."

(6) To the foregoing paragraph there is one exception: When a statement is unequivocally associated with a particular time in the past, the tense used must indicate this. Although it is correct to use the present tense—that is, the tense of the original direct quotation—in such a sentence as, "He is sick and tired, he said, of graft in the police force," it is necessary to use the past tense in one like this: "He was sick and tired, he said, and asked to be excused from testifying." Another example of a statement associated with a particular time in the past: "He was glad, the speaker said, to see so many friendly faces." These past-tense usages, it should be emphasized, are exceptional.

(7) Phrases like "according to" and "in the opinion of," when used in past-tense contexts, are equivalent to "he said." When they appear at the beginnings of sentences they govern the subsequent verbs; when they appear anywhere else they are considered to be mere parenthetical interpolations and do not govern the verbs.

(8) The tense of the dominant verb in a sentence does not necessarily and indiscriminately govern every other verb in the sentence. Sometimes clauses are interpolated or added almost as if the writer were taking you aside and revealing information quite outside the context of the rest

of the sentence. In such sentences the verbs of these clauses go their own way. Example: "George M. Haskew, water engineer, *said* the main reservoir of the Plainfield Union Water Company, which *supplies* [not supplied] many communities in that area, *was* full for the first time since early June."

What amounts to an amplification of Point 1 evolved from the following sentence in a dispatch: "Mark T. Shaw . . . has charged that French trade associations nullify efforts to introduce competitive productivity into France." An itchy pencil changed "nullify" to "had nullified." In so doing, the copy editor also changed the meaning, making the nullification completely antecedent to the charge. If the governing verb is in the present perfect tense ("has charged") it should be regarded as if it were in the present tense ("charges") so far as the subsequent verb is concerned. Thus, "nullify" should have been allowed to stand.

Here is another example: "He *gives* [present tense] no indication he *plans* [present tense] to run for office." "He *has given* [present perfect] no indication he *plans* [present] to run for office." A change in the subsequent verb would occur, however, if the governing verb were in the past tense: "He *gave* [past] no indication he *planned* [past] to run for office."

That forest isn't really so confusing after all. Yet, to judge by this example, writers and editors must walk, not run, through it: "There were signs today that some European members of the Atlantic alliance might raise the question of who pulled the trigger on intermediate-range missiles at bases the United States intended to establish on the Continent."

As written by the correspondent and as printed in the first edition, it was "pulls" (and "intends"). But then a copy editor had second thoughts and decided that this was not a normal sequence of tenses—which, indeed, it was not. He made the two changes and thereby sacrificed clarity to the mechanical application of a rule of grammar. If he feared he would be unable to sleep that night unless the tense sequence was normal, he might have made it "who would pull" or "who was to pull." But the tense change he decided on was the worst possible revision. All of which leads to this suggestion: Normal sequence of tenses is desirable except when it produces obscurity or ambiguity.

Here is an example of outright ambiguity: "Some believed that the same issue would be raised again when the name of Japan was presented this year." Does everything in the sentence refer to the past, or does some of it refer to the future? "Is" instead of "was," although a violation of normal sequence, would have made the meaning unmistakable.

**SERIES.** *See* "enumeration."

**SOONER.** A comparative adverb or adjective is followed by "than," except in the usage of the gray flannelmouths of Madison Avenue, where a cigarette is merely smoother, a detergent is merely better, a coffee is merely "coffee-er"— but not *than* anything. It should come as no surprise, then, that "sooner" should be followed by "than." Yet a common solecism is to substitute "when" for "than," as in this example: "No sooner had the inquiry been announced when it became known that eighty-nine Eastern and Western railroads were appealing . . ." The error arises from thinking of "no sooner" as if it were "scarcely" or "hardly."

Incidentally and irrelevantly, when we say "no sooner" we usually actually mean "a little sooner." And a little sooner is an Oklahoma baby. Where does that leave us?

**SPLIT INFINITIVE.** There will be no argument here with the general validity of Miss Thistlebottom's dictum against splitting the infinitive. However, boldness is commendable when one has to be split.

For example: "Señor Peron told the visiting Congressmen that in the second five-year plan he hoped to at least double Argentina's agricultural production." If you make it "hoped at least" it could mean "hoped" rather than expected; if you put the "at least" after the infinitive it might suggest a contrast between agricultural and industrial production.

Here is another example: "Spring, which was a little late this year, is expected to more than make up for its tardiness today." Once in a great while a situation like this arises.

When you are satisfied that the price of not splitting is either ambiguity or clumsiness, don't flinch—split.

It should not be necessary to emphasize that in general the split infinitive is undesirable usage. But apparently it is necessary, for here are two that appeared in one story: "Specialists . . . were unable to definitely identify representative specimens from the site." (Why not: "to make a definite identification" or "could not definitely identify"?) "Congress tightened up quarantine laws to allow the Department of Agriculture . . . to thoroughly search cargoes from abroad . . ." (The "thoroughly" could be placed after "abroad" or dropped altogether.)

Splitting also seems unnecessary in this sentence: "At the minimum, the conference here will provide a diversion that will permit Egypt to quietly drop her violent opposition to the Turkish-Iraqi treaty . . ." How about a slight recasting for smoothness, such as "retreat quietly from"?

**STREET.** There is sometimes confusion about whether to use the singular or the plural of the word "street" when two streets are mentioned in a phrase. You should say "from one street to another street" (singular) as in "the pavement is torn up from 79th to 86th Street." But "between 79th and 86th Streets" (plural). It's that simple.

**SUBJUNCTIVE.** (1) Much ink has been impressed on paper in arguing whether the subjunctive mood is alive, asleep, dying or dead. Little will be said here on the subject, except to point to one situation in which the subjunctive is indisputably alive: in expressing a condition either contrary to fact or purely hypothetical ("if I were in your shoes"). The indicative mood may well be used for other conditional clauses; *e.g.,* "The racket consisted of the distribution among motorists of courtesy cards, which a driver would give to a motorcycle policeman if he *was* stopped for a traffic violation." But the indicative is incorrect in this example: "In talking with Government functionaries in East Germany, one becomes quickly aware that they are much concerned as to what would happen if Germany *was* united."

(2) "Justice Felix Frankfurter issued a dissenting opinion today that looked as though it was going to stop on page

5 . . ." "As though" is exactly equivalent to "as if," and the full form of this sentence would be: "Justice Frankfurter issued a dissenting opinion today that looked as it would look if it *were* going to stop on page 5." In the full form, of course, "was" is impossible, and it is equally impossible in the sentence cited. By the way, this writer has always had a preference for "as if" over "as though," not only because it is shorter but also because it makes sense—which "as though," when you analyze it, does not, though it is idiomatic.

**SWITCHING VOICES.** "Quartz Cut Without Touching It." Normally, switching from the passive voice to the active or vice versa within a sentence is not good practice. What makes this headline worse is that there is also a switch of subjects—from "quartz" to "anyone." This is an example of swapping horses in midstream and finding too late that there is only one horse.

**THAT.** *Conjunction.* When may the conjunction "that" be omitted? You will search books on English usage in vain for any uniform, much less helpful, guidance on the subject. The reason probably is that in the vast majority of instances the inclusion or exclusion of "that" is optional and a matter of idiom, which means how it sounds to one speaking English as a native tongue. There are two situations, however, where the inclusion of the word seems to be definitely indicated. One is a sentence in which a time element intervenes between the verb (if it is other than "said") and the clause. The following sentence, for example, would have been better if a "that" had been inserted after "today": "President Adib Shishekly announced today opposition elements had attacked government troops . . ." The other situation calling for inclusion of "that" is one in which a long passage separates the verb from the clause. A good illustration is the third sentence of this paragraph beginning, "The reason . . ." Aside from these two circumstances, however, you'll have to play it by ear.

Notice how the reader is led off on a false scent in the following sentence, and then must backtrack: "The Army disclosed today a document that 'apparently contained secret information' on the Army's roles and missions has been discovered 'in the hands of unauthorized persons.' " Inclusion of "that" after "today" is definitely needed.

Here is another undesirable omission of "that": "Mr. Brownell said a District of Columbia grand jury returned the indictment last Oct. 13, but that the District Court had kept it sealed pending the arrival of Mr. Onassis . . ." When you have "but that" or "and that" introducing a second clause it is surely preferable to insert "that" ahead of the first clause. Matter of tidiness.

**THAT AND WHICH.** "That" is better used to introduce a limiting or defining clause; "which" to introduce a non-defining or parenthetical clause. Getting away from the grammatical gobbledygook, we might take this as a rule of thumb: If the clause could be omitted without leaving the noun it modifies incomplete, or without materially altering the sense of what is being said—or if it could be reasonably enclosed in parentheses—it should be introduced by "which"; otherwise, by "that." For example: "The Hudson River, *which* flows west of Manhattan, is muddy." (A non-defining clause; it could be omitted or parenthesized.) But: "The river *that* flows west of Manhattan is the Hudson."

"That" clauses outnumber "which" clauses, but this does not mean that you can have a "which" burning. This sentence is incorrect: "Mrs. Patty Miller . . . was killed upon being thrown out of her car that had skidded into collision with another vehicle . . ." The car has already been defined by the word "her," so that unless Mrs. Miller had two cars, the clause is not a defining one and the "that" is uncalled for.

There are two exceptions to the use of "that" to introduce a defining clause. One is when the demonstrative and the relative come together as in this sentence: "The latent opposition to rearming Germany is as strong as that that has found public expression." Idiom dictates making it "that which." The second exception is when the relative follows a preposition (*e.g.*, "of which," not "of that").

**TIME ELEMENT.** A usage that seems to be peculiar to newspapering tends to put the time element ahead of the verb in the lead sentence. The practice is undesirable because, for one thing, it is contrary to normal idiom (you don't say

"I today went to the dentist") and, for a second thing, it gives too conspicuous a position to an element that, while necessary, is unimportant.

Sometimes, however, this kind of positioning of the time element is inescapable, as in: "Sweden's Supreme Court today increased to three years' hard labor a sentence of twenty months passed earlier by lower courts on a Communist town councilor . . ." But such situations are extremely rare. Normally an effort should be made to slip the time element into the sentence somewhere after the verb, inconspicuously and naturally.

Keeping in mind that word "naturally," examine this sentence: "The United States described the Czechoslovak fighter-plane attack on two United States jet planes over West Germany Tuesday as a 'provocative incident' today and warned the Communist Government in Prague that . . ." The editor in this case hopped out of the frying pan right into hot water.

Two sentences in which the time element is out of place:

(1) "On May 25 Frankie suffered multiple injuries in an automobile accident in his home town and has been in a cast from his hips down for the past twelve weeks." The second part of the sentence does not read properly out of "on May 25," which should be shifted elsewhere.

(2) "He said Mr. Symington had desired to leave the Government for a year and a half." And then return? Put the final phrase after "desired."

**UNATTACHED MODIFIERS.** These usually take the form of dangling participles, but dangling adjectives can produce the same effect. The error arises, of course, from not putting the noun in direct contact with the word or phrase that is supposed to modify it.

Unattached participles do not always appear at the beginnings of sentences; *e.g.*, "His release Saturday night after being held hostage more than seventy-eight hours came . . ."

Here's another specimen, and this one sets some kind of record by having two unattached modifiers in a single sentence: "Unbeaten thus far this year, the victory was his seventh in a row and his tenth since last dropping a decision last September."

Following are some juicy samples of dangling modifiers:

"Sitting here on the balcony of a small hotel, with the breeze blowing softly off the Aegean Sea below, the college world of New Haven, with its classrooms, its football weekends and its fraternities, seems eons away." And its English courses—how far away do they seem?

"Developed by scientists at the Argonne National Laboratory . . . , Admiral Strauss asserted that the new device . . ." Yes, sir, the A.N.L. builds men.

"Although definitely extinct, Professor Daevey said it had not been too long ago that the moa was floundering around his deathtrap swamps." Dangled into extinction?

"Small and sallow, her huge dark eyes and mane of hair were her only real beauties." Those small huge eyes, that sallow mane.

"As reconstructed by the police, Pfeffer at first denied any knowledge of the Byrd murder." The cops must have really taken him apart.

"Lying astride the Quebec-Labrador boundary . . . , a prospector looking for gold found the ore in what is known as the Labrador Trough . . ." Prone to error.

"Standing before an electronic device that sorted eggs by color, the President's eyes popped." Dangling exophthalmos.

"A Phi Beta Kappa graduate of Dartmouth, Pat Weaver's head is said to burst with ideas . . ." What did Dartmouth do with the rest of him?

**UNIQUE.** *See* "incomparables."

**WHAT.** "What looks like two supersize golden bird cages . . . have been erected overnight." "What" is a tricky word. It may be either singular or plural. To determine which it is, the writer must ask himself what the word stands for. In the sentence quoted here it clearly does not stand for "a thing that" but rather "things that"; therefore the verb should be "look."

**WHICH.** (1) The use of "which" to refer to the whole idea of a preceding clause is frowned upon by the ultra-finicky, but may be regarded as permissible when not ambiguous. It tends to be ambiguous when the "which" follows a noun, as in this sentence: "Laboratory animals don't catch the disease, which hampers research." It would be better to make it "which fact" or to reconstruct the sentence.

(2) A frequent solecism is illustrated here: "These decisions were announced . . . today by Minister of Commerce John McEwen, who introduced a bill to give them effect and which was taken to the second reading stage." Take it as a rule of thumb that "and which" must be preceded by another "which" clause. The sainted Mr. Fowler acknowledges the existence of such a rule of thumb but sets forth some exceptions to it. Valid or no, his exceptions would require so careful a weighing of the factors pro and con that you'd never make a deadline. So just follow the rule of thumb; it will never let you down. *See also* "that."

**WHO.** (1) *"And who."* Just as it is a good idea to precede an "and which" clause by another "which," the same treatment should be given to "and who." For example: "Opposition politicians, including many arrested last month by President Shishekly after an uprising in the Jebel ed Druz area, *and who* were freed after the general's ouster, met today . . ." In *Modern English Usage* Mr. Fowler goes round and round to specify certain circumstances under which, in cases like this one, the first "who" may be omitted. But, to lift one of his passages unashamedly out of context, he comes out here: "If he [the writer] had foreseen that a relative clause was to come (& not to foresee is carelessness), he could usually have paved the way for it by throwing his first expression into the same form." The crucial phrase is the one Mr. Fowler parenthesizes; in written language it is carelessness not to foresee what is coming, whatever it may be in spoken language. Therefore if there is an "and who," let it be heralded by a predecessor "who."

(2) *Ambiguous antecedent.* A "who" clause preceded by designations of two individuals can often be ambiguous and sometimes even libelous. Example: "John Brown, attorney for Smith who is charged with stealing $48,000 in union funds . . ." The writer or the editor apparently recognized the pitfall here, and thought to avoid it by omitting the comma after Smith, intending thus to tie the clause closely to that name. The comma is necessary, however, if the punctuation is to be correct. The only ways out of the difficulty are either to insert an identification ahead of the

"who" (*e.g.*, "the former union leader") or to make the "who" clause a separate sentence. The need is for precision.

(3) *"Who" for "that."* "The State Senate tonight considered coming to the rescue of salt water fish who were being terrorized by Martian-appearing swimmers . . ." These fish apparently are almost who-man. "Who" is reserved for persons or personified animals. Make it "that."

**WHOM.** "For 'Whom' the Bell Tolls" is a division of *Winners & Sinners* reserved for the type of error exemplified by this sentence: "William Z. Foster . . . whom Federal Judge Ryan ruled is not physically fit now to be tried . . ." The error arises, of course, from failure to notice that the pronoun is not the object of the first verb but the subject of the second. Make it "who." "But the disputants differed diametrically as to whom they thought might turn out to be the violator." Here it is not the pronoun that is the object of the prepositional "as to," but rather the whole clause, and in this clause the pronoun is the subject. Therefore, "who." Following is a similar error involving the word "whomever": "He called on the party to close ranks behind whomever was nominated . . ." "Whomever" is not the object of the preposition "behind"; the object is the entire clause. Within that clause the pronoun is the subject of "was nominated" and therefore should be "whoever."

# Helpful Hints for
# Hatchet Men

"Hatchet men," as here used, is the playful *Winner & Sinners* designation for copy editors, who are otherwise and less accurately known as copy readers. The label suggests the manner in which writers sometimes regard those anonymous super-critics who modify their cherished prose.

Modifying prose, however, is only one of the functions copy editors are paid to perform. They are also responsible for checking on the accuracy of information, detecting inconsistencies or unanswered questions, removing libelous or unobjective statements, making the writing adhere to standards of good English usage and good taste, seeing to it that stories are clearly and logically organized and bringing the spelling, punctuation, capitalization and typography into conformity with the newspaper's style rules. All this constitutes the function of editing.

Beyond that the copy editor also has the task of writing the headline for every story he handles. This task is discussed in the next chapter.

The present chapter treats of editing pure and simple, neither of which editing ever is. Indeed, if it does nothing else, this chapter illustrates how complex and many-faceted is this indispensable function. And it is indispensable in any publishing enterprise, newspaper or otherwise.

## ITCHY PENCIL

Traditionally, if not actually, the relationship between the copy editor and the reporter is akin to that between a mongoose and a snake. It would be unfortunate if this were the reality. Both have important functions in the production of the newspaper, although the functions are quite different. The reporter's are essentially creative, the editor's critical. If the editor's work is not to be destructive, he must ponder any change he makes in copy. It is always important to conserve space and to set things right, but it is equally important not to change meaning or to destroy the flavor of the writing.

*Winners & Sinners* has had occasion to compare some stories as written for The New York Times with the versions as printed. In one of them a correspondent said that Khrushchev and Bulganin "do not have tuxedos but they will travel." The editor made it: "They do not have dinner jackets but they will travel." In what kind of ivory tower does that editor dwell? Another reporter wrote that Vassar alumnae, gathering for a reunion, brought with them sixty-six husbands, many of whom had been classmates elsewhere, and then said that the men "greeted one another with discreet whoops and held subsidiary reunions of their own." The editor changed it to, "numbers of them held reunions of their own." While the change is not catastrophic, it does alter the feel of the sentence; it makes the reunions appear to have been planned, formal parts of the occasion.

It is always well to weigh the caliber and care of the writer. Some writers brush words onto their canvases with gentle precision and the utmost feeling for color; others spray them on and leave them to drip. Expert editors know which are which. It is a good thing, when editing the work of a careful writer, to hesitate over every change and to try to determine why he wrote as he did. The change may still be desirable, of course, but it will then not be made on the basis of a blind following of "rules." And reporters will be less likely to regard copy editors as a pack of mongee—er . . . mongoo— . . . as just one mongoose after another.

*-w&s-*

Itchy pencils on the copy desk can cause damage, minor or major. If the reporter writes "Shots by the police touched off the rioting," and the copy editor changes the verb to "precipitated," the damage is minor. Yet the editor has removed a trace of color to no purpose, and has accomplished nothing except to perplex the writer.

More serious is tinkering that introduces an outright error. For instance, a reporter wrote: ". . . Gen. Mark Clark's Fifth Army reached Rome after a bitter nine-month campaign in Italy," and the copy editor made it "campaign up from the 'toe' of Italy." The fact is that the Fifth Army began its campaign at Salerno, which is a fur piece from the quote toe unquote of Italy. Why not verify the facts before making the change? But, more important, what was the need for the change in the first place?

An itchy pencil on a copy desk is a menace. Even if it does no actual damage to a story, it makes a reporter wonder whether his copy is in safe and sure hands. That kind of worry can be destructive of a writer's morale.

Here are additional illustrations:

A correspondent, discussing the economy of southern Italy, wrote: "The small bourgeois population, deprived of its sources of income, is largely unemployed and restless." The copy editor changed "small" to "petit," thereby altering the meaning. Why assume that the correspondent is so unintelligent he would not have written "petit bourgeois" if he had meant that?

-*w&s*-

A reporter wrote: "At his news conference on May 11, President Eisenhower was asked . . ." The copy editor made it: "At his press interview . . ." The change was for the worse; the President's regular conferences are not restricted to the press, but include radio and television men as well.

-*w&s*-

Another reporter wrote: "Istanbul was mentioned as the probable site." The copy editor, trying to be helpful, inserted "capital of Turkey." Ankara is the capital, as any Turkish schoolboy knows.

-*w&s*-

In a story about the decay of 10 Downing Street a correspondent wrote: "Any British decision dealing with venerable buildings is accompanied by ceremony. Prime Minister Macmillan did not whistle in a construction firm to put the old homestead right." The desk changed "whistle" to "call." Why? "Whistle" lends color, perhaps even humor, by suggesting a swift, impulsive action; "call" flattens it out.

*-w&s-*

As edited, a story said: ". . . the three ministers function like a well-drilled basketball or soccer team, passing the ball quickly and surely from hand to hand." But the correspondent had written "from one to the other." Anyone who knows any-thing about soccer knows it is illegal for any player except the goalkeeper to use his hands. Why the change? To make mat-ters worse, the head said, "Allied Officials at Berlin Toss Ball from Hand to Hand Like Well-Drilled Soccer Team."

## IT SHOULDN'T HAPPEN

In *Winners & Sinners,* the heading "It Shouldn't Happen" applies to inaccuracies and inconsistencies, two of the flaws in stories that copy editors are supposed to detect. If they overlook such errors, it is bad. If they make such errors them-selves in the process of editing or of writing headlines, it is inexcusable.

Every time a story contains an "it shouldn't happen" it means that an editor has fallen down on the job. These errors usually originate with the reporter, but they are the final re-sponsibility of the copy editor. One doesn't like to attribute them to ignorance, so let's set them down to either sloth or inattention. For example:

". . . he traveled on to The New York World where he spun journalistic yarns until 1932." The World died in 1931.

*-w&s-*

The story and head both referred to "Sturges," Kentucky. The gazetteer, which should be only a few steps away from even the most distant copy editor, would disclose that it's "Sturgis."

*-w&s-*

"Within an hour Judge Davies had signed a summons asking for a temporary injunction against the Governor's use of troops, demanding that it be delivered 'forthwith.' " It is elementary that a summons does not ask for anything except an appearance.

*-w&s-*

Second paragraph: "The President and his partner, Norman Palmer . . ." Sixth paragraph: "All of them outdrove the President and Mr. Norman . . ." If the editor is alert to his work he should constantly be checking to see that the story is self-consistent, that it doesn't refer to Mr. Palmer at one point and to Mr. Norman at another.

*-w&s-*

The Connie Mack obituary that appeared in the first edition said, in reference to the 1905 World Series, "He [Mathewson] beat the Athletics three times, all shutouts. Bender won the only game for Philadelphia, 3-1. In this series the losing team was blanked in every game." The copy editor evidently noticed that the last sentence conflicted with the previous one. His solution was to delete the final sentence in the last edition. He would have done better had he checked the facts. The score of the game Bender won was 3-0.

*-w&s-*

Headline the first day: "Girls' Nation Elects President." Headline the next day: " 'Girl's Nation' Officials Greeted by Eisenhower." And the story: ". . . 100 girls attending 'Girls Nation' . . ." Lucky the story didn't go on another day; the desk was obviously running out of variations.

*-w&s-*

"The Marine Band from the royal yacht . . . played 'I'm Going to Wash That Man Right Out of My Hair' and other songs from Rodgers and Hammerstein shows." Two that come to mind are: "There Is Nothing Like a Lady" and "June Is Bursting Out All Over." (P.S.—The name of the song, which the copy editor should have checked, is "I'm Gonna Wash That Man Right Outa My Hair.")

-w&s-

"The Rio Grande is no more regional in the usual connotation of that word than the shot at Bunker Hill heard around the world was regional." The globe-girdling bang was at Concord. (And it was heard *'round* the world.)

## SLEEPY-TIME EDITOR

The errors just cited are representative of the "it shouldn't happens"—fortunately not numerous—that creep into any paper. All, as you see, were preventable. The plea here is for all editors to drink more black coffee, take more Benzedrine, slap one another in the face with cold towels—anything to stay awake.

But, alas, the copy editor sometimes does enjoy a snooze along with the reporter. The reporter writes something in haste or in preoccupation, and the editor, his mind perhaps on the headline he is about to write or on the novel he hopes to write, allows it to ride uncorrected. Following are samples of what happens when the editor dozes, selected from the "Sleepy-Time Editor" department of *Winners & Sinners:*

*Broken-field runner.* "Twelve shoppers on a crowded Brooklyn thoroughfare were injured yesterday . . . when a 65-year-old woman lost control of her car, mounted the curb and ran for forty feet among pedestrians on the sidewalk."

-w&s-

*Bumpers, gentlemen!* ". . . it lets mechanical sweepers in where the old-fashioned street cleaner was breaking his back to sweep the litter from under miles of cars parked hub to hub."

-w&s-

*Fleeting moment.* ". . . he said that 104 United States

citizens visited his country between 1953 and 1954." When was that?

-*w&s*-

*Anachronism.* "We, on our part, believed, and most of us still believe, that Nasser could have been dealt with and the canal kept as an international waterway without the use of the antique, nineteenth-century methods of ships, airplanes and guns." Will you ever forget Prince Albert flying those ol' crates by the seat of his striped pants?

-*w&s*-

*Too bad.* "A college friendship that began a year ago ended in matrimony yesterday . . ."

-*w&s*-

*Two-dimensional length.* "The one-story building was 75 × 100 feet in length."

-*w&s*-

*Fast ship.* Sentence in a story about the docking of the liner United States: "At 9:12 A.M. the new speed queen was fast."

-*w&s*-

*Naturally.* "Sheriff Tidwell said a leopard had been spotted . . ."

-*w&s*-

*Live dangerously.* "Safety prevention was the important subject of a gathering yesterday morning at the Hotel Lexington." To top it off, the dozing copy editor wrote the subhead: "Discuss Safety Prevention."

-*w&s*-

*Busy Natalia.* "Natalia now works in a ten-bed clinic

housed in a squat wooden structure near the main administration buildings. Half the beds and most of her time are devoted to increasing the farm's population."

-w&s-

*Meet Mr. Sea.* "Nicely acted throughout by a ship-shape little cast, featuring Sterling Hayden in the title role . . ." The title of the picture? "The Eternal Sea."

-w&s-

*Improper name.* Granted there are many organizations with odd names these days. Still you'd expect that alarm bells would be touched off in a copy editor's brain by this one in a dispatch telephoned from Toronto: ". . . the United Higher Servants, the worldwide Jewish migration agency . . ." It should have been United Hias Service. Moral for reporters: Spell out all proper names on the phone. Moral for copy editors: Be suspicious.

-w&s-

*He should of stood on first.* "No Chicago player got farther than second base, and that was John Goryl, who doubled in the fifth with one out."

-w&s-

*That's what television does.* "It is not that these people will not or cannot read English, they just won't, Mr. Lovick declared."

-w&s-

*How to avoid overloading of a boat.* "To avoid overloading of a boat, have the weight evenly distributed."

-w&s-

*Architectural innovation.* Subhead in a story describing

the new Beverly Hilton Hotel, "Floor-to-Ceiling Walls." Why didn't anyone ever think of those before?

## DICTUMS FOR DESKMEN

Here, in alphabetical array, are categories of specific helpful hints for copy editors, ranging from broad matters of taste to narrow matters of punctuation.

### *ATTRIBUTION*

The ultimate in attribution of statements in a story is the apocryphal filler piece, "The moon is 238,000 miles from the earth, according to The Associated Press."

Short of that absurd extreme many unnecessary attributions are inserted into stories by overzealous copy editors. The zeal is commendable when it rescues a story from editorialization. But sometimes an attribution can be erroneous and harmful. In a dispatch about the West German Social Democratic leader, Erich Ollenhauer, the correspondent had written that "according to well established fact" the Social Democrats were prepared to form a coalition with the Christian Democrats if Adenauer stepped aside. The desk man, editing hastily, struck out the quoted phrase and substituted "he said."

This sort of thing can be damaging. If a correspondent has, for example, been told something off the record and the copy desk pencils in a phrase of attribution, it not only might embarrass the correspondent but also could dry up a carefully cultivated news source. Be sure not to develop a mania for attribution that leads into error.

However, in stories dealing with touchy subjects, the need for attribution poses a difficult problem for both reporter and copy editor. The problem is to turn out a smooth-reading story and at the same time be sure that every statement that does require qualification has it. Sometimes the problem is acute, as it was in one of the first stories reporting information received in this country concerning Khrushchev's speech downgrading Stalin. The dispatch contained something like twenty-five qualifying attributions—almost one to a paragraph. This makes for encumbered reading. Is there an alternative?

It is frequently possible to construct the story so that the matter requiring attribution is all in one section. Then this section can be introduced with some such blanket sentence as, "Mr. Khrushchev's speech is reported to have made these points." To make matters absolutely clear, the section can in addition be followed by a sentence reminding the reader that the foregoing material was attributed—a sentence like, "Such is the gist of the speech as reported here."

If the summary section lends itself to numbered paragraphs or to a series of paragraph marks, so much the better.

It will not always be possible, of course, to follow the plan just outlined, but it is a device worth considering to avoid the monotony of repeated qualifiers.

## BAD TASTE

"Don'ts" for the avoidance of bad taste would make a list of incalculable length, and it is not proposed to embark on one. But a few cautions should be noted.

*Matters of religion.* A story related that Bishop Sheen was embarrassed when he caused a plane departure to be delayed because he had overlooked having his passport validated. The head said: "Sheen, Temporarily, Lacks Peace of Soul." *Don't* go fooling around with religion or any of the appurtenances thereof. (*See also* "religion.")

*Physical afflictions.* Another story concerned a "cookout" at which little deaf girls served frankfurters. The head said "Deaf Girl Scouts Know Hot Dogs Go Without Saying." *Don't* deal lightly with physical afflictions.

*Death and injury.* A third story was about a 14-year-old boy who was seriously injured when a chemical experiment he was performing at home caused an explosion. It was headlined: "Boy's 'Lab' Goes Boom." *Don't* try to be funny or featurish when death or serious injury is involved.

*Blood, sweat and dirt.* Filth, stench, gore and the purely animal functions normally meet with little hospitality in the news columns. There are rare exceptions. A bowel movement may be mentioned if it belongs to a President recovering from a heart attack. If the nation is at war, it may be advisable in an occasional descriptive story to let the home folks know that the lads at the front are not vying for Boy Scout merit badges in woodcraft.

Generally, however, such details are ruled out on the grounds of repulsiveness and redundancy. Accidents and violent crimes, for example, usually spill blood. Likewise, if detectives find a couple of decaying bodies in a car, this sentence in a report of the event is out of order: "When the detectives opened the door of the car they were assailed by an unpleasant odor."

Remembering that the paper usually accompanies the morning eggs and coffee, writers and editors must apply the Times-honored test: Is it fit for breakfast-table reading? Here a little squeamishness is a good thing.

*Outrageous details.* A reader complained, not without some justification, about the "almost do-it-yourself descriptions" of infernal machines in news accounts. An unnecessarily detailed description appeared in a story of a bomb explosion at Pennsylvania Station. A Cyprus dispatch about the finding of a bomb in Sir John Harding's bed described an unusual detonating mechanism. And a story about the acid attack on Victor Riesel contained a gratuitous couple of sentences that seemed to suggest that alkali would have done the job better. Even if there is no evidence that such publicity abets these kinds of outrages, let's play it safe and avoid too many details.

*Race, belief, national origin.* People in the news should not be identified by race, color, religion or national origin unless such identifications are pertinent in the news context. Although "Negro" in a segregation story and "Hungarian" in a refugeee story are perfectly proper, in contexts where such designations are not relevant they tend to be invidious. We should not write of an American, "O'Rourke, a lean, white-haired, red-faced, blue-eyed Irishman of 57 . . ." "Irishman" may seem to slip through the typewriter innocuously, but you wouldn't dream of writing, "Carmine De Sapio, a tall, gray-at-the-temples, dark-spectacled Italian." Identifications of that kind are irrelevant and, conceivably, offensive.

## COMMAS

Let us pause to consider the lowly comma. If we regard it as a mere flyspeck with a tail, that may account for some of the capricious uses (and non-uses) of it that appear from time to time. Following are some examples illustrating where commas belong and do not belong.

*With nonrestrictive phrases.* (1) "The luncheon was in honor of the three new Council representatives from Australia, Cuba and Yugoslavia . . ." Without a comma after "representatives," the meaning is that three new representatives are replacing three old ones. A comma (perhaps, preferably, a dash) would have brought out the correct meaning: that representatives of the three countries were new to the Council.

(2) A sort of reverse of Example 1: "The right to the title, 'Boy Wonder of American Politics,' slipped a bit further today from Richard M. Nixon." Delete the commas here. If you know when to use "that" and when to use "which"—and you should (*see also* "That and Which," Chapter 3, "Syntax Sinners")—the distinction between Examples 1 and 2 will be obvious; it is the distinction between a nonrestrictive or nondefining phrase, and a restrictive or defining phrase.

In elaboration of Examples 1 and 2 above, observe these usages: The photo caption said, "Andrei Y. Vishinsky . . . shown with his wife and their daughter, Zinaida, after they arrived here . . ." The story said, "The Soviet statesman, who was accompanied by his wife, his daughter Zinaida and his usual three burly bodyguards . . ." Both versions cannot be correct. If Mr. Vishinsky has only one daughter it should be written, ". . . his daughter, Zinaida." If he has more than one it should be written, ". . . his daughter Zinaida." The point was effectively illustrated in the remainder of the sentence from the story: ". . . he was a passenger aboard the Cunard liner Queen Mary." A comma after "liner" would indicate there was only one Cunard liner.

(3) This is a kindred, but more unusual, situation: "Mrs. Anna Roosevelt Boettiger, only daughter of the late President Roosevelt, disclosed today plans for her third marriage to Dr. James Addison Halstead . . ." Surely she's not marrying the same man for the third time. Put a comma after "marriage."

*For parenthetical purposes.* ". . . as the lips and skin of the mask are in natural colors, the inventor says a very lifelike illusion is created." Insert a comma after "says" to set off a parenthetical phrase.

The following sentence illustrates the reverse of the previous example: "This morning, some sources said, the total death count might reach more than 400 . . ." No parenthetical phrase in this case, as is proved by the use of "might" (governed by "said") rather than "may." Therefore remove the commas. (*See also* "Parenthetical Phrases," Chapter 3, "Syntax Sinners.")

*Mischievous commas.* University professorships bearing the names of distinguished persons seem to trouble the composing room and therefore need watching by copy desks. One example: "David M. Potter, William Robertson Coe, Professor of American History at Yale, was speaking on . . ." The comma after "Coe" is ridiculous. Sillier yet is this example: "Dr. Woodward . . . is Morris Loeb, Professor of Chemistry at Harvard."

*For phrases with a common termination.* A situation that sometimes causes punctuation trouble occurs when two or more phrases have a common element, only one of which is expressed; *e.g.*, "Many, if not most, copy editors use pens." The trouble usually is failure to insert a comma ahead of the expressed common element (in this case, "copy editors"). But here is a sentence in which both required commas have been omitted: "His achievements . . . had not saved him from suggestions that he was at bottom only a Southern as distinguished from a national politician." Insert commas after "Southern" and "national."

*In erroneous combination.* Following is an incorrect combination of punctuation: "Should the Government of Jordan collapse, how is the United States to prevent it becoming a part of Egypt and a rallying point for the most violent forms of Arab nationalism?, the British ask." The combination of interrogation point and comma is impossible. Delete the comma. Incidentally, make it "prevent its becoming" or "prevent it from becoming." (*See also* "Fused Participles," Chapter 3, "Syntax Sinners.")

*In place of dashes.* Commas would help this sentence: "Physicists at Columbia University are delving into the mysteries of the forces within the nucleus of the atom—source of atomic energy—with a powerful new tool—a beam of mesons —the sub-atomic particles believed to serve as the 'cosmic cement.'" The dashes simply confuse the sentence. Use commas except after "tool," and see how orderly it all becomes.

## CUTTING STORIES

When a copy editor must reduce the length of a story, he tends to divide its contents into categories of "hard" factual matter and "soft" color, background or interpretation. Not infrequently, however, some of this "soft" material may be more enlightening than "hard" minor facts. A story about a Lincoln life mask put on display contained a description of how such masks are made, intended to explain the peculiar appearance of the one being exhibited. In the cutting process the editor eliminated all this material, leaving only the facts about the opening of the exhibition. These facts had been printed the day before in the future tense. The cutting thus made the story routine and virtually worthless.

A correspondent writing about the attitudes of Rhodesians at a royal reception included this informative bit of psychological insight: "A solid bloc of whites took the attitude that African chiefs in their ritual tribal regalia might have been all right, but they frankly resented the recognition granted to Negro 'intellectuals' in European clothing. The other section of the whites was equally firm in its hostility to this 'sahib' attitude." In trimming the lengthy story after the first edition, the copy editor deleted just one paragraph, and this paragraph was it. The passage was not "hard," but it was a mighty good piece of helpful observation. The episode proves that you cannot mechanically classify only immediately apparent facts as "hard" and everything else as "soft." It's a difficult chore, this cutting of stories, and there is no sterner test of an editor's skill.

One form of space-saving that the copy editor practices constantly is elimination of useless words. Tight editing—using the fewest words necessary to communicate the thought—is imperative in the newspaper. It is not alone a matter of achieving simple, forceful writing, although that is primary. It is also a matter of conserving space, which even on the largest newspapers is a desperately important consideration.

Wasteful locutions written by the reporter out of habit and passed by the copy editor out of inattention have been cited in the chapter on "Words That Need Watching." They occupy precious space and mar the landscape of crisp, tight writing.

In the following three examples, which alert copy editing should have caught, suggested substitutes are enclosed in parentheses:

"Three teen-age youths were arrested in the Bronx early yesterday *in connection with* (in) the shooting of two youths."

"No other Communist country has had a similar trial of police officials . . . *with the exception of* (except) Yugoslavia . . ."

"The car . . . had to be towed seven times *during the course of* (during, on) the trip."

In each of these examples the substitution of the shorter form would have saved an entire line of type. Trivial? Try a little arithmetic. If each of forty copy editors saved only five such lines a night the total saving would be about a column from this source alone. It seems like a worthwhile economy when you consider that in addition you are improving tired writing.

## EXCLAMATION POINTS

The question of when to use the exclamation point is raised by the following lead: "It was bound to happen sometime! A bull got into a china shop here yesterday." A comment appropriate to this usage appears in the Fowler brothers' book, *The King's English:*

"When the exclamation mark is used after mere statements it deserves the name, by which it is sometimes called, mark of admiration; we feel that the writer is indeed lost in admiration of his own wit or impressiveness."

Like other punctuation marks, the exclamation point is often indispensable to convey proper meaning. For illustration, if a gent comes home sossled at 2 A.M. and says to his wife, "Evenin' precious; how'sh my li'l honeybunch?" her monosyllabic reply may have three meanings, depending on punctuation: (1) "Well." (She's feeling okay.) (2) "Well?" (I'm waiting for an explanation, buster. And don't call me honeybunch.) (3) "Well!" (You're a fine spectacle, you miserable creature!)

Obviously the exclamation point indicates strong emotion. Also it may signal an interjection, excited feeling and sometimes irony. But what place, pray, have any of these in detached, objective news writing? Let us, therefore, assume the exclamation mark to be guilty until proved innocent.

## FIGURES

The copy editor should always check figures in a story. Not only are they the most common source of factual error; they also provide the kinds of mistakes most glaringly obvious to readers. When a piece of copy refers to Charlotte V., 27, who has a son, 12, and then goes on to say that before the baby was born Miss V. was 17, the editor should detect that something is wrong.

It is even worse when an editor repeats a reporter's error in a headline, as in "716 Die in Christmas Accidents, 3-Day Rate is 1 Every 9 Minutes." It doesn't take an Einstein to establish that 1 every 9 minutes is approximately 7 every hour, 168 for a day and 504 for 3 days. Perhaps an appropriate punishment for an editor who passes such errors should be to compel him to answer, in longhand, every letter that comes to the newspaper from a triumphant reader pointing out—and it's always in these terms—"how the mighty have fallen."

Another example: "Records showed that in the last eighty-six years it rained nineteen times on Oct. 21. The odds are, therefore, 4½ to 1 against rain." A "Constant Reader" of *Winners & Sinners* suggests that we keep this reporter away from the crap tables. He observes that "the odds, out of 86 possibilities, are 67 favorable to 19 unfavorable, or 3½ to 1, with an extra half-point for the house."

*A footnote on figures:* "Though actual figures will not be available until today, Irving Gitlin, C.B.S. director of public affairs, estimated that about 10,000,000 persons had heard Mr. Khrushchev on television and radio. Normally 5,000,000 persons tune in to the 'Face the Nation' program." "Actual figures" of TV and radio audiences will not be available "today" or at any other time in the foreseeable future. The best that is ever available is a disputable estimate. Nor can we say that "normally 5,000,000 persons" tune in to a given program; this, too, is only a guess. Such figures should always be presented as estimates, preferably attributed to their source.

## FOREIGN LANGUAGES

(1) Translation of foreign phrases in news copy seems to pose a minor problem. A correspondent wrote from Puerto Rico: "Streamers over roads, pennants atop important buildings and huge electric signs all read, 'Bienvenida a la Fiesta Casals.'" The copy editor apparently felt that there was need to translate the Spanish, and there can be no quarrel with that. However, he proceeded to strike out the Spanish and substituted, "Welcome to the Casals Festival." With this decision there *can* be a quarrel, because the story then left the impression that the signs were all in English.

(2) In another story the quotation in the original language was likewise desirable, but for a different reason. Dean Acheson was asked to comment on the death of Senator McCarthy and, according to the story, "he quoted a Latin phrase which he translated: 'Say nothing about the dead unless it is good.'" In this situation, omitting the well-known Latin "De mortuis nil nisi bonum" makes the newspaper look completely unlettered. Surely you wouldn't duck "C'est la guerre" and say a man quoted a French phrase meaning "That is war," nor would you duck "Gesundheit" and say that when his wife sneezed the man used a German word meaning "health."

What is called for, of course, is judgment; and that in turn requires a moment of thought.

(3) Needless to say, renderings in a foreign language should be accurate: ". . . he began, 'Ladies and gentlemen,' then he repeated that salutation in French—'Madames et Messieurs.' That was as far as he went in French, however." It was not quite far enough.

## FOREIGN NAMES

Foreign names—particularly Spanish personal names—are a little difficult to handle if you don't know how. Obviously the desk man who edited a story about a visit to New Jersey of Puerto Rican legislators did not know how. In a first reference the story mentioned Luis Segarra Micheli; in a second reference the original copy called him Mr. Segarra Micheli, but an itchy pencil shortened this to Mr. Micheli, and that was a mistake.

Theoretically, every Spanish last name is a combination of the family names of the father and the mother. Thus if George Burns and Gracie Allen were natives of a Spanish-speaking country, their son's name in its fullest form would be Ronaldo Burns y Allen (that "y," which is a tough one to get through the composing room, means "and"). In Latin American countries, the "y" is not generally used, so the name would be Ronaldo Burns Allen. Sometimes the owner, for personal reasons, prefers to use only the father's name, but even if he doesn't, the name still may be properly reduced to Ronaldo Burns. If the father's name is a very common one like Gonzalez, the son may prefer to use both names as a distinguishing mark, and such a preference should be respected.

The only other complication that arises is that Latins often have a second given, or middle, name. If our friend of a few lines back were Ronaldo Antonio Burns, the father's name would, of course, be evident, but if it were Ronaldo Michel Burns—where Michel looks like either a given name or a family name—the copy editor might have some trouble determining which one was the family name. In that event he must find out either from a reference book or from the reporter. What he must not do is guess.

## HYPHENS

Hyphens are necessary evils. They should therefore be used only when necessary. One such necessity is avoiding ambiguity; another is avoiding absurdity.

*In compound adjectives.* Without a hyphen this headline is ambiguous: "False Jailing Claim Delayed." What was meant was "false-jailing claim."

Here are two situations in which hyphens can avert absurdities: "They have enabled the five-inch gun crew to iron out kinks in its fire control system . . ." One more hyphen is needed to make that crew man-size. "The former President will speak to small business men . . ." Make it "small-business," to indicate the phrase is a single adjective.

On the other hand, the head, "U.S.-Egyptian Ships Collide," suggests that two ships, each jointly owned by the United States and Egypt, collided. A hyphen is used to compound two elements. When it is desired to omit an "and" in a headline the comma should be used. Incidentally, that desire should be suppressed whenever possible.

*Suspensive hyphen.* Missing links are evident in this sentence: "The change in Administration attitude is reflected in pre and post satellite letters . . ." "Post-satellite" requires a hyphen. "Pre" is not a word in itself but a prefix; therefore it, too, requires a hyphen—a suspensive hyphen. Hence, make it "pre- and post-satellite letters." Or, if you don't like the awkward appearance of this arrangement, you can get around it—and in newspaper practice you probably should—by writing "pre-satellite and post-satellite letters."

Here is a similar misuse: "The paintings include land and seascapes . . ." Since a hyphen cannot be used after "land" ("landscapes" is not a hyphenated word), you would have to write it in full—"landscapes."

## INSERTS AND BRACKETS

(1) Some copy editors, when confronted with the need to put an insert into a story or include bracketed information—two forms of interpolation often necessary—become as panicky as a guest holding the last inch of a cigarette in a plushy room without ash trays.* What do they do? They just drop the insert anywhere.

For example, a Washington dispatch said that Senator McCarthy presided over his last committee hearing "in typical fashion," and elaborated this with one paragraph relating that he had heard a few friendly witnesses, and a second reporting that others had resorted to the Fifth Amendment. An insert came over the wire telling when the hearing had begun, when it had ended and when it would resume. The editor wedged the insert in between those two paragraphs, disrupting the thought that was being developed.

On another occasion, a feature story about the new Prime Minister of South Africa opened by saying that as a boy he

---

* Incidentally, the resourceful Drew Middleton came up with a solution to this predicament in the presence of the author at a Dulles press conference in the Ambassador's Residence in London. He produced a British penny, which, of course, comes in the large economy size. The idea is that you stub the cigarette out on the coin and put the butt in your pocket. Then you either dispose of it at the first opportunity or, more likely, have it pressed into the pocket next time the suit goes to the cleaner's.

used to leap on the backs of ostriches and often was shaken off, but would jump on again and again until he got his free ride. This led up to a paragraph saying: "In his political career Mr. Strijdom has overcome falls with the same single-minded iron determination." A requested insert giving the preferred spelling and pronunciation of "Strijdom" arrived. You've guessed it; the insert was placed so that it neatly derailed the train of thought.

It should not be necessary to labor the point that all that is required in placing an insert is a glance fore and aft to see what is going to happen to the story when the insert appears in print.

(2) Two other facets of background or explanatory matter call for a word of counsel.

First, explanatory matter that seems to require repetition over a period of days not only should be kept brief—so as not to crowd news out of the story—but also should not be presented in the same words day after day. Carrying this out demands ingenuity on the part of the writers and editors, but it is not an impossible task.

Second, overzealousness in bracketing explanations can sometimes irritate the reader. Here are examples of bracketing in the text of a press conference with Jim Hagerty that are needful because the name references would be meaningless otherwise:

"Q.—Milton [Dr. Milton S. Eisenhower, the President's brother] is not coming, Jim? A.—There is a possibility that Milton and Ruth [daughter of Dr. Eisenhower] will come over . . ."

On the other hand, in the text of a Dulles press conference, what is gained by bracketing "Konrad" into "Chancellor Adenauer" or, when the Secretary refers to "the German Foreign Minister," in bracketing "West" ahead of it? Bracketing should be confined to elucidating what might be obscure.

By the way, how is this for elucidation: ". . . their use so often amounts to just a hopeless antemortem [after death] gesture"? Big help.

(3) Two other points require attention when matter is bracketed into a dispatch. The first is to make certain that the story resumes smoothly after the bracketed matter. A Rome dispatch about evidence as to the date of Jesus' death cited Daniel's prophecy of the "seventy weeks" in the Bible.

Next came a bracketed paragraph quoting the passage from Daniel. The story then continued, "The eminence of the author of this new theory . . . ," leaving momentarily unclear whether or not it was Daniel who was meant.

The second point that needs watching is the time element in a bracketed passage. Such passages, since they are written locally, are not governed by the dateline of the dispatch, and the time elements should therefore be the same as those in a local story. Thus, for a morning paper this usage in a bracketed paragraph is incorrect: "He picked up two more delegates in Kansas today, The United Press reported . . ." To make things completely clear to the reader, the best idea is to substitute the day of the week for "today" or "yesterday."

## PARAGRAPHING

(1) When a copy editor imposes his own ideas of paragraphing on an official document he may distort its meaning, or at least the authors of the document may think he has done so. The safest rule to follow is this: A written document presented in the news columns as a text should be not only complete but also in the exact form of the original, and this includes the paragraphing.

In the reprinting of a speech, however—even though it is written in advance—long paragraphs may be broken up. No violence is done to the original in such an event since an orator does not speak in paragraphs, and his hearers are not aware of where paragraphs begin and end.

Paragraphing by reporters in their own copy is, naturally, not sacrosanct. Yet if the reporter has knitted together a rhetorical unit, due attention should be paid to that unity. In the desire for short paragraphs—and news writing demands shorter paragraphs than are the norm elsewhere—the editor should not hack the copy into little bits.

The following paragraph, which admittedly was too long, was broken up by the editor as indicated by the slant marks (/)—did you know they are called virgules?—inserted below: "When oil went to war in 1941, soft coal took up the slack./ Idle road-building machinery was put into strip-mine areas to gouge out the top soil and then the easily mined surface veins./ Soft coal increased its production from 350,-000,000 tons a year to a wartime peak of 650,000,000 tons and kept the wheels of industry turning./ But the easily mined seams are now nearing exhaustion./ Coal cannot be dug out with road scrapers now. Unless there is a sound mining industry in being there can be no major expansion of industrial production . . ."

The whole paragraph could readily and naturally be broken into two, beginning a second paragraph with the "but" idea, if not with that word. It is a question whether chopping apart related ideas, as was done, is not a hindrance rather than a help to the reader.

(2) Often several itemized paragraphs are introduced by an incomplete sentence; the paragraphs that follow are intended to complete the sentence. But through shortness of memory on the part of the writer and the editor, the intention is not always fulfilled. For example:

"The terminal communique of the ninth Council session recalled that it had:

"1. Endorsed a report . . .

"2. Accepted a build-up . . .

"3. The infrastructure program was adopted . . .

"4. An agreement was reached . . .

"5. Nonmilitary aspects of the organization were again emphasized . . ."

Paragraphs 3, 4 and 5 do not, of course, complete the partial verb "had." At the very least the parallelism should be maintained. But at best the incomplete clause or verb is a poor way to introduce a listing, because it compels the reader to look back to the introduction or keep it in mind—something that the writer and the editor themselves are obviously not always capable of doing.

## RELIGION

In religious matters, as indeed in all other matters, the news columns advocate nothing. They do respect all religious beliefs, but the line between respecting and endorsing is not always easy to draw. Here is a statement that is unexceptionable: "Miss Day will pray for the money to St. Joseph, whom she credits with meeting the bills through good-willed people all these years." On the other hand, here is a statement that is dubious: "Of the total sent to her in response to her prayers to St. Joseph, patron saint of workers, $1,500 was received yesterday." Here the corrective is to take account of the views of those who might believe otherwise. A peril, of course, lies in going so far in this direction as to appear skeptical. Intelligent carefulness, however, will keep things in equilibrium.

## REPORTERS AS NEWS FIGURES

A reporter filing a dispatch will sometimes refer to "this correspondent" in the happy expectation that his monicker will grace the top of the story. But if the by-line is ruled out, a sentence like "A police officer told this correspondent . . ." makes the reader look around in a fruitless effort to see who the correspondent is. In a situation like this the copy editor should remove "this correspondent," and just let the police officer "say" whatever he has to say.

Which leads to another and related point. Newspapermen are prone to write, "The District Attorney told reporters . . ." Now it is true that the reporters are the D.A.'s immediate hearers, but the D.A. is really telling the public, not the reporters, who, after all, are only a handful of votes. Representatives of the press should keep in mind, humbly, that they are reporters of affairs, not participants in them.

## SCIENCE

Science has taken the center of the stage. One reason advanced to explain why it has not done so earlier is that the cultural climate of the country has been unfavorable and that the egghead has been downgraded.

The press has a part in both reflecting and producing the cultural climate, and thus shares responsibility for it. Most of all, a serious paper that is assumed to be an intellectual leader carries an important part of this responsibility. It must be knowledgeable, not naive, and surely not ignorant. Three letters from *Winners & Sinners* readers make points on this general subject.

The first, from a geologist, suggests that the magic word "scientist" is being overworked and that the press should specify what kind of scientist is involved: physicist, chemist, biologist, geologist or what have you.

The second, from a physician, complains that the terms

"scientist" and "technician" are used as if they were interchangeable. The terms are not, of course, synonymous.

The third letter, from a paleontologist, points to this statement in a story about the National Academy of Sciences: "The academy is a private nonprofit organization of 550 scientists dedicated to the furtherance of science and to its use for the general welfare. Membership is by election in recognition of research accomplishments." To describe the Academy thus, says this writer, is true enough, but it is as if one were to describe the Philharmonic as "a group of gentlemen who play fiddles and other instruments."

Or, as the waiter said, looking scornfully at the 12-cent tip for a $1.20 lunch, "It's correct, but it's not right." Newspapers should try to have savvy about science.

## STYLE

Newspaper style rules are devised to avert typographical anarchy. They are also intended to instill confidence in the reader that the newspaper's right hand knows what its left hand is doing and that, as is not the case in piano playing, they are doing the same thing. Sometimes too much piano playing goes on. Here are several examples:

"Cuba's political strife took eight more lives today, bringing the death total to 21 for the last forty-eight hours and to about sixty for this month." That "21" in conjunction with the spelled-out numbers is completely illogical.

On the subject of spelling, have a look at this: "The children were served hot chocolate and donuts." You won't find "donuts" in *Webster's New International Dictionary*.

This sentence raises another small style matter: "The prairie hen, also commonly known as the pinnated grouse and to science as tympanuchus americanus . . ." Proper scientific usage calls for capitalizing the genus and lower-casing the species. Therefore, it should be "Tympanuchus americanus."

With a justifiable smirk, *The New Yorker* reprinted a passage from a story about the members of the Yankee baseball team who were caught off base in a party at the Copacabana night club in the middle of the fifth. The passage said: "Mr. Bauer, a long-ball hitter, was dropped to eighth in the Yankee batting order. Mr. Berra was withdrawn from the line-up altogether, while Mr. Mantle trotted out to his regular place in center field."

Now it is true that Times style calls for the use of "Mr." in the general news columns before the name of anyone who has not been tagged out by the law. In the sports columns, however, "Mr." is not used at all. But copy editors in either category should not follow style rules blindly; in fact, they should not do anything blindly. The use or non-use of "Mr." should never call attention to itself. Thus, if ball players appear in a close context with ordinary citizens who are designated "Mr.," they, too, should be called "Mr." But when they shed their mufti they shed their "Mr."

So, although it was Mr. Mantle who was a member of the night club party, it was (yes, in the same story) Mantle who trotted out to center field. Rules of style are never a substitute for good judgment.

## TIME ELEMENTS

(1) *Advance stories.* The press agencies occasionally employ this formula: ". . . Arthur S. Genet said in a *prepared address* at the convention of the National Association of Motor Bus Operators." The intention is to show that the story is based on a speech released to the press before its actual delivery. The formula does not say this, however; it says merely that the address was a prepared one, in contrast, perhaps, to an extemporaneous one. It should read, "an address prepared for delivery at the convention." But even this phraseology should not continue into an edition appearing after the speech has been delivered.

Another example: A first edition story, written in advance of the fact, said, "The Russians left the New York International Airport, Idlewild, Queens, last night . . ." So what happened? A bomb scare delayed the departure for four hours and instead of leaving "last night" they left "today." And for all the reporter could have foretold, they might not have left until tomorrow, or might even have been blown to bits. The correct way to handle such a story is to write that they were "scheduled to leave last night," then change the sentence when the plane takes off. Don't take chances on the future.

(2) *Midnight datelines.* A practically impossible dateline is the one carried on this dispatch: "Cleveland, Oct. 31 (AP)

—The Newspaper Guild here struck The Cleveland Press at midnight tonight after a deadlock in wage negotiations." If the reporter waited until midnight for the strike to materialize —and that is the implication of his dispatch—he could not possibly have filed his story until after midnight—that is, Nov. 1. Alert editing would have changed the dateline to Nov. 1 and the time element in the story to last night. Small point? But are newspapers supposed to be correct only in large matters?

## QUOTATION MARKS

A piece about Maj. Gen. Robert W. Grow illustrates the overuse and abuse of quotation marks. They were used thus: the "goat" of this incident; his various "contacts"; intelligence "agents"; tact, distinction, dignity and "brains"; open "squabbles"; "live wires"; and "spoils" system. Of "contacts," "agents," "squabbles" and "spoils," nothing need be said beyond observing that the writer apparently did not realize he was using normal English words in a normal context and that the quotation marks were quite out of place.

The remaining words raise a point about taste in writing. The news columns of a serious newspaper are usually written at the level of what might be called standard English. Occasionally it is desirable to descend to the vulgate level to select a word or phrase that is slang. But when we do this, we should descend, not condescend. If the slang conveys the thought in the desired manner it requires no apologetic quotation marks. The only explaining that is necessary is to your own conscience, to be quite certain that the slang is the best possible way of expressing the idea.

To illustrate further: One story on page 1 said that "the watchdog committee . . . is trying to determine whether there was a political fix in the case," but another story in an adjoining column spoke of an offer "to 'fix' a wage dispute." The latter story also referred to "a man with an 'in' to the Detroit teamster chief" and to "charges of 'planting' a former Secret Service agent on the Senate committee's staff." Three of these four examples illustrate the unnecessary use of quotation marks. If it is desirable to use slang—and there is no gainsaying that the word "fix," at least, qualifies, since there is no synonym—the slang should be used without the apology of quotation marks.

Here is another example of unnecessary timidity: "Bans Planes Towing 'Ad.'" "Ad" is a recognized colloquial word for advertisement. There is no more need to quote it than there is to quote "homer" on the sports pages.

For a different reason, quotation marks are undesirable in this headline: "Text of Speech by Stevenson Giving 'Facts' on His Part in Hiss Case." A commendable effort toward impartiality has here gone astray. In trying to avoid implying acceptance of the Stevenson statements as facts, the copy editor has actually implied that they are not.

## QUOTATIONS

A correspondent of *Winners & Sinners* inveighed against the practice of breaking into and out of quotations several times in one sentence. "This practice," he said, "raises and lowers the attention level of the reader in much too rapid succession, thereby tending to tire and confuse him."

Here is an example of what he has in mind: "He [Bidault] added that the Communist acceptance of the United Nations plan for the repatriation of ill and disabled war prisoners in Korea through an 'about-face' was 'no surprise,' in view of the previous 'gestures' apparently made 'deliberately' to show progress toward 'easing the situation.'"

Quoting a pungent or significant word or phrase to point up what a speaker said is all to the good. But to quote a collection of nondescript items, as in the cited sentence, is pointless and, what is worse, annoying. Unadulterated quotation or unadulterated paraphrase does a smoother job.

Two other words of counsel about the handling of quotation marks may be appended. Regardless of usage in other kinds of writing, which are read leisurely, the following methods will help speed the newspaper reader on his way. First, set out a quotation as a separate paragraph introduced by a colon. Second, if a quotation begins midway in the quoted sentence, close it as soon as a period is reached and then, if more is to be quoted, reopen with new quotation marks and insert "he went on" or "he continued" or the like. These devices will make things plainer for a reader who is holding the newspaper in one hand and pouring the coffee with the other.

# Head-Hunting

Writing headlines is an art—and a difficult one. The difficulty lies in the extreme space restriction. It is not possible to fit more than a few short words into a headline, and so the problem is one of cramming large ideas into small spaces.

A common impression among the non-journalistic laity is that the reporter writes the headline for his story. Except on the smallest newspapers, this is not the fact. Not only is it desirable to have the news judgment of another person brought to bear on any piece of news, but also, as a practical matter, the reporter is not in a position to decide the "play" of his story—that is, the place of importance it is to receive in the paper and the size head it is to carry. This is a job for supervising editors, who see the paper as a whole. In then carrying out their editorial decisions, it is the copy editor who writes the headline. This he does after he has performed the first, and in many respects the most important, part of his function—the editing of the copy.

The excerpts from *Winners & Sinners* contained in this chapter do not constitute a basic text on the art of headline writing. They were written for professionals, most of whom are well acquainted with the underlying techniques. Yet this material does touch on all the fundamentals, and the examples do contain sufficient reminders of essentials to enable the novice to avoid errors, or at least to question himself and come up with the right answer most of the time.*

Beginning with a five-point check list designed to measure the headline against a yardstick of obviously desirable re-

---

* This seems to provide a cue for a commercial plug: For a basic course in headline writing, see *Headlines and Deadlines,* by Robert E. Garst and Theodore M. Bernstein (New York, Columbia University Press, Third Edition, 1961).

quirements, this chapter then moves on to structural and technical details of head writing, next to the treatment of feature heads and finally to examples of headline writing at its best. Here again names of winners are included.

## A CHECK LIST OF FLAWS

The writing of headlines calls for craftsmanship. Not everyone can do it well, and copy editors therefore usually take deserved pride in their work. But in the scramble of getting to press they sometimes put up with heads that fall short of the best possible product. To combat this tendency, *Winners & Sinners* has, over the years, suggested five questions that can be used to detect headline deficiencies:

(1) *Is the head accurate?* For instance, does the story say, "Two children were rescued in a Queens fire yesterday when their mother dropped them twenty feet into the arms of policemen," while the head says, "Mother Drops Children 20 Feet to a Fireman"?

(2) *Is the head as complete as possible?* If the Board of Estimate has taken two routine, foreordained actions, does the head include only one—"15-Cent Bus Fare on Private Lines Approved by City"—when it might include both— "City Board Raises Private Bus Fares and Council Pay"?

(3) *Is the head specific?* A generalization is usually less understandable and less interesting than a specification. For example, "Witnesses Tell of Plane Crash" would be less meaningful to a reader than "Two Saw Planes Crash Near Grand Canyon."

(4) *Does the head focus on the news point?* Does it reveal the point that differentiates the story at hand from other, similar ones? If the story is about an off-duty probationary fireman who rescues two boys from a fire, is it sufficient to say, "Fireman Rescues Two Little Boys," or might it not be better to say, "Rookie Fireman, Off Duty, Saves Two"?

(5) *Finally, is the head clear and unambiguous?* One head, speaking of the British Christmas season, said: "Only Snows Are Decorative as Buying Spree Raises Demands for Currency." It was unclear because the "as" connected two ideas that really had no connection. And it was ambiguous in its opening phrase; what was meant was, "The Only Snows Are

Decorative Ones"—that is, artificial ones. Naturally, not every head can be perfect, but many can be improved by the simple expedient of a second thought, a second look.

Items 1 and 2 in the check list—accuracy and complete-ness—require no elaboration. The three other items will be discussed in order.

## HEADS IN THE CLOUDS

*Is the Head Specific?* "Be specific" is the chief guide to be kept in mind in writing headlines. A head that says, "Inspec-tion Plan Offered to City," is a deadhead; that is, it says virtually nothing. The story on which this head was used described a plan for periodic inspection of multiple dwellings; what was needed in the headline was a key word or phrase giving a clue to the subject matter. Such a key word would be "dwellings" or "homes" or "housing." Why not, "Periodic Checks on Housing Asked"?

*-w&s-*

This head has a key word in it, all right, but is too general: "College Leaders Study Problems." The story was mainly about burgeoning enrollments. How about "Educators Study Big College Rolls"?

*-w&s-*

Illustrating once more how a little extra effort makes a vague head precise: "Rear-End Crash a Major Problem" (First edition). "Rear-End Crash Big Road Hazard" (Final edition).

*-w&s-*

The headline, "Huge Princeton Tract Donated for Develop-ment as Arboretum," contains a characterization and is inferior to "81-Acre Tract Donated, etc." A general characterization may sometimes sound opinionated ("Vast Expenditures," for example), but in any event it is better to *be specific* and let the reader draw his own conclusions. In the present instance it may even be questioned whether eighty-one acres is "huge" as parks go.

*-w&s-*

Here's a dramatic illustration of the way a head can be improved by following the elementary guide to be specific: "U.S. Calls Polio News Good; Cites Drop in the Death Toll" (First edition). "No Child Died of Polio in '56 Who Had All 3 Salk Shots" (Final edition).

*-w&s-*

*Deadheads.* The term "deadheads," as has been indicated, may be applied to headlines that give the reader no clue to the subject matter of the story. For instance: "Not Yet Bound by Pact." The story was about Australia and the International Wheat Agreement. Obviously, "wheat" was the key word needed in the head.

Here's another example: "President Backs $10,000,000 Drive." The drive was one for funds for medical schools, and the word "medical" was the *sine qua non.* "President Asks Aid for Medical Study" would certainly have done the job better, if not perfectly.

Except in rare feature stories, the reader should not be driven to reading the bank of the head or the story itself to find out the bare minimum—the basic news of the piece. Otherwise the headline defeats its own purpose and is mere decoration. The trick lies in simply prying out the key word or phrase and then working it into the head, one way or another.

Examples of deadheads:

> "Projects Held Valid"
> "Symposium Scheduled"
> "Basic Aims Held Vital"
> "Identification Is Urged"
> "Open Hearings Set"

This head says something so obvious that it almost says nothing at all and hence comes close to being a deadhead:

"Canadian Chrysler's Expansion Aimed at Increasing Auto Output." Remember the immortal head, "Stairs Are Necessary in a Two-Story House"?

## WHAT'S THE POINT?

*Does the Head Focus on the News Point?* The headline "Connecticut Reds Seek a New Trial" seems to be satisfactory on the face of it. But what the copy editor neglected to ask himself was, "What is diffcrent about this story? What sets it apart from similar stories?" The difference, the element that constituted the unusual news, was the defendants' novel legal claim that they were entitled to demand trial without a jury. The head, then, might well have said, "Reds Claim Right to Non-Jury Trial." True, headlines must often be batted out in great haste. But there is usually another edition, an opportunity for a second and better thought. Why not seize the opportunity?

Here's another example of a weak surrender to a challenge. The story was about a man who, over a period of several months, had won a Brooklyn woman's confidence by pretending to help wounded veterans, and then robbed her of $24,000. The first edition head said, "Brooklyn Woman Robbed of $24,000." Notice how the rewritten version attempts to include the unusual angle: "Confidant Steals a Woman's $24,000."

*-w&s-*

Even shorts—brief stories carrying small heads—are not too insignificant to deserve less than the best headlining that a copy editor can give them. Shorts undoubtedly have a high degree of readership. Therefore they should not be brushed off with an "it's-good-enough" attitude. A headline like "Man Perishes in Fire" can be accounted for only by undue haste or indolence, but it cannot thereby be excused. A moment's consideration of two elementary headline precepts—that a head should be specific and that it should tell one story and no other story—would have convinced the copy editor that he could turn out a better head, *e.g.*, "Brooklyn Fire Kills Seaman." How could that extra moment have been better spent?

## SAY ONE THING, SAY IT CLEARLY

*Is the Head Clear and Unambiguous?* Since the headline is intended for the hurried reader, it should deliver its message so that it may be grasped, and grasped correctly, at first reading.

The copy editor who headlined a story about drunken pedestrians was too easily satisfied when he wrote, "Drunks Termed Traffic Hazard," because the reader would assume he was talking about drunken drivers. Giving it the old college try could improve it: "Drunken Walking Adds to Auto Toll."

*Two-Faced Heads.* Two-faced heads are headlines that are susceptible of two different readings. Here is a sampling of them, each of which illustrates a different cause of ambiguity.

1. "G.O.P. Races Hard to Win in Florida." The word "races" can be construed as either a noun or a verb.

2. "Ives Will 'Take Off Gloves' After Tomatoes Fly Upstate." Improper time sequence; the tomatoes had already flown when this head was written.

3. "Egyptian Vessel Struck in Jersey." Collision? No, labor trouble. The verb can mean two different things.

4. "Waves to Train in Maryland." Silly until you realize that "Waves" refers to those sailorettes.

5. "Roosevelt Named Envoy to Vatican." The meaning intended was that of the past tense, active voice. This one headed a background story recounting some history. It was particularly unfortunate because on the facing page was a continuation head on the current story, which read, "Gen. Clark Named Envoy to Vatican" (present tense, passive voice).

6. "Holland Visits Mexico." Names can sometimes cause trouble; this head referred to Henry F. Holland.

Two-faced heads can be avoided by taking a little more care, a little more time. When you finish writing a headline, read it over twice. Read it first for the meaning you intended —that is, the way any sensible person would read it. Then read it a second time for the meaning that that jackanapes, the perverse customer, might conceivably get out of it. If both are possible readings, chuck it.

Illustrating further how names can be bothersome:
"Nehru Is Grateful for New U.S. Grant"

"Crooks Re-elected by Stock Exchange"

"Hope to Do 6 Shows on Radio-TV Weekly." It referred, of course, to Bob Hope.

"Senator Long in Line." It referred to the gentleman from Louisiana.

"Windsor Greets Duchess of Kent." The Duke? No, the city in Ontario.

"Tito's Birthday Hailed. Relays Carry Nation's Greetings to President 62 Today." Sounds as if temperance has come to Yugoslavia.

*-w&s-*

Flies can be a nuisance all year round. Witness:

1. "Flies to Receive Nobel Prize"
2. "Fly to Attend Venice Art Show"
3. The same sort of thing in reverse: "British Fly Plague Blankets 100 Miles." You have to read that one a second time—which is what the copy editor should have done, and then discarded it.

*-w&s-*

Miscellaneous examples of two-faced heads:

"Anna Russell Hit as Opera's Witch"

"Atoms Foe Starts Fast"

"Developers Scan Virgin Far North"

"Surgery in Heavy Seas Follows Dash by Cutter"

"Japanese Ships Can Crab Meat"

"Smoking Chief Cause of Fire Deaths Here"

"Lawmakers Hope to Pass Water, Other Bills in Trenton Tomorrow"

"Fur Factor in Fatal Fall." This was about a money-lender in the fur trade. Aside from the ambiguity of the word "factor," the alliteration, whether intentional or un-intentional, was out of place.

"Fencers Club Victor." Where's your sportsmanship, lads?

"Egypt Restricts Sales to Britain." And only Britain?

"Dolls Sent to Flood Homeless." The Betsy Wetsy variety, obviously.

*-w&s-*

Misuse of a word can give a headline an unintended meaning, as this one shows: "Westport Refuses Army's Bid to Clear

Snow From Its Street." The chief trouble here is that the noun "bid" means primarily "offer," whereas what was intended was "request."

-w&s-

Free association is a psychological fact of life and it can trip a reader trying to grasp a headline. The trouble becomes acute when, in addition, words are used that can have more than one meaning. For instance: "Fleet Backs Buoy Andover Eleven." "Fleet" in conjunction with "buoy" is bound to have a nautical association for many readers. But perhaps the basic trouble with that jumbled head is that each of the first three words can be a different part of speech from what is intended.

To take another example: The word "draft" can mean several things. Put the word "military" with it and you suggest the idea of conscription. But this is not what was meant in the head, "Military Drafts Wider Protests on Defense Cuts." It doesn't do to argue that the head wouldn't make any sense if the first two words were taken to denote conscription. Of course it wouldn't, but this is further evidence that the reader will have to go back and start over. This he should never have to do, because the function of the headline is to convey the message swiftly. Lesson: Always read your head over for wrong associations or double meanings, and be sure it's instantly clear.

*Headlinese.* Headlinese ranks high as a cause of obscurity. It is the tortured, sometimes almost unintelligible language that occasionally appears in inexpertly written heads. It can result from the unusual use and piling up of nouns employed as adjectives, from overuse of the comma to replace "and," from ambiguous use of words, from the injection of odd coinages not found in normal speech or writing and from unreasonable extensions of meanings given to handy short words. It is caused not by any perverse desire of the headline writer to be cryptic, but rather by his desperate need to fit size 7 ideas into size 2 spaces.

The sad examples that follow are presented with diagnoses attached:

"24-Hour Strike Halts Italy Mail, Railroads." The use of the noun (Italy) where the adjective (Italian) would be normal should be a last-ditch expedient in a head. So should the use of a comma to replace "and." Two last ditches in a single head are too much of a retreat.

"G.O.P. Senators Hit Nehru for Airlift Ban, Hint Aid Halt." Note the headline gimmicks that appear here: the strictly headline abbreviation "G.O.P.," the overworked headline word "hit," the unusual adjectival use of the noun "airlift" and the uncommon phrase "aid halt." Any one of these would be acceptable by itself in a head. It is the piling up of the gimmicks that makes the head a wide departure from normal English into the language of headlinese.

"Moody Death Aids Ferguson Chance." Again two uses in a single head of a noun where an adjective or a possessive is indicated.

"Cage Star Is Hurt in Auto Crack-Up." "Cage Star" would be bad enough on the sports pages; it is inexcusable in the general news columns.

"Jews Score Bard Fete on Play." Not to keep you guessing, the story was about the protest of a Jewish group over inclusion of "The Merchant of Venice" in a Canadian Shakespearean festival.

"Mrs. Zaharias Fit for Texas Surgery." Special technique in the Lone Star state?

"Price Index Rises, First in 3 Months." What does "first" refer to?

"Tax Rises Mark Shifts by States." Difficult to grasp. Note that every word in the head except "by" can be either a noun or a verb. Correction: "By" can be both a noun and a verb, too.

*-w&s-*

In normal speech or writing, the word "self" would never be used as it is in this head: "Berserk Father Kills 6 and Self." It therefore may be classed as headlinese and should be ruled out except when it is inescapable. The foregoing head might have said: ". . . Kills 6, Ends Life."

*-w&s-*

"Dulles Explains on Yalta Papers." "On" is a nice short word, but it can't be used indiscriminately.

*-w&s-*

Short words are, of course, tools of the headline writer's trade. But a tool can become dulled by overuse and twisted by misuse. Such a dull, twisted one is the word "hit," which appears in heads as a synonym for everything from striking physically to being mildly critical. In this example its use is definitely out of place: "Teachers College Hit on Curriculum." (Notice, incidentally, that an additional result is a two-faced head.)

The short word "aide" is perfectly good, but tends to be overused; "bid" also gets a big play from head writers, and, of course, there are many others in this category. The counsel here is not to stop using the short words; that would be wholly unreasonable. It is rather to save them as weapons of last resort, to explore first for other ways to win the battle.

*-w&s-*

*The New Yorker* carried this squib: " 'Many Seen Failing to Enjoy Their Jobs' (Headline in *The Times*). They might at least keep out of sight." This raises a question about the use—let's say the overuse—of the word "see" in headlines.

In normal English (which is what headlines should approximate as much as possible) the use of "see" in the sense of "regard" or "consider" is not common. It is a possible locution, but not a likely one, to say, "The psychiatrist saw many persons failing to enjoy their jobs." Let us confess, then, that this use of the verb "see" is not normal but is instead a headline convention, a kind of special license. It is employed either to introduce into the head a necessary attribution of a statement or to avoid the tentative "may." But, having said this, let us then recognize that the license should not be abused. Since "see" is a conveniently short word, the license *is* abused, with the result that the word appears far too often.

Moreover, the offense is sometimes compounded when the headline writer tries to impose another license on top of the original one. Examples: "Soviet Deserters See Army Ally of West"; "Robert Ryan Seen Miss Booth Co-Star." In these headlines the necessary word "as" has been improperly omitted. Remembering that "see" as used here is synonymous with "view" or "regard," would you say "Soviet Deserters View Army Ally of West" or "Robert Ryan Regarded Miss Booth Co-Star"? The answer, it is to be hoped, is no.

Another caution: Don't use the word "see" when it could be read in its literal sense and thus produce a two-faced head, as in this example: "More TV Football Seen This Season." Or this one: "Savant Sees Man Cruising in Space."

An odd use appeared in a head on an archeological story: "Negro Visits in 900 to Americas Seen." What does the verb mean in this headline? Actually observed? Obviously no. Forecast or foreseen? No again. Considered or regarded? No. Then what?

*-w&s-*

The word "hold," while not so strained in its headline uses as "see," is likewise subject to overuse. And, believe it or not, the two appeared together in a single head: "Official Seen Held by Reds." Any day now we'll probably get the combination in reverse: "Missing Man Held Seen in Oshkosh."

*-w&s-*

Talking about headlinese and "held," what does the word mean here: "Little Success Is Held for Swiss Plane Plea"?

Another caution about the word "held" is in order: A report that a sister of Dr. Charles Laughead had petitioned a court to declare the physician mentally ill carried the head, "Dr. Laughead Held Ill." "Held" often has the special meaning of a judicial ruling. In this headline its use could have suggested that court action had already been completed. As a matter of fact, it had just been begun.

## STRICTURES ON STRUCTURE

*Top and Bank.* If the top of the headline begins with a verb—and it would be better if it didn't—the subject of that verb must be the first word or phrase of the bank. This is incorrect: (Top) "Seeks to Restore Whitewall Tires." (Bank) "Rubber Shortage Is Over, Ban Is Causing Black Market, Industry Leader Says." The bank should have begun with "industry leader."

*-w&s-*

*Verb in Bank.* If the bank of a head begins with a verb, the assumption is that its subject is the same as that of the top. This one is improperly framed: (Top) "Inflation Spreads to Umbrellas in Balloon-Like Plastic Model." (Bank) "Can Be Turned Inside Out . . ."

*-w&s-*

*This Kind Is Lousy of Head:*
1. "Early Sale Impends of Yankee Stadium"
2. "Disposal Is Urged of Ex-Peron Papers"
3. "Operator Buys Home on King St. Built by Astor From the Assumption Nuns."

*-w&s-*

*Tense and Time.* The convention whereby the present tense is used in a headline to describe action in the past is upset when a past-time element is introduced into the headline. The convention then calls attention to itself and is incongruous. Examples: "Soviet-West Trade Drops 50% Last Year." "Buying of Machine Tools Turns Higher in January." When a past-time element appears in the head the only thing to do is use a verb in the past tense.

A time-element complication arises also in headlines on late-breaking stories. News events may be unresolved at the moment of going to press, but editors should constantly keep in mind that the paper will usually not be read until many hours later, by which time the events are likely to have been completed. Therefore, headlines should not suggest continuing or future action in rapidly developing situations. It is disconcerting to a reader to pick up his paper at breakfast and read "Floor Battle On" in a headline about a national convention, when he is quite aware that the convention delegates ended their battle and went to bed hours before. Similarly he would be puzzled to read at 9 A.M. that "Speech Is Awaited; President Will Address Delegates, Introduce a Standard Bearer," when the actual event took place many hours earlier. In such situations headlines should be confined to developments that are already wrapped up, and should be phrased to suggest past action; for example, "Floor Battle Waged" instead of "Floor Battle On." An exception, of course, is a situation in which it is certain that the events will still be in progress when the paper is read; "Coal Strike On" in these circumstances is unexceptionable.

*-w&s-*

*Verb in Subordinate Clause.* "Play's Translator Claims Spirit More Believable Than 'Hamlet' Ghost." In a headline of this kind it is necessary to include the verb of the subordinate clause—"is." The reason, briefly, is that in clauses following certain verbs of "saying," inclusion of the verb is the only way to indicate quickly that the next noun is not, as would be expected, in the objective case, but in the nominative case—it is the subject of the clause. (Incidentally, for a comment on the above use of the word "claims," consult Chapter 1, "Words That Need Watching.")

*-w&s-*

*Auxiliary Verbs.* The passive voice, when used in a head without its auxiliary verb, sometimes causes fleeting puzzlement. This is because it may appear to be the past tense of an active verb. For instance, "Surgeons Left Towel, Ex-G.I. Voted $7,500." Nor does it make any difference whether the passive is a regular one—"Soviet Engineers Offered Lebanon" —or a so-called false passive—"Lebanon Offered Soviet Engineers." It is the absence of the auxiliary ("is" or "are") that causes the trouble. Admittedly the confusion is only momentary, but anything that makes the reader stumble or retrace his steps defeats a chief purpose of the headline: to tell the story swiftly.

*-w&s-*

*Head and Story Should Match.* In headlining a sermon story it may be quite all right to come out boldly and say, "Bishop Opposes Sin," instead of playing it safe with "Bishop Says He Opposes Sin." But in dealing with sensitive subjects and controversial characters a greater degree of caution and strict objectivity are imperative. The headline should say no more than the story. Thus if a Russian makes a speech deploring world tension it is not proper to headline the story, "Russian Favors End of 'Cold War.'" A better version would be, "Russian Says He Favors End of 'Cold War,'" or, "Russian Speaks Against 'Cold War.'" It should be kept in mind that we do not know what people think; we know only what they say they think.

Here is a misleading head: "Anti-Polio Vaccine Guaranteed by Salk." What Dr. Salk guaranteed was the safety of the inoculation—not, as the head would suggest to most readers, its effectiveness. The treatment of disease is one of the subjects in which special caution and conservatism are indicated.

A final note on conformity of headline and story. Letters and comments of readers indicate that they find few things more irritating than to read something in a headline that does not appear in the story. Checking the head against the story should be as much a matter of routine for the copy editor as it is for a flier to verify that his flaps are unlocked before a take-off.

Although the head should not, as a rule, contain something that is not in the story, there are, of course, exceptions: (a) shorthand references that are perfectly obvious, like "G.O.P.," and (b) phrases or ideas in feature heads where the headline writer may take the bit in his teeth, provided he does not gallop too far afield.

-*w&s*-

*Continuation Heads.* Among the exasperations that afflict readers, to judge by a letter or two, is the unfindable continuation of a page 1 story—unfindable because the jump head says something different from the front page head. For instance, a reader complained about this instance: "A Nautical Look Adorns Coliseum" (main head); "Motor Boat Show Draws Big Crowd" (jump head). Understandably, it is not always possible to repeat the main head exactly. If it is not possible, the next best thing is to repeat the first line at least. If even that is not possible, the key word or phrase of the main head must be repeated. Violations occur most often when the main head is changed at the last minute and there is no time to make the jump head conform. But opportunity almost always knocks twice; there is usually another edition.

## FEATURE HEADS

Feature heads can be the spice of the newspaper when they come off. But when they don't, they can be pure vinegar. Moreover, if they are used inappropriately, they can damage the paper by seeming smart-alecky.

*Straining.* Brightness in a headline is, of course, desirable if it is appropriate to the story and if it isn't far-fetched or labored. Straining for cleverness may also strain the reader's patience and not produce the best possible head.

For example, on a story about a tobacco man who over-planted his Federal allotment and was not permitted to market the excess for charity, this head appeared: "U.S. Bars Tobacco Road to Good Samaritan Deed." Not only is the head obscure, but the phrase "tobacco road" is misleading. Similarly misleading is the head, "Mrs. Luce Quotes Saga of an Ancient Mariner," on a story about her recitation of the words of a sixteenth-century naval commander. A straightforward dispatch on *Pravda's* appeal for more and better movies did not call for a feature head, much less this rhymed concoction: "Better Films, Pravda Pines, Needed on Russian Vines." Finally, a story about Greek sheep that allegedly violated the Albanian border produced what must surely have been the most labored pun of the year: "Albania Now Rams Charge at Greece." Let's have brightness by all means, but let's also have rightness.

In tackling any feature story, headline writers should ask themselves whether the story really needs a clever head or whether simply telling the facts of the story will not be sufficiently featurish. When the Governor denounced as a waste of money a bill merely changing a "who" to a "whom" in an existing law, the copy editor thought of a grand combination pun: "Never Ask the Governor for Whom the Bill Tolls." But wouldn't restraining himself have been better than straining? Wouldn't a straight recital of the facts have been preferable?

Also, when a couple were married aboard a tender in Gibraltar Bay the copy editor wrote the headline, "A Tug into Nuptials." Aside from the fact that a tender is not a tug, the head is less interesting and less informative than one simply setting forth the unusual fact.

On a routine story about Safety Week this head essayed brightness that was uncalled for: "Be Safe or Drop Dead." In the same category is this one: The lead said, "A St. Bernard was rescued today by an 11-year-old boy." The headline writer (a lily-painter, if there ever was one) came up with, "Variation on Old Theme." What could have been better than simply telling the story: "Boy Saves a St. Bernard"?

*Puns.* After the rhyme, the pun is the most available (not necessarily best) tool for the headline writer who is striving for brightness. A pat pun is a legitimate ornament, a strained pun is little better than a parasite. But how can you tell the difference? Admittedly it's largely a matter of taste and opinion, but there are two suggested tests: First, both the double meanings should be appropriate; second, the reader's reaction should not be a wince followed by a sickly smile, but rather a double take followed by a pleased smile or—if you're lucky—by a guffaw. At the risk of outraging contrary opinions, this corner will cite some examples:

Strained, or wince, type: "Middies to Have One Bell of a Time Today for Wringing Out the Cadets on Gridiron."

Pat type: On a story about a delayed letter: "Post, but Hardly Haste" (Jacob S. Badiner). On a story about a repulsive Himalayan goat at large in the Chappaqua area: "This Tahr Nobody's Baby" (Frazier Dickson).

Okay, lads, fire away.

*-w&s-*

A play on words is legitimate in headlines, as it is anywhere else, if it is appropriate and contains meaning. If it lacks both these qualities, however, it becomes a mere game. For example: A skin specialist said that daily bathing was the worst thing for your skin, especially when you used soap, and the copy editor wrote the head, "Doctor Calls Daily Bath Just a Lot of Soft Soap." In view of the fact that "soft soap" is a colloquial phrase denoting flattery, what meaning does that headline contain? It is a purely idle play on words. On the other hand, here is a head that has meaning, and includes a perfect, if not brilliant, play on words: "Nervous Passenger Gets a Brake—Now He, Too, Can Stop the Car" (Sherman Davis). Notice that the head not only puns but actually tells the story.

-*w&s*-

If a correspondent writes about a Bulgarian radio series and applies to it the American characterization of "soap opera," which has very little to do with soap in any case, that is enough to send a headline writer galloping off in all directions with, "Bulgaria Washes Out Soap Opera; Red Wrath Lathers Fickle Heroine." A dispatch reports the chartering of the Firehouse Nursery School, and this somehow suggests to an editor the head, "Ladder of Success." Or a TV review of a George Gobel show impels a desk man to write, "A Merry Christmas in Gobel-dygook." All of these are mere toying with words. They bear little relation to a really good pun like this one on a story about an imbibing Kris Kringle: "Santa Claus Carries Load a Bit Too Far" (Sherman Davis). Notice that in this headline there is more than a simple fooling with words; there is a genuine, amusing double meaning, and the head tells the story. Admittedly, beauts like this are hard to come by, but they surely do not result from let's-try-anything tactics.

-*w&s*-

When Ira Henry Freeman wrote this sprightly lead, "From now on it's Lüchow's, not Luchow's, and the addition of the little umlaut over the 'u' spells all the difference between an old-fashioned German restaurant and a chop suey palace," John S. Radosta produced a really sparkling pun in this head: "Umlaut Spells Difference in Chow on 14th Street." A triple meaning, when you think about it.

-*w&s*-

A word about puns on names. If someone's name lends itself to a pun, you can take it as certain that you are not the first one who has thought of it, and that the pun has been made *ad nauseam*. Take, for example, the Cleveland pitcher Herb Score. What could be more obvious or cornier than a picture caption reading: "The Winning Score"? Even worse is a pun on a name in which there is no double meaning and therefore no point: "A Word to Mrs. Wise." Another example: Pat Boone appeared on a TV show, and this produced the head, "No Boon to TV." Convinced?

*-w&s-*

A footnote about rhymed heads. For every rhyme there should be a reason. A story about a reptile, quoting the "Ode Tuatara," properly inspired a rhymed head: "Zoo 'Fossil's' Plight Now Is Set Aright" (Paul L. Havely). But . . . avoid rhymes when they are not suited to the subject matter of the story, and watch out for unintentional rhymes like this: "Austrians Afraid G.O.P. May End Aid."

*-w&s-*

A second footnote, warning about unwanted rhythm. "Stocks Seesaw, Fall a Bit More; 5 Million Shares Change Hands." Was the writer aware of the assonance there and the beat of the oompah bands?

## TROPHIES OF A HEAD-HUNTER

*Toughies.* A common complaint of copy editors is that the only headlines to win recognition are the bright feature heads, whereas a straightforward, unspectacular head often represents a brilliant meeting of a tough challenge, but commands no praise. This is altogether true. The explanation is simply that the toughies emerge from a struggle known usually only to the copy editor and God, and they do not bear the marks of the battle on them. Here are a few:

An involved thought, smartly expressed: "Ehrenburg Shoots Own Dove of Peace" (Robert S. Crandall).

Packing a lot of information, this difficult head is made to look easy: "Captives Seize Plane in Air, Flee Bolivia" (Gordon N. Havens).

A large idea successfully compressed into small space: "Warren Puts Hope in Ideas, Not Bombs" (Jerome V. Keating).

Deft writing conveys much information: "Dio Pleads Fifth; His Voice, on Tape, Ties Him to Hoffa" (John F. Wicklein).

A double-barreled idea embraced in very limited space: "Zhukov Lauds U.S. While Warning It" (Robert Simpson).

Here is a headline in which the copy editor passed over the obvious surface development to get at the underlying substance of the story: "Dean Pike Rejects a 'White' Divinity.'" Then, in the bank: "Refuses a Color-Line Degree at Sewanee and Declines to Preach Baccalaureate" (Grover C. Loud).

Discerning selection of detail: "50 Dead in Wreck of London Trains. Christmas Packages Litter Fog-Bound Crash Scene" (Sherman R. Miller).

*-w&s-*

*Bright Heads.* "Boys Hang Their Socks for Santa on His Chin" (Jerome V. Keating).

"Sutton Poesy in Re Cash Is No Like of Ogden Nash" (Paul L. Havely).

"6 Scientists Climb on Limb of Future" (Socrates K. Butsikares).

"Mocktail Tixing Kilt. Cocktail Mixing Tilt Won by—Who Won 'At Ol' Thing Anyway?" (John Stephenson).

"Auto Men Are Told to Get Out and Push" (Arnold Blom).

"Trades Stars for Stripes. U.S. Sergeant in Germany Was Once a General in Kashmir" (Foster Hailey).

"Room for Improvement. India's Vice President Finds U.N. Meditation Hall Little Used" (Robert S. Crandall).

"Churchill Kneels to Queen and Arises as Sir Winston" (John S. Chalmers).

"Poison Ivy Gives Scouts an Outing to Remember" (Robert D. Dinsmore).

"Twin Bronze Bell Men at Herald Square to Get Two Weeks Off for Bad Behavior" (Willard B. Crosby).

"Soft You Now, Richard III, Friends Gather to Battle 'Lies' Long Fouling Your Name" (Werner M. Wiskari).

"5% Rail Increase: Is It Fare Enough?" (John Hess).

"M'Sorley's Hears 'Time, Gentlemen'" (James E. Darby).

"Army's Pigeons to Turn In Wings" (James J. Tuite).

"F.T.C., Finding an Ocean of Difference Between Parfum and Perfume, Cites 3" (John Hess).

"Broadway to Give Its Regards to Cohan; Statue Will Remember Him at Duffy Sq." (William P. Luce).

"Zoo's Food Costs Increase $9,300, and That Ain't All Hay Either" (Alden Whitman).

"Bees Follow 'Line,' or So Say Russians" (David L. Lidman).

"Judge Rules It's No Crime to * ! * / at the Police" (S. Lee Kanner).

"Ezier Speling Bil Skors in Kommuns" (Robert Simpson).

"Houz That Agen? Police Misspell Caution Sign to Make Drivers Take Notice" (Arnold Blom).

"New Trombone S-l-i-d-e-s to Side, So Precluding the Forward Conk" (John Stephenson).

"Vanishing A's on Facade Puzzle N tur l History Museum People" (Elizabeth Wade Boylan).

"Horse Goes Bathing at L.I. Beach Despite Nays of Some Residents" (Richard W. Haitch).

"Outdoorsmen in Gray Flannel Suits Rub Natural Shoulders at Vacation Show" (Thomas F. S. Buckley).

Listed that way, the headlines look easy. What is not evident to the newspaper reader, but is constantly vexing to the headline writer, is the necessity for conforming to a foreordained typographical pattern, for painfully counting units to be sure that the head, set in the prescribed type, will fit into the prescribed space. Often—discouragingly often—the copy editor comes up with an idea for a head that is a natural, only to find that it will not fit. It is then that his ingenuity, his resourcefulness and his patience face a test. But when, at last, he hits upon the thought and the phrasing that are just right, the sense of achievement and of craftsmanship is immense.

Thus does the copy editor cap the work of the reporter. The editor fashions his headline, not to tease the reader into the story and so perhaps compel him to fritter away time on something in which he has no interest, but on the contrary to save him time by providing a quick, attractive précis of the reporter's work. The reporter in turn, as has been set forth in earlier chapters, should be intent on conveying information swiftly, clearly and precisely. The two—reporter and editor—when working as an effective team realize the true and only valid purpose of the press: to inform the public.

# Appendix

To illustrate some of the points made throughout this book, and particularly in the chapter titled "Storytelling," a handful of news stories from The New York Times are reproduced here.

They in no sense constitute a collection of "best" stories, although all are of high quality. Many other reporters have produced pieces of the same fine caliber. These were selected because they seemed to be excellent examples of the types of writing indicated by the categories in which they appear. As their subject matter shows, they were not written yesterday; but stories of similar merit undoubtedly were, and can be found in the paper on your breakfast table today. Newspaper craftsmen are continually producing creditable pieces of writing like these despite the harrying pressures of distracting environment and insistent deadlines.

All the news articles appended are reproduced in full, except for Milton Bracker's satellite story and Meyer Berger's snow story, from which tail-end details have been omitted.

## Innocents Abroad: How-People-Live Stories

### BRITISH ARE LOSING TASTE FOR BEER; SALES FALL AS THE POPULATION RISES

#### By DREW MIDDLETON

LONDON, July 31—The British are going off the beer. The race that has quaffed brown October ale and ordered the landlord to fill the flowing bowl until it runs over is slowly but steadily cutting its intake of beer, ale and allied beverages.

The men who make and serve the nation's drinks are worried by a decline in sales, especially in beer. This decline, it is suggested, is part of a general change in British social customs accelerated by prosperity and prices.

In a country that produced the proverb, "Bread is the staff of life, but beer is life itself," the cut in beer drinking borders on the sensational.

Back in 1900, when the population of the United Kingdom was about 38,000,000 and the sun never set on the British Empire, the British got through 36,000,000 barrels of beer a year. In 1953, when the Commonwealth had replaced the Empire and the home population had risen to more than 50,000,000, just under 25,000,000 barrels was brewed.

There are thoughtful beer drinkers who see an ominous connection between these two sets of circumstances. Publicans and other students of human nature offer a variety of reasons for the decline in beer drinking.

One is that rationing, imposed by war and austerity, weakened beer and drove many to gin and rum.

But the alcoholic content of ordinary draft beers has increased with the return of prosperity. Brewers are again making "special" ales, two or three pints of which will blow a soft hat through a concrete ceiling.

Nevertheless, the British drank 40,000,000 gallons less of beer in 1954 than in 1953.

Traditionally the drink was a pint of old and mild, or mild and bitter, or ale. Nowadays bartenders report an increased demand for bottled beer—there are nearly 2,000 brands on the market—from persons whose fathers regarded bottled stuff as sissy.

The most popular bottled drink is brown ale. A barmaid summed up the brown-ale drinker as, "A nice fellow, you know, but not what we used to call a drinking man. The sort of a man who used to queue at the shops for his wife. Pushes the pram."

This fellow, she added disdainfully, drinks a couple of bottles of brown ale and goes home.

There are parts of Britain where the drinker sticks to his "pint of draft." Not long ago in the north a reporter saw two men get through six pints each in the course of an evening.

### High Cost a Factor

The high cost of beer has helped reduce consumption.

Prices for a pint in London run from a shilling and 6 pence
(21 cents) for brown ale to 2 shillings and 10 pence (about
40 cents) for some of the stronger brews. These are London
prices. The pint is tuppence (2⅓ cents) less in the provinces
generally. But everywhere there is a tax of 9 pence (10½
cents) a pint.

Publicans blame television and other attractions for the
decline in beer drinking and, in fact, all public-house drinking.

"Bloke used to come in after his tea and have three or four
pints with the boys," said a man who runs a London pub, as
his father did before him. "He used to bring his wife on
Saturdays and she'd have gin and something or maybe a port
and lemon. Nowadays he's at the dogs (dog races) or they're
both watching the tele (television)."

The tea referred to is not the skimpy afternoon variety but
the British workingman's evening meal at which tea washes
down lots of heavy food.

Half a century ago the corner pub was the workingman's
club and almost his only means of regular entertainment. But
horizons have widened.

The farm laborer or steel worker can spend his money on
television sets, new furniture, new clothes that were beyond
his father's pocketbook. Most of these are bought on "the
never-never" (installment system) and they leave less money
and less time for "the local" (public house).

### Tobacco a Serious Rival

Tobacco prices have outstripped those for drink. But consumption rises. Sociologists assert that all but drunkards, faced
with a choice between the two, will buy cigarettes or pipe
tobacco and spend what remains for beer. These days there
isn't much left.

Soft drinks have cut into the beer trade, but not as much
as was expected at the end of the war. The British will drink
something like 250,000,000 gallons of soft drinks this year,
about double the pre-war figure, but publicans say that consumption is confined to groups that never were serious beer
drinkers.

Since prices for gin, whisky and rum and other spirits,
which are called "shorts" in London pubs, have risen with
beer, national consumption of these drinks has not risen

appreciably. Many who before the war had whisky and soda before going home now are content with a bottle of brown ale.

### Young Are Drinking More

Young people, however, are drinking more. Sir Hugh Lucas-Tooth, Under Secretary for the Home Office, recently revealed in the House of Commons that convictions for drunkenness rose from 2,995 in 1953 to 3,336 in 1954 among those aged 17 to 21.

National military service, which like television serves as a handy whipping boy for viewers-with-alarm, is blamed by many. Youths go off to the services at 18 and develop a taste for beer once the paternal eye is withdrawn, it is charged.

But a likelier cause of the trouble is the increased earnings of young people still living at home. There are plenty of young men making more in a week than their fathers made in a month thirty years ago.

Publicans are disturbed by the increase in teen-age drinking.

"Come in with their loud clothes and their larks and give a quiet, family place like mine a bad name," one said. "Told 'em straight last time they was in to get out and stay out. Don't know what the country's coming to."

-*w&s*-

## PAKISTANI REGIME HAVING HARD TIME

*Tempers Short, Hours Long*
*As Suhrawardy Copes*
*With Fasting Period*

### By A. M. ROSENTHAL

KARACHI, Pakistan, April 9—Prime Minister Hussein Shaheed Suhrawardy is performing some skillful but almost desperate political juggling to keep his seven-month-old Pakistani coalition government from falling.

Keeping a coalition from collapsing into the mutual distrusts that are its component parts is a strain any time. But this is the month of Ramadan, when Moslems fast from sunup to sundown, and that makes for some especially difficult and short-tempered days in Karachi.

The National Assembly of Pakistan meets in a chamber that looks like a teak-lined well. The combination of coalition and Ramadan often gets the better of parliamentary order.

Abdul Wahab Khan, Speaker of the House—a man with a great, white, patriarchal beard—keeps order by out-shouting the members. But the members are masters at the art of waiting until the speaker draws his breath. Then they get in the broad insult.

## A Politic Suggestion

The Minister for Parliamentary affairs, a dapper man, dressed, like most members, in Western clothes, suggests that the House meet from 6 to 8 in the evening, hours when Pakistanis say evening prayers and break their fast.

The Speaker is about to say something when an Opposition member rises, raises an accusing arm toward the Minister and shouts: "He does not even pray, not to talk of fasting!"

Time to talk politics, then, is at sundown when temperature and tempers fall. Politicians, like the rest of their countrymen, listen to the holy men chanting the sundown prayer. Then Pakistanis mutter a prayer, eat a date, sip some water and sit down with a sigh to the huge meal that will have to do them until next sundown.

But even with the sweeter tempers of the evening nobody denies that Pakistan is going through another of the crises that have become almost a political way of life for her.

## Small Group Shares Offices

The major trouble, as it was last year and the year before that and every year since national independence a decade ago, is that politics in the country is still a process of shifting of offices among a small group of men. There has never been a national election and nobody really holds the people's mandate.

Mr. Suhrawardy is probably the most adroit politician Pakistan has produced. But his Awami League is only a minority in Parliament and the whole coalition appears to be restless.

Mr. Suhrawardy needs the votes of the Republican party to stay in office. President Iskander Mirza is one of the major powers behind that party.

Many members of the Republican party are furious that Mr. Mirza dissolved the West Pakistan Legislative Assembly, which they had controlled. There were desertions within the West Pakistani unit of the party and Mr. Mirza decided that the time had come for him to use his powers to take over.

The Republicans seem to have decided to swallow their anger and go along with the President and Prime Minister. But their resentments remain.

To add to the trouble, Mr. Suhrawardy finds himself at odds with the leaders of his own party. They have been agitating for more self-rule for East Pakistan, something the Prime Minister feels could lead to destruction of the country. Mr. Suhrawardy needs the Awami League leaders and they need him, to share in the benefits of office.

People close to Mr. Mirza say that all this shows Pakistan is not ready for democracy unless it is of the "controlled" variety. Young Pakistani intellectuals say that democracy has not failed, that it simply has not been given a real chance.

-w&s-

## POLES GRUMBLING OVER SLOW GAINS

*Women in Warsaw's Queues*
*Waiting for Scarce Butter*
*Typify Nation's Task*

### By SYDNEY GRUSON

WARSAW, May 7—A young mother engaged in the eternal queue's chatter outside a delicatessen shop in Nowy Swiat said, "Maybe it will be better after a while."

"For you young people perhaps," replied an old woman, "but not for me. I haven't much time left."

It was a little after 1 P.M. They had been waiting with a hundred others since 11 A.M., protected from the cold drizzle only because the delicatessen is in an arcade. All over

Warsaw there have been similar queues, and presumably similar conversations, for nearly two weeks.

The queues are for butter. Butter has suddenly become a symbol of the discontent, malaise and impatience of the people of this weary capital. At best butter is difficult to find. Sometimes it is impossible. According to reports, things are no better in the countryside.

No one knows why butter has disappeared from the shops. Lacking an official explanation, people make up their own in the increasing bitterness over the difficult economic situation.

### Lots of Whys in Poland

"Why is there no butter?" a reporter asked as he took a place in the queue.

"Why?" replied a woman. "That's what we ask. There are lots of whys in Poland."

The answer that a taxi driver gave was the one most frequently heard—and the one that made least sense.

"It's gone for the festival," said the taxi driver. The festival was not further identified, but he meant the gathering of youth planned for Moscow in July. This was the kind of remark heard all the time in Poland during the worst days of the Stalinist era. Its popping up again was a measure of the disillusionment setting in here.

The taxi driver, chortling, recited a couplet in another comment on the situation. "Staline, Staline, oddaj, swinie," he said. Translated, it goes, "Stalin, Stalin, return our pigs," another hangover of the not so long ago when whatever evil befell Poles was attributed to the Russians.

Some people say butter is short in Warsaw because great quantities have been sent to Poznan and other western areas to quiet workers' unrest there. Another explanation on the streets is that peasants now find it more profitable to sell milk than to make butter.

Many people go back to a speech made some months ago by Wladyslaw Gomulka, who became the hero of the people of the queues when he defied the Russians last October and was restored as the Polish Communists' First Secretary. In that speech M. Gomulka advised the Poles to save butter imports by eating lard. Now some people say butter is being deliberately withheld to make people buy up lard supplies.

Not only butter has been short recently. There is difficulty in getting meat as well, and sometimes vegetables and even milk, though peasants now are paid 2 zlotys (8 cents) a liter for it instead of the 90 groszy (3½ cents) paid when milk deliveries were compulsory.

## Patience Wearing Thin

A hard life has become increasingly harder, people say, though no one contends he is worse off economically than before M. Gomulka came back. Thankful though they are for the increased freedoms that M. Gomulka symbolizes, the Poles seem less and less inclined to heed his pleas for patience and sacrifices in return for hope of a better life in the still unsighted future.

This impatience tinged with despair, most noticeable among the women who must work and tend houses as well, has seeped into industrial workers. No other explanation is possible for the spate of strikes and strike threats with which the Government and the ruling Communist party have been faced in the last two months.

"Before we had no money and could not talk," said a middle-aged engineer. "Now we have no money but we can talk. That is better, of course—" and the sentence trailed off.

It is in the queues and among the underpaid workers that the credit of confidence given to M. Gomulka last October is running out. How to check the run is a problem for which no one seems to have a solution at this moment.

-w&s-

## CHANGES MARKED IN CZECH CAPITAL

*Gaiety Gives Way to Worry
—Goods Are Plentiful but
Quality Appears Poor*

### By ELIE ABEL

PRAGUE, Czechoslovakia, March 2—The winter sun slants down on Wenceslas Square, bestowing a little light but very little warmth on the wind-blown shoppers in the center of Prague.

The River Vltava (Moldau) winds through the old city, its hundred spires blurred by overhanging fog, past the monstrous Stalin statue on the embankment and under the carved stone saints of the Charles Bridge.

Take away the granite Stalin, the Soviet flags, the Communist mottoes in subdued neon lights downtown, and the face of Prague is as it must have been twenty years ago, in the last days of Thomas Garrigue Masaryk's First Republic.

Yet a great deal has changed. The hotels swarm with young Egyptians in civilian dress, wearing air force blue trench coats. It is a fair guess that they are fighter pilots being trained in Czechoslovakia to fly MIG's.

## Russian Visitors Noted

Stocky Russians, their nationality given away by their flapping bell-bottomed trousers, sip tea in the lounge. Their mission here is unknown, and they seem to speak only with one another.

Gaiety is a stranger here, worry a constant companion. An old Czechoslovak friend politely refuses to call on an American visitor in his hotel room.

"I'll meet you outside in the street," he explains gravely. "Nowadays there are always some formalities."

Compared with the capitals of other Communist states, Prague is a city of abundance. Store windows are loaded with consumer goods. Street crowds are warmly if not stylishly dressed.

But an hour or two of comparison shopping discloses that the quality of goods in the shops is low by Western or prewar Czechoslovak standards. And the prices are high.

A badly cut suit of clothes, the fabric stiff with cheaper substitutes for wool, costs an industrial worker 700 crowns, or more than two weeks' work. According to the Government's own statistics, average wages are 1,200 to 1,300 crowns a month.

Square-toed women's shoes, designed to make the most graceful foot look clumsy, are 300 to 400 crowns. That is the equivalent of one week's earnings for a skilled worker.

But many office clerks and secretaries receive no more than 800 a month.

At the unrealistic rate of exchange maintained by the State Bank of Czechoslovakia, the plainest pair of women's shoes on display costs $30 to $40.

Coffee is 17 to 21 crowns for 100 grams, or about 85 to 105 crowns a pound. Even if you apply the special tourist exchange rate this translates into $4 or $5.

There are many more automobiles here than in Belgrade, Bucharest or Warsaw, some earmarked for sale to private citizens. But the price of a small Czech-built Skoda is 27,000 crowns, or the equivalent of fourteen months' pay for a hard-coal miner, the aristocrat of present-day Czechoslovakia.

According to Svobodny Slovo, former Socialist newspaper, 30,961 Czechs and Slovaks had their names on waiting lists to buy automobiles as of last Dec. 31. Each application was backed by a virtually irrevocable deposit of 20,000 crowns.

### Worker's Rating a Factor

There is the Communist merit system with which to contend. Allocations of automobiles are made on the basis of a worker's rating in his factory. Shock workers have first call.

Take the case of a Czechoslovak machinist known to this correspondent. His name is fifty-first on his factory's list of deserving workers. This particular factory is allotted ten automobiles a year. At that rate, the machinist should get his Skoda by 1962, other things being equal, as the mathematicians say.

Supporters of the Communist regime say price comparisons are misleading because they do not take into account free medical care, cheap rents and street car fares. There is some merit in this contention. A young engineer proudly showed an American visitor through his drab but comfortable two-bedroom apartment in a new housing development on the outskirts of Prague. His rent, 215 crowns a month, amounts to 10 per cent of his salary.

The national health plan was started back in the days of the First Republic, a point the Communists carefully ignore. Moreover, Czechoslovak doctors today are so overworked that the quality of medical care often suffers.

-*w&s*-

## MADRID SERENOS KEEP NIGHT PEACE

*City's Street Watchmen Are
A Beloved Heritage of
The Middle Ages*

### By BENJAMIN WELLES

MADRID, May 11—Americans visiting or living in Madrid often can be found late at night clapping their hands in unison, rapping on glass doors with rings, keys or coins, or calling out "sereno" at the tops of their voices.

They have fallen afoul of one of the heritages of the past that lingers on virtually unchanged in twentieth-century Spain.

The "serenos," or night watchmen of the streets, usually are elderly ex-soldiers or functionaries who deserve well of their government. They have been granted the right to patrol the streets at night and to assist the police in maintaining law and order.

Clad in the semblance of a uniform and equipped with three-foot staves that they rap sharply on the sidewalk to signal their arrival or to attract their colleagues' help, they are a symbol of a bygone age. But they also are a much-loved element of Madrid life.

### Doors Are Locked Early

Here front doors of apartment houses are closed and locked by the house porters at 10:30 P.M. Until daylight, entry—or what is more problematic, exit—is limited to those with keys or to those fortunate few who can attract the attention of the sereno.

Legion is the number of unwary Americans who have had dinner in the apartment of a Spanish or foreign friend here and who, having bid their hosts goodnight, have descended to the ground floor to find themselves locked in.

If the local host has forgotten to send down a servant to unlock the front door, there are two alternatives. Either one returns and asks for the front door key or one hammers on the glass or wood doors to attract the sereno. If he is in the next block or around the corner, the wait is long and sobering.

In a matter of two, ten or perhaps fifteen minutes, the sound of shuffling feet will be heard, the clap of the three-foot stave on the sidewalk will signal his approach and the doors will unlock. The foreigner will then be released with many a smile and a bow. A 1-peseta (2-cent) tip is the normal reward for this highly welcome service.

The sereno dates from the Middle Ages—when the unlit streets of Spanish cities were patrolled by watchmen. At regular intervals they cried out the time, adding—if the night was clear—"todo sereno!" (all clear).

Although their cries are silenced, the serenos still circulate through the night watching over commercial premises, releasing trapped Americans, or calming—with more or less force—the noisy or the "gamberros" (hooligans) against whom the Madrid press regularly inveighs.

The pay of the serenos is nominal and they live on tips or small monthly contributions of about 30 pesetas from householders over whose premises they watch. As a quasi-police force, the serenos deal sternly with rowdies and many an inebriate has found their three-foot staves are not just for appearances.

-w&s-

# Explain, Explain, Explain: An Expository Story

## THE ANTE IS BILLIONS

*A Study of the Gigantic Poker Game
With the Status of Sterling at Stake*

### By EDWIN L. DALE JR.

WASHINGTON, Sept. 26—A gigantic poker game, with billions of dollars and the reputation of the world's most widely used currency at stake, is quietly being played out in the world's financial centers.

On one side of the table, with a large pile of chips and good cards, is the British Government. On the other side, with a smaller pile but with some hoped-for resources in the background, are several thousand private traders, banks and corporations.

This great poker game has been the dominating topic of conversation at this week's meeting of the world's finance ministers in their role as governors of the International Monetary Fund.

The "speculators" group is gambling that if it can hold out long enough it will force Britain to devalue the pound, simply by forcing a sort of "run" on Britain's gold and dollar reserves. If devaluation could be forced, they would profit by many millions of dollars.

The British Government, its spokesmen have emphasized, has no intention of devaluing. In 1949, when the pound was devalued from $4.03 to $2.80, there were genuine economic benefits to be gained from devaluation. This time there are few, if any. Britain's prices, in general, are not out of line with a rate of $2.80 for the pound, and British exports are the strongest in history.

### Odds in Britain's Favor

Only if the speculators and other factors drove Britain's reserves down almost to the vanishing point could devaluation be forced.

The best single method the speculators have of winning the game is to persuade others that a devaluation is possible. As long as the world's traders and bankers think of this as a possibility, the pressure on sterling and the drain on reserves will continue. But if the speculators fail, their gamble will have cost them substantial sums of money.

The odds, in the view of the world financial experts gathered here this week, are strongly in the favor of the British Government to win the game. But the odds are equally strong that at the next clash between these giant forces the British will be less assured of victory unless they can conquer their economic problem at home.

Both sides in the current game—which should be settled in a matter of days or weeks—have strong allies. The British ally, a somewhat belated one, is the Government of West Germany.

A large part of the "run on the pound" has been by people who expected West Germany to increase the value of the Deutsche mark. Indeed, it seemed for a while that the British Government itself would stand to benefit by a higher value for the mark.

But the British decided some weeks ago that their main interest was clearly in a stable mark, to halt the speculation. The Germans, for their own reasons, gradually decided that the mark should stay where it was.

Just prior to this week's meeting here, the Germans and the British agreed to announce jointly to the world that their currencies would not change in value. It had been said before, but with somewhat less conviction.

The Germans intend to stick by their decision. This fact alone is a severe blow to the speculator side. But the speculators have allies, too—in a sense unwitting allies. They are hundreds of thousands of the world's traders, who indulge in a game called "leads and lags."

Suppose you are an American importer of British automobiles. You normally pay your bills, say, in ninety days after shipment, buying the necessary sterling with dollars at that time.

You hear rumors and read reports that sterling might be devalued. So you delay your payment as long as possible in the hope that sterling will be cheaper when you have to pay the bill. That many fewer dollars flow into Britain's reserve for the month.

Or suppose you are a British importer of United States cotton. You, too, hear talk of devaluation. So you accelerate your payment, lest, if you wait the normal ninety days, a bale of cotton will cost more in your own currency. That many dollars flow artificially out of the British reserves this month.

This "leads and lags" item is the truly huge factor in the poker game. No one really knows how big it is, but it might have a short-run effect of as much as $1,000,000,000 on the British reserves.

The crucial point is that it can be only short-term. Eventually the American importer must pay his bill. The British cotton importer who pays this month will not make a payment next month that otherwise would have been made.

### British Resources Cited

That is why, if the British can hold out, as the experts here almost unanimously believe they can, money will start to flow back into the British reserves. Not all the losses caused by the current crisis—and they may already be in excess of $500,-000,000—will be recouped. Some people who ordinarily hold sterling for "working balances," and who sold it quickly on the devaluation rumors, may never fully repurchase it with marks or dollars. But at least the "leads and lags" item will be almost entirely recouped.

The British can match an extremely large bet by the speculators. They have something under $2,000,000,000 in reserves (the figures will not be out for a few days), plus $500,000,000 to be drawn from the United States Export-Import Bank, plus $731,000,000 they can draw at any time under a "stand-by" credit from the International Monetary Fund.

That is why they are expected to win.

But, there may be another crisis (this one was touched off by the partial devaluation of the French franc). The basic root of lack of confidence in sterling is insufficient sterling reserves. And the root of insufficient reserves is a persistent failure of the British to earn enough surplus in their trading with the world.

The surplus the British are earning is barely enough to cover the investments they make overseas in the Commonwealth countries, and thus the reserves are not increased.

If, by tough policies at home, Britain cannot so improve her trading position as to build the reserves, at the next crisis the speculators will try again. Next time, the British may not have such extra resources as the Export-Import Bank loan and the Monetary Fund credit.

*-w&s-*

# A Clear, Tightly Written Political Dispatch

## MOLLET WINS TEST ON ALGERIA FUNDS BY WIDE MARGIN

### *Paris Assembly Compromise Gives Premier Discretionary Loan and Tax Powers*

### By ROBERT C. DOTY

PARIS, July 28—Premier Guy Mollet won a vote of confidence from the National Assembly today on a plan to finance France's campaign of pacification in Algeria by taxation and borrowing.

It was the twenty-fourth time in six months that Premier Mollet had given the Assembly the choice of supporting him or voting him out of office. He won by the comfortable margin of 273 to 163, with only the extremes—the Communists and right-wing Poujadists—voting against him.

The vote was preceded by a week of parliamentary debate and corridor maneuvering between those who favored taxation for economic reasons, and those who urged borrowing for fear of the political consequences of taxation.

The Government urged taxation in the belief that this would withdraw money from circulation more broadly and thus reduce inflationary pressures on prices. It was contended that funds subscribed to Government loans came mostly from an investors' surplus and so were not withdrawn from the money competing for limited goods.

### Loan Plan Called 'Gamble'

Paul Ramadier, Minister of Finance and Economic Affairs, characterized the Assembly loan proposal as a "gamble" and insisted that the plan be supported by authority to tax. The Assembly-approved compromise left the Government a large measure of discretionary power.

When the measure is approved by the Council of the Republic, advisory second chamber of Parliament, the Government will be authorized to raise 150,000,000,000 francs ($248,000,000), approximately half the cost of maintaining 400,000 troops in Algeria this year.

It may use either a Government bond issue or a series of tax increases on personal business and corporate incomes or a combination of both.

In parliamentary circles the borrowing authorization was being referred to as the "alibi-loan." By giving the Government borrowing power many Deputies obviously hoped to acquire a "lightning rod" to turn voter wrath. If the loan is undersubscribed, as most observers believe it will be, and the Government is forced to resort to taxation, the politicians can argue that the public was given a chance to lend rather than pay.

Premier Mollet reaffirmed his Government's program for settlement of the Algerian rebellion. He spoke in the Pantheon on the anniversary of the death of Jean Jaurès, regarded as the founder of French socialism.

-*w&s*-

## Color Stories

## ARMY LAUNCHES U.S. SATELLITE INTO ORBIT; PRESIDENT PROMISES WORLD WILL GET DATA; JUPITER-C ROCKET PUTS UP 30-POUND DEVICE

*Roars Up in Florida*
*Tense 15-3/4 Seconds*
*After It Is Fired*

### By MILTON BRACKER

CAPE CANAVERAL, Fla., Jan. 31—The United States' first earth satellite was borne spaceward tonight on a tremendous golden jet that roared its way across the sky from the base of the Army's Jupiter-C rocket.

At 10:48 P.M., after an agonizing fifteen and three-quarter seconds between the actual firing command and the lift-off, the giant rocket lit up the night with a seething burst of flame and gradually accelerated directly upward from the pad.

As the Jupiter-C gained speed, it emitted a violent roar that filled the entire area.

Never wavering on its course, the rocket rose faster and faster, cut through a layer of overcast and reappeared as a steadily diminishing spark burning its way out of sight.

### Tracking Stations in Action

From the vicinity of the Cape, the launching appeared perfect. Radio-tracking stations went into action at once.

Searchlights picked out the Jupiter-C before launching so as to reveal clearly its unusual conformation.

As soon as the rocket got off the ground, the Air Force, which is in charge of the Missile Testing Center here, distributed information on it to newsmen.

These data said the Jupiter-C was about 68.6 feet long, and the pointed cylindrical satellite case containing the scientific instruments was 80 inches long and 6 inches in diameter.

The weight of the satellite proper was 18.13 pounds, and the final stage of rocket after burn-out weighed 12.67 pounds, giving a total weight of the satellite of 30.8 pounds.

The "payload" instruments weigh about 11 pounds exclusive of the protecting steel case, which weighed 7½ pounds, the Air Force said.

"The satellite and final stage rocket were designed to remain together and circle the earth as one unit," the Air Force said. "The satellite is not designed to be recovered."

One of the most dramatic phases of the count-down came at eleven minutes before the firing, when the cluster of solid rockets making up the second and third stages of the Jupiter-C began to revolve rapidly.

This rotation, imparted by electric motors, was to stabilize the second and third stages of small solid rockets in the event that one of them fired before any of the others.

As the count-down got down to time zero—the firing time—the servicing structure, or gantry, moved back on its rails and its lights went out.

This left the Jupiter-C exposed in a great silvery brilliance with a red light flashing in warning and a claxon moaning ominously.

As the firing command neared, a deadly silence fell on those who were watching.

In the glare of the searchlights, a stream of liquid oxygen could be seen venting like a lavender cloud from the side of the seventy-foot rocket.

At three seconds after the firing command, the fuel tank was pressurized.

Seven seconds later a boom that had fed dry ice to the rocket's battery system dropped away.

At fourteen and one-half seconds after time zero, after the priming fuel had ignited almost invisibly, the main stage engine came to life with an immeasurable thrust of flame in all directions.

A great orange cloud of fire illuminated the base of the rocket. But quickly it subsided as the moment of lift-off occurred and the jet no longer had the launching stand to punish.

With thousands of eyes following it, the rocket dug into the night and accelerated as its sound loudened.

Spectators on near-by beaches pointed and craned their necks and cried, "There it is!" and began to cheer.

Others insisted they could follow it even farther and argued with one another as to exactly where it had disappeared.

Within a few minutes of the launching, the following statement by the Department of Defense was issued through the Air Force Missile Test Center, which takes in the Cape Canaveral launching site:

"As part of the International Geophysical Year, a satellite launching program, the Army launched a multistage test rocket at 10:48 o'clock tonight at Cape Canaveral, Florida.

"It is too early to determine whether or not the satellite is in orbit.

"All additional information will be available at the National Academy of Sciences, Washington, D. C."

### Count-Down Is Swift

The progress of the count-down was remarkably swift and efficient in contrast to the heartbreaking delays encountered for four days of last week when the Navy tried to launch its Vanguard.

From X minus 80 minutes tonight, down to the time of the

actual launching, there was only one substantial hold—at X minus 45 minutes.

Since it was known that the earliest the Army hoped to fire the rocket was 10:30 P.M., it actually lifted from the pad only eighteen minutes behind its best possible schedule.

*-w&s-*

## 13.5-INCH SNOW PARALYZES CITY; SCHOOLS CLOSED, BUSINESS DROPS; TRANSIT SNARLED IN NORTHEAST

*4-Day Toll Is 125;*
*State of Emergency Is*
*Declared in Suffolk*

### By MEYER BERGER

NEW YORK, March 20—Winter spread a snow carpet 13.5 inches deep between 11 A.M. Sunday and early last evening in a last unmatronly pet. It left an icy footing for spring, which is due at 10:11 A.M. today.

The storm blanketed states all the way from West Virginia to Maine. It came in with strong winds and temperatures that never climbed out of the 20's. It left tremendous drifts in the countryside, and in main urban avenues it veiled skylines, tufting skyscrapers and steeples with enormous white caps.

The deep snows isolated many communities in Suffolk County, and Sheriff William C. McCollom last night declared a state of emergency in the county. The county's Civil Defense force of some 14,000 persons was alerted to stand by "because of the increasingly acute situation in Suffolk County." One of the critical problems facing communities there was the inability of food trucks to make deliveries.

The Associated Press reported that the two snowstorms of the week-end—the first started Friday morning and ended after midnight—cost at least 125 lives. Most of the deaths occurred when snow-blinded drivers skidded, or when persons with weak hearts took up snow shoveling.

The Friday snowfall had deposited 4.8 inches on city roofs

and pavements, but this had melted down to about a half-inch when the Sunday storm came howling in. This under-carpeting was like armor—sheer ice—and the second storm soon covered it. With the snowfall that tapered off last night the pile-up in city streets measured a full fourteen inches.

Up and down the coast the picture was pretty much the same—trains delayed, buses stalled in snowdrifts, thousands of motorists stranded overnight on major highways, city traffic thrown off schedule, countless commuters unable to get to their jobs. Schools were closed. Factories and offices shut down at noon or soon after to permit their hands to struggle back to their homes.

Ships moved cautiously into harbor, feeling their way through the dense snow curtain with their radar. Ferryboats from the Battery to Staten Island used their electronic feelers, too. Hundreds of take-offs and landings were canceled at local airports. The skies, though, were hardly less silent than the metropolis that moved on footfall-deadening white.

The storm "officially" ended at 9:05 o'clock last night, when the last of the swirling flakes hit the ground, according to the Weather Bureau. The main bluster, however, was about over around 6 P.M., although, as Weather Bureau officials noted, it was "still spitting" two hours later.

Department stores, specialty shops and almost all other establishments that had hoped for an Easter windfall had only a trickle of shoppers, and despair was evident. Rough estimates placed the possible loss of business at $150,000,000. There was fear that it might be days before roads were clear.

The Sanitation Department put 8,000 men and 2,000 pieces of equipment onto the snow-choked streets. Cardinal Spellman gave special dispensation of Lenten fast and abstinence to the 8,000 workers, because they were compelled to labor under extraordinary conditions amounting to hardship.

The Weather Bureau in New York pointed out that the storm had sharper teeth than earlier snows. Yesterday, according to Ernest J. Christie, meteorologist in charge, was the coldest March 19 in the bureau's eighty-five years of meteorological records. Not once in the day did the thermometer go to 30, and that has happened only twice before in the last sixty years. At 5 o'clock last night, as the snow thinned a little, the reading was 22 degrees.

## But Not a Blizzard

Curiously, neither Mr. Christie nor his aides, all hard put to keep up with the flood of inquiries about the storm, would call the great snowfall a blizzard. A blizzard, they explained patiently, is a "violent, extremely cold wind laden with snow" that is "mostly, or entirely, picked up from the ground."

Even after the snow had seemed to stop—the winds kept tearing at deposits on skyscrapers and dwelling roofs and blowing them off in fine powder—there was little relief for the pedestrian on city streets. The gusts took great mounds from one side of broad avenues and highways, and wickedly blew them to the opposite side in beautiful, fantastic patterns.

The winds, as the snows ended, were still whining at around twenty-five to thirty miles an hour and the weather men seemed to think they might maintain that velocity through the night, possibly into early this morning. They were expected to drop after daybreak, possibly down to fifteen miles an hour.

Today the temperatures are expected to stay in the 20's until mid-afternoon, when they may rise to the middle 30's. The outlook was for fair weather through today.

For those who could lift their heads to the cutting flakes and ice-bits, there was a kind of beauty all about, in town. Back yards were done in weird sculptured effects wherever trees or bushes made foundation. The skyscrapers' tops, almost lost in the upper storm, were dreamy looking structures, seen through the blowing snow curtain. Bridges and steeples wore lovely winter lace.

The impact on the city's millions was amusing where it was not tragic. New Yorkers, who rarely walk when buses or cabs are to be had, found themselves suddenly afoot—and in deep, drifted snow. The early risers took the mid-roadway where fuel trucks had broken trail. Then, as traffic picked up, the later risers floundered down narrow paths on the sidewalks or plowed through the drifts at either side.

Funerals were delayed, courts found themselves without juries and, in some cases, without judges, prosecutors or defense attorneys. City ambulances could not enter deeply drifted sidestreets, so internes and drivers had to carry patients a half-block or more to get them aboard. Passengers entering the city by railroad, bus and ship could get no taxis. Barely a handful were in the streets.

Almost every hotel in the city was filled by mid-afternoon yesterday. The commuters who had made it to the city, but were afraid they could not get back home, swamped the desks to register. Midtown hotels reported they could have filled 1,000 to 1,500 more rooms than were available. They also reported that many comparatively small dinner parties had been canceled. Large banquets, arranged months in advance, went on as scheduled, to thin attendance.

### Buses Many Hours Late

Train and bus delays were universal in New York and in all major cities that lay under the great snow cover. One Trailways bus from Raleigh, N. C., limped into the Midtown Bus Terminal eleven hours late, fringed and bearded with icicles. Two buses from Norfolk arrived, after a tough pull, ten hours late, and they, too, wore snow and ice shrouds. The passengers were none the worse for the experience. Ninety-five percent of the long-haul runs scheduled at the Midtown Terminal were taken off the boards as the snow grew deeper and deeper.

*–w&s–*

# Index

A, an, 97-98, 104-5
  *see also* Articles
About, in approximation, 8; misused, 8
Accused, *see* Alleged, Accused, Suspected, 9
ADJECTIVES
  misused as adverbs, 106
  multiple, 105
  placement with verb, 110, 130-131
Admit, overstatement through misuse, 8
"Advance planning," 8
ADVERBS
  misused for adjectives, 105-6
  placement of, 105-6
Aggravate, misused, 8
AGREEMENT, subject and verb, 116-117
  *see also* Collectives, 107-8; Each, 109; and None, 115
"Ahold," 8
Air, misused as broadcast, 9
*Alcometer*, 22
All-around, all-round, 9
All right, alright, *see* "One Word, Two Words," 38
Alleged, misused, 9
Allusion, misused for reference, 10
*Ambiguity*, 132-133
American Press Institute, 84
Among, between, 106-7
Anachronism, misused for paradox, 10
And
  replaced by comma in headlines, 168
  with "which" and "who" clauses, 132
And/or, 10

Another, misused, 10
  *see also* Other
ANTECEDENTS
  of relative pronouns, 98-99, 132-33
"Any and all," 10
Anyway, any way, 10
Appear, *see* Show, 46
*Appendix*, 181-203
Around, used superfluously, 16, 46
  *see also* All-around
ARTICLES
  before consonants, initials, 104
  misuse of definite for indefinite, 11
  omission of, 97-98, 104-5
As, *see* Like, 114-115
"As the crow flies,"
"As the result of," 11
"As well as," *see* "Both . . . as well as," 14
Ask, *see* Request, 43
Assassin, misused, 11
Assert, *see* Claim, 17
Attack, used euphemistically, 11
"At the present time," 7, 11
Attorney, misused for lawyer, 12
*Attribution of statements*, in newswriting, 142-43
Audience, misused for crowd, 12
Awhile, *see* "One Word, Two Words," 38

"Back and forth," *see* "Remand back," 43
*Bad taste*, in newswriting, 143-144

Balding, baldish, 12

Bandit, misused, 12-13

Bastion, misused, 13

"Bear by the tail," *see* "Bull," 15

Because, *see* "Reason . . . because," 42

Because of, *see* "Due to," 109-110

"Before in the past," a redundancy, 13

Below, used unnecessarily, 13

*Berger, Meyer,* (news story in Appendix), 200

Between
and among, 106-7
with each, every, 107

Bimonthly, biweekly, 13

"Bid in," 13

Bisect, misused, 13

Blame, misused with on, 13-14

Boat, inaccurately used, 14

Boost, misused for raise, 14

Both . . . and, proper placement of, 107

Both . . . as well as, misused for Both . . . and, 14

*Bracker, Milton,* (news story in Appendix), 197

Bridegroom, *see* Groom, 28

Bring, misused for carry, 14

"Bring to a head," 14

Brown, Charles H., 91-92

"Bull" ["by the horns,"] misused, 15

Burgermeister, Burgomaster, 15

Burglary, misused, 15

Business, misused for profession, 32-33

Buyers, misused for customers, 15

By, misused for from, through, with, 15

"By means of," 15

Cablegram, misused, 16

Cannot, can not, *see* "One Word, Two Words," 38

Carry, *see* Bring, 14

Casket, a euphemism, 23-24

Celebrants, celebrators, 16

Center, misused with around, 16

"Chain reaction," 16

Chair, misused as verb, 16

*Characterization* in newswriting, 66

"Check into," 16-17

Chord, misused for cord, 17

Citizen, misused for [British] subject, 17

Claim, misused, 17

Clergy, *see* Rector, 42, and Reverend, 43

Client, misused for patient, 17

Coffin, *see* "Euphemisms," 23-24

Cohort, misused, 17

*Coined titles,* 17-18

Coke, misused as generic term, 18

COLLECTIVE NOUNS, 107-8

Collision, misused for impact, 18

Combine, misused as noun, 18

COMMA
appositives, 145
for parenthetical purpose, 145
for phrases with a common termination, 146
in erroneous combination, 146
in place of dashes, 146
misused in headlines, 168
with nonrestrictive phrases, 145

COMMUNICATION IN WRITING, 55-102

Company, *see* Firm, 25

*Comparison*
incomparable, 114
incomplete alternative, 114

"Complected," complexioned, 19

COMPOUND WORDS, *see* Hyphens, 151-52

Comprise, comprised of, 19

Concern, misuse as noun, 19
  *see also* Firm
*Concrete versus abstract writing*, 77-83
CONJUNCTIONS, *see* Like, 114-115; and That, 128-129
  *see also* And
"Conspicuous by their absence," 19
Consuls general, correct plural, 19
Contemporary, *see* Modernistic, 35
Continually, continuously, 19-20
CONTINUED HEADS, 174
Contractual, correct spelling, 20
Copperud, Roy H., 61
COPY EDITING, 134-160
  cutting stories, 147-148
  "don'ts," 143-144
  "helpful hints," 142-160
  hyphens, 151-152
  inaccuracies, inconsistencies, 137-142
  inserts and brackets, 152-154
  matters of style, 157-158; of taste, 143-144
  paragraphing, 154-155
  punctuation, 144-146, 159-160
Country, *see* Nation, 36
  *see also* "Pronouns for Countries," 122-123
Crescendo, misused for peak, 20
CUTTING STORIES, 147-148

*Dale, Edwin L., Jr.* (news story in Appendix), 192
DANGLING MODIFIERS, 103, 130-131
Data, datum, 108
"Deadheads," (in headline writing), 164-165
Declare, *see* Claim, 17
Dentifrice, correct spelling, 20
Deprecatory, depreciatory, 20
Deplane, 21

Develop, *see* Discover, 21
Diagnose, misused, 20
*Dictionary of American-English Usage,* 107
"*Dictums for Deskmen,*" 142-160
Different, misused, 21, 108-109
Dig, misused for drill, 21
Dilemma, misuse of, 21
Dimensions, *see* Proportions, 41
Dis-, in combination, 21
Discover, misused for develop, 21
Disinterested, misused for uninterested, 21
Distinct, *see* Separate, 45
DISTORTIONS AND INJUSTICES, INADVERTENT
  in newswriting, 67-69
*Dominican Republic,* correct usage, 21-22
"Done," as a colloquialism, 22
*Doty, Robert C.,* (news story in Appendix), 196
"Double duty" words, 109
Down, *see* "Up, down, and out," 51-52
Drugs, misused for narcotics, 22
Drunk, misused for drunken, 22
*Drunkometer,* misused as generic term, 22
"Due to," 109-110
During, *see* "In the course of," 20
"Dutch uncle," 47

Each,
  placement with verb, 110
  used with between, 107
Each other, misused, 110
EDITING
  *see* Copy editing
EDITORALIZING IN NEWS STORIES, 65-66
-ee, indiscriminate use of as suffix, 22
Either . . . or, agreement of verb with, 110-111
*Ellipsis,* misused, 111

Emote, misused, 22-23

Enormity, enormousness, 23

Enthuse, a colloquialism, 23

*Enumeration*, grammatical pitfalls in, 111-112

"Equally as," 23

EUPHEMISMS, 23-24, 31-32

Everyone, *see* Pronouns

Ex-, misplacement of, 24

Exclamation points, 148-149

"Explain, explain, explain," 69-71

"Falsely fabricate," 25

Farther, further, 25

Fewer, *see* Less, 33

Figuratively, *see* Literally, 34

*Figures,* checking, 149
  *see also* About, 8

"Finalize," 25

"Fire," a colloquialism, 25

Firm, misused for company, 25

"Fixin's," 25

"Flatly," 25-26

Flaunt, flout, 26

"Folks," 26

"For the purpose of," 7

Foreign names and phrases, translation of, 75, 150-151

"Forelady," 26

Fortuitous, fortunate, 26

Founder, misused, 26

*Fowler, H. W.,* 23, 24, 101, 105, 107, 111

"Frankenstein," 26

Fulsome, misused, 26-27

Further, *see* Farther, further, 25

FUSED PARTICIPLES, 112-113

Gambit, misused, 27

Gendarme, overused, 27

Gender, misused for sex, 27

GENDER OF NOUNS
  *see* "It and She," 30; "Pronouns for Countries," 122-123

GERUND, *see* "Fused Participles," 112-113

"Gild the lily," 27

"Got," as a gaucherie, 27-28

GRAMMAR

Adjectives
  misused as adverbs, 105
    multiple, 105
    placement with verb, 110, 130-131

Adverbs, 105-6

Articles,
  before consonants, initials, 104-5
  misuse of definite for indefinite, 11
  omission of, 97-98, 103-4

Clauses,
  restrictive and nonrestrictive, 129
  subordinate, 173

Conjunctions, 114-115, 128-129

Ellipsis, 111

Infinitives, split, 126-127

Nouns,
  collective, 107-8

Participles,
  dangling, 103, 130-131
  fused, 112-113

Prepositions, 120-121

Pronouns,
  for animals, countries, 30, 121-123
  relative, agreement with antecedents, 98-99, 132 133

Punctuation,
  comma, use and abuse, 144-146, 168-169
  exclamation points, 148-149
  hyphens, 151-152
  quotation marks, 159-160

Sentence structure,
  and intelligibility, 104
  length and reader comprehension, 83-92
  *see also* "Double Duty words" 109

GRAMMAR—*Continued*
  Tenses, sequence of, 123-126
  Verbs,
    agreement with subject, 107-9, 110, 115-116
    auxiliary, 173
    in subordinate clause, 173
    (*See also* "Words that need watching, uses undesirable in writing," 7-54, "Helpful Hints for Hatchet Men," 134-160, and "Syntax Sinners," 103-133.)
Groom, misused for bridegroom, 28
*Gruson, Sydney,* (News story in Appendix), 186

Hardly, a built-in negative, 45
"HEAD-HUNTING," 161-180 [discussion of headline writing]
HEADLINE WRITING, 161-180
  check list of flaws, 162-163
  continuation heads, 174
  feature heads, and their pitfalls, 175-176
  good heads, examples of, 164, 178-180
  specific hazards: ambiguity, "deadheads," "headlinese," obscurity, "two-faced" heads, words with double meaning, 166-171
"Head up," *see* Up, 51-52
Healthy, misused, *see* Boost, 14
"HELPFUL HINTS FOR HATCHET MEN," 134-160
Hike, misused, *see* Boost, 14
Hitherto, misused for theretofore, 28
Hold, misused, 171
"Hopeful optimism," 28
Housetop, *see* "Rooftop," 44
Hurt, used archaically, 28
HYPHEN USAGE, 151-152

"If and when," 28
Imply, misused for infer, 29
Include, used inaccurately, 28-29
*Incomparables,* 114
Individual, misused for person, 29
Infantry, 29
Infer, 29
INFINITIVES, SPLIT, 126-127
*Informing the People,* [book], 91-92
"In order to," 7, 29
Inquiry, *see* Query, 41
*Inserts and Brackets,* 152-154
"In the course of," 20
Intrigue, misused, 30
It, use and misuse, 30

Judge, misused for justice, 12, 30
"Joined together," 30
Jurist, misused for judge, 12
Justice, correct usage re Supreme Court, 30

Kidnap, misused as noun, 31
Kilowatt, kilowatt hour, 31
"Kind of a," 31
Knot [Naut.], misused, 31

Lady, misused for woman, 31-32
Laid, lay, 114
Last, latest, 32
Late, [meaning deceased] used redundantly, 32
Latter, misused, 32
"Lawmen," 33
Lawyer, *see* Attorney, 12
LEADS, NEWS STORY
  attributing quotations in, 58-59
  cluttered, overloaded, puzzling, 56-57, 59-63, 80, 81-85
  direct, 58-65
  "double-barreled," 62

good, examples of, 58-60, 63-65

simplifying, 61-62

superfluous, 60-61

Leave [alone], misused for let, 33

Less, misused for fewer, 33

Like, misused as conjunction, 114-115

"Lit into," 33

*Litotes,* 37

"Lit up like Christmas trees," 34

Literally, misused for figuratively, 34

Livid, misused as vivid, 34

"LOADED WORDS AND PHRASES," 66-67

Longshoreman, *see* Stevedore, 47

Masterly, masterful, 34

"Matinee performance," 34

Mayoralty, misused as adjective, 34

Means

 *see* "By means of," and "Ways and means"

Menial, misused as unskilled, 35

METAPHORS, mixed, 100

*Middleton, Drew,* (News story in Appendix), 181

Minion, misused, 35

Militate, *see* Mitigate

Minister

 *see* Rector, 42

MISUSED WORDS, PHRASES, 7-54

Mitigate, misused for militate, 35

*Modern English Usage* (Fowler), 23, 24, 101, 105, 107, 111

Modernistic, misused, 35

MODIFIERS, UNATTACHED, 103, 130-131

"Mortgage burning," 35

"Mortician," 23-24

"Nab," 36

NAMES

 faulty abbreviation, 21-22

 foreign, 150-51

 *see also* Plurals, 40

Narcotics, *see* Drugs, 22

Nation, misused for country, 36

Nauseated, nauseous, 36

Navy Department, misused for Department of the Navy, 36

"Near-record," 36

Neé, misused, 36

Neither . . . nor, agreement of verb with nouns, 110-11

Nerve-racking, "nerve-wracking," 37

NEWSWRITING, 55-102

 *see also* "Copy editing"

*Nicholson, Margaret,* 107

None, singular and plural usage, 115-116

NONRESTRICTIVE MODIFIERS, 129

 and comma usage, 144-145

Not only, misplacement in sentence, 116

"Not too," 37

Now, *see* "At the present time," 11

NUMBER, agreement between subject and verb, 116-117

*Numbers,* checking, 149

Officer, policeman, 37

"One and the same," 37

One another, misused, 110

*"One idea, one sentence,"* discussion of, 83-92

"One of the," 37

ONE WORD, TWO WORDS distinctions in meaning, use, 38

Only, correct placing of, 118

Oral, *see* Verbal, 52

Other, misused, 38

Over, misused, 38

Out, *see* "Up, down and out," 51-52

*Overrefinement*, 118-119

PARAGRAPH LENGTH, 92, 154-155

PARENTHESIS, PAREN-THETICAL PHRASES, 98-99, 119-120, 156-158

   *see also* "Inserts and Brackets"

Parliamentarian, misused, 38-39

PARTICIPLES

   as adjectives, 120

   dangling, 103, 130-131

   fused, 112-113

"Pass away," 24

Pastor, *see* Rector, 42

People, misused for persons, 39

Per, when preferable to each, 39

"Personal friend," 39

"Pinch hitter," 39

*Play on words, see* Puns, 176-178

"Plead innocent," 12

Plenty, misused for very, 40

PLURALS OF NAMES OTH-ER NOUNS, 19, 40

   *see also* Collectives, 107-8; Street, 127; and What, 131

Point [noun], used superfluously, 40

Predicate, misused verb for base or found, 40

Premise, misused for premises, 40

Preparatory [to], misused for before, 40

PREPOSITION AT END OF SENTENCE, 120-121

Present, *see* "At the present time," 11

Presently, misused to mean now, 41

Preventative, preventive, 41

Priest, *see* Rector, 42

Profession, *see* Law, 32-33

PRONOUNS, PERSONAL, 30, 121-123

   for animals, 30

   for countries, 122-123

Proportions, misused for dimensions, 41

Proposition, misused as verb, 41

Protagonist, misused, 41

Proven, 41

Punctuation,

   commas, use and abuse, 144-146, 168-169, 222-223

   exclamation points, 148-149

   hyphens, 151-152

   quotation marks, 159-160

*Puns,* effective and bad, 176-178

Pupil, 41

"Put the blame on," *see* Blame, 13-14

Query, misused for inquiry, 41

QUOTATION MARKS, use and abuse, 159-160

QUOTATIONS, 98-99, 159-160

   editorial style for, 159-160, 209-211

   foreign-language, translation of, 150

   partial, 99-100

"Quote," 41

Ravish, misused for ravage, 42

"Reach should exceed grasp," *see* "Gild the lily, 27

"Reason . . . because," 42

Rector, 42

Reference, *see* Allusion, 10

Refute, misused for dispute, 42

Relatively, misused, 42

*Religion,* news treatment of, 155-156

"Remains," a euphemism for body, 42-43

"Remand back," 43

Replica, misused, 43

REPORTING
  characterization in, 66
  direct leads, 58-65
  distortion and injustice, un-
    witting, 67-69
  essential small items in, 72-
    75
  interpretive, 65-66
Request, with for, 43
Restrictive and non-restrictive
  modifiers, 129
Result, *see* "As the result of,"
  11
"Reverend," incorrectly used as
  title, 43
"Riding a tiger," *see* "Bull," 15
Rob, misused, 43
"Rock 'n' Roll," 43-44
"Rooftop," misused for house-
  top, 44
*Rosenthal, A. M.*, (news story
  in Appendix), 184
Row [noun], as overstatement,
  44
RULES, STYLE, 157-158
Russian, *see* Soviet, 47

Safe, *see* Vault, 52
"Sahara Desert," 44
Sandhog, misused, 44
Save, misused for except, 44
Say, faulty substitutes for, 17,
  102
Scarcely, a built-in negative, 45
*Science*, news treatment of, 156-
  157
See, misused, 171
"Self-confessed," 45
"Senior citizens," 45
SENTENCE STRUCTURE,
  and intelligibility, 104-5
  length and reader compre-
    hension, 83-92
  "one idea, one sentence," 83-
    90
Separate, used superfluously, 45
SEQUENCE OF TENSES,
  123-126

*Series, see* Enumeration, 111-
  112
Service, misused for serve, 45
Sex, *see* Gender, 27
Shambles, misused, 45
*She, see* "It and She," 30, "Pro-
  nouns for Countries," 122-
  123
Ship, *see* Boat, 14
Shipper, misused for ship-own-
  er, 45-46
Show [verb], misused for ap-
  pear, 46
Shut, *see* "Up, down and out,"
  51-52
"Sierra Mountains," 46
"Simple reason," 46
Site, misused for a building, 46
Size, used redundantly, 41, 46
"Skirt around," 46
"Small in size," 46
Some, misused with statistics,
  46-47
  *see also* About and Over
Sometime, *see* "One Word, Two
  Words, 38
Sooner, incorrectly combined
  with "when" for "than,"
  126
"Sort of a," *see* "Kind of a," 31
Soviet, misused, 47
*Speech reporting*, 81
"Spell out," 47
Spiral, misused to mean rise,
  47
SPLIT INFINITIVES, 126-127
*Statistics*, checking, *see* Figures,
  149
*Statistics*, interpretation, 71
Stevedore, 47
"Stick up for," 47
STORYTELLING, 55-102
"Strangled to death," 47
Streamlined, misused, 48
Streets, correct plural usage,
  127
Stress, misused, 48
Student, misused for pupil, 41

STYLE, RULES OF, 157-158

Subject [British], *see* Citizen, 17

SUBJUNCTIVE, correct use of, 127-128

Succeed, used superfluously, 48

*Superlatives*, 98

Suspected, misused, 9

"Swap," 48

*Switching voices*, 128

"SYNTAX SINNERS," 103-133

"Talkathon," misused as generic term, 49

Target, overuse of, 48

TECHNICAL TERMS, interpretation of
  *see* "Explain, Explain, Explain," 69-76; and "Answered Questions," 76-77

"Teleprompter," misuse as generic term, 48-49

That, as conjunction, when to omit, 128-129

That and which, distinction between, 129

The, *see* Articles

Theretofore, *see* Hitherto, 28

*Time*, placement of, in newswriting, 129-130, 158-159
  and tense, in headline writing, 172-173

*Titles, see* Coined Titles, 17-18

Total, a total of, 49

"Toward the ground," 49

"Tow-headed," 49

Transpire, misused for happen, 49

Trigger, misused for cause, begin, 49-50

Trio, indiscriminate use of for three, 50

Truculent, frequently an overstatement, 50

"True facts," 50

Try, colloq. as noun, 50

"Try and," misused for "try to," 50

"Two-faced" heads, 166-167

-type, misuse, overuse as suffix, 50-51

"Unanswered questions," 71-76

UNATTACHED MODIFIERS, 130-131

Underwater, *see* "One Word, Two Words," 38

Unique, *see* Incomparables, 114

Unknown, misused for undisclosed, 51

Unprecedented, risk in use of, 51

Up, down and out, used unnecessarily, 51-52

VERBS
  agreement with noun, *see* Collectives, 107-8; Each, 110; Either . . . or, 110-111; None, 115-116
  auxiliary, 173
  in subordinate clause, 173

Verbal, misused for oral, 52

Veritable, used unnecessarily, 52

-ward, a misused suffix, 52

Warn, misused for charge or say, 53

"Ways and means," 53

*Welles, Benjamin,* (news story in Appendix), 191

What, when singular, when plural, 131

"Whether or not," 53

Whence, misused with from, 53

Which, misused, 131-132
  *see also* "That and Which," 129

Whir, misused, 53

Who
  with ambiguous antecedent, 132-133
  misused for "that," 133
  preceded by "and," 132

Whom, misused for who, 133

Widow, *see* Late, 32

Windfall, redundant use of, 54
-wise, suffix misused, 54
"WORDS THAT NEED
    WATCHING," 7-54
"Worst to worse," misused for
    "worse to worst," 54
WRITING HEADLINES, 161-
    180
    check list of flaws, 162-163
    continued heads, 174
    "deadheads," 164-165

feature heads and their pit-
    falls, 175-176
good heads, examples of, 164,
    178-180
specific hazards (ambiguity,
    "headlinese," obscurity,
    "two-faced" heads, words
    with double meanings,
    166-171
top and bank, 171

Zoom, misused 54

From simple arithmetic through calendars—the
world-famous best seller that takes the mystery
out of one of the most fascinating sciences.
Formerly $6.95. Now only 95¢.

# MATHEMATICS
## FOR THE
# MILLION

### COMPLETE NEW EDITION WITH ANSWERS

# Lancelot Hogben, F.R.S.

Illustrated by J. F. Horrabin

**95016 / 95¢**

If your bookseller does not have this title, you
may order it by sending retail price, plus 10¢
for mailing and handling to: MAIL SERVICE
DEPARTMENT, Pocket Books, Inc., 1 W. 39th
St., New York, N. Y. 10018. Not responsible
for orders containing cash. Please send check
or money order.

Published by POCKET BOOKS, INC.